W9-CHO-676

CONNECTIONS
English Language Arts

Grade 6

Perfection Learning®

Editorial Director:	Sue Thies
Editors:	Andrea Stark, John T. Ham
Proofreading Coordinator:	Sheri Cooper
Art Director:	Randy Messer
Designers:	Tobi Cunningham, Emily Adickes
Contributors:	Carmel McDonald, Jen Yocum

Reviewers:

Karen Dierks
Media Specialist, ESL certified
ELA and Social Studies
Shawnee Mission Schools
Overland Park, Kansas

Danielle Emery, M.Ed.
Secondary ESL Coordinator
Lewisville, Texas, ISD

Lauri Garbo, M.Ed.
English Department
Gulf Coast High School
Collier County School District, Florida

Carmel McDonald
Instructional Coach
Paragon Charter Academy
Jackson, Michigan

Matthew T. Meldrum
Secondary Language Arts Curriculum
    Specialist
Austin Independent School District
Austin, Texas

Lisa Scribellito Milligan, MA.Ed.
Special Education/Reading
    /ELL Teacher Ed
White High School
Jacksonville, Florida

Kendall Mott
DL Spanish Instructor
Region 5 Education Service Center
Beaumont, Texas

Shelli Shaw
Instructional Officer for Secondary
    Reading Intervention
Katy Independent School District
Katy, Texas

JoAnn Williams
Secondary ELA/Reading Interventionist
Alief Independent School District
Houston, Texas

© 2019 by Perfection Learning®

Please visit our website at: perfectionlearning.com

When ordering this book, please specify:
ISBN: 978-1-5311-2711-4 or **R7342**
ebook ISBN: 978-1-5311-2712-1 or **R7342D**

All rights reserved. No part of this book may be reproduced, stored in a retrieval system, or transmitted in any form or by any means, electronic, mechanical, photocopying, recording, or otherwise, without the prior permission of the publisher. For information regarding permissions, write to: Permissions Department, Perfection Learning, 2680 Berkshire Parkway, Des Moines, Iowa 50325.

2 3 4 5 6 7 BB 23 22 21 20 19 18

Printed in the United States of America

Contents

Unit **4** **Essential Question** Why should you protect Earth
and its creatures? 307

Read, Reread, and Read Again

Welcome to *Connections!* Think about an amazing movie you have seen—one you couldn't stop thinking about when you left the theater. Have you talked about the movie with your family or friends? Have you watched the movie again after first seeing it in the theater? Do you see something new each time you watch it?

Complex texts are like movies. You can't grasp all of the details in one read. Each time you read, you'll discover something new.

Connections will encourage you to develop a habit of reading a text several times. With each read, you will dive deeper into the text. You'll move from key ideas and details to discovering how authors create meaning by using special types of language to communicate their thoughts. With each read of the selections in *Connections*, you will be asked to focus on a central question: *What? How? Why* or *Why Not?*

First Read Focus on *What?*

What are the key ideas?

Ask: What is this mostly about? Which ideas are most important?

Who is writing and why are they writing?

What words or phrases stand out as important?

Second Read Focus on *How?*

How does the writer support his or her purpose?

Ask: How do details develop the central idea?

What special types of language (figurative language, repetition, rhyme) does the writer use to create meaning?

How do the sentences/paragraphs in the text relate, or fit together? How does the structure of the text emphasize the ideas? Do I see causes/effects? problems/solutions? claims/reasons?

Third Read Focus on *Why* or *Why not?*

Why is this text important or meaningful to me—or to others?

Ask: What can I learn from this text that will help me understand the world?

What can I learn that will make me a better writer?

Why is (or why isn't) this nonfiction text convincing? Why is (or why isn't) this work of literature meaningful?

How does this text connect to other texts? Where have I seen this theme before? How do other presentations of this text (movie, artwork, etc.) or ideas in this text communicate the theme in similar or different ways?

Learning to read and reread texts for meaning will make you a confident, successful reader as you encounter ever more challenging texts.

Unit 1

Essential Question
How are friendships built and broken?

Welsh composer and musician Joseph Parry died more than one hundred years ago, but his poem about friendship lives on.

New Friends and Old Friends

Make new friends, but keep the old;
Those are silver, these are gold.
New-made friendships, like new wine,
Age will mellow and refine.
Friendships that have stood the test—
Time and change are surely best;
Brow may wrinkle, hair grow gray,
Friendship never knows decay.
For 'mid old friends, tried and true,
Once more we our youth renew.
But old friends, alas! may die,
New friends must their place supply.
Cherish friendship in your breast—
New is good, but old is best;
Make new friends, but keep the old;
Those are silver, these are gold.

GOALS

- To make inferences based on textual evidence
- To analyze the plot and theme of a memoir
- To identify claims, reasons, and evidence in an argument
- To compare and contrast ideas from multiple texts
- To analyze how key ideas are developed in nonfiction texts
- To understand how elements of a play reveal theme
- To write an informational essay on the qualities of a strong friendship

The lines in this poem remind you that friendship is precious, and something to be treasured. The words *best*, *test*, *cherish*, *renew*, *silver*, and *gold* have positive connotations that make the reader ponder the value of friends in their lives.

Friends can lift your spirit and break your heart. Unit 1 will explore the topic of friendship from different points of view with narratives, nonfiction articles, and a play. By the end of the unit, *you* may have a different view of the importance of friendship in your life.

©Perfection Learning® • No Reproduction Permitted

Chapter 1

Using Evidence to Support Inferences

Preview Concepts

How do two people begin and build a friendship? How have you met your lasting friends? Place a check mark in the chart below that show ways you have met, or could meet, friends. Add your own ideas to the blank rows in the chart.

CHAPTER GOALS

In this chapter you will:

- cite textual evidence when making inferences about texts.
- understand how authors develop characterization.
- analyze how dialogue and dialect are used to develop characterization.

	Living in the same neighborhood
	Being on the same team for a sport
	Playing in the same band
	Singing in the same chorus
	Meeting online while playing video games
	Being in the same classroom
	Meeting through other friends

PREVIEW ACADEMIC VOCABULARY

characterization

dialect/register

dialogue

inference

standard English

textual evidence

Share your answers with a partner. Discuss which ways are most likely to result in a friendship that lasts. Summarize your conclusions from your discussion in the space below.

©Perfection Learning® • No Reproduction Permitted

Making Connections

Charlotte's Web by E. B. White is a classic title about friendship. In the beginning, eight-year-old Fern is Wilbur's best friend as she convinces her father to let her keep the newborn piglet as a pet. However, Wilbur soon grows too large to keep as a pet, and he moves to the Zuckerman farm. Here, Wilbur wants nothing more than to find a friend.

Read this excerpt. As you read, underline details about friendship.

"Well," he thought, "I've got a new friend, all right. But what a gamble friendship is! Charlotte is fierce, brutal, scheming, bloodthirsty—everything I don't like. How can I learn to like her, even though she is pretty and, of course, clever?"

Wilbur was merely suffering the doubts and fears that often go with finding a new friend. In good time he was to discover that he was mistaken about Charlotte.

Look at your underlined details. In your own words, how does Wilbur characterize friendship? Do you agree? Explain.

> **MAKING CONNECTIONS**
>
> In this chapter you will cite textual evidence to support your inferences about characterization.

First Read: Citing Textual Evidence to Support Inferences

The following excerpt is from Christopher Paul Curtis's novel *Bud, Not Buddy*.

Objective: As you read the excerpt, underline words and phrases that help you make inferences about the setting (when and where the action is taking place), the situation, and the relationship between the two main characters. Use the My Thoughts box to record your inferences.

excerpt
Bud, Not Buddy
Chapter 8
by Christopher Paul Curtis

	My Thoughts

1   Something stepped on a little stick. As soon as the twig cracked my eyes snapped open and I was wide awake. I held my breath and kept as still as I could. Whatever it was that was sneaking up on me knew I'd woked up 'cause it stopped

5   moving and kept as still as it could too. Even though my head was still under my blanket, I could feel two eyes staring at me real hard, and I knew these weren't critter eyes, these eyes made the hair on the back of my neck raise up the way only human bean eyes can do.

10   Without wiggling or jiggling around too much under my blanket I got my fingers wrapped around my jackknife. Right when I was ready to push the covers off of me and start running or stabbing, whoever it was that had been watching jumped right on top of me. I was as trapped as a roach under a

15   dishrag! . . .

    It was Bugs!

    When I tried to talk it felt like I had to suck all the air out of Flint, I finally got breathing right and said, "Doggone it, Bugs, it *is* me! You nearly scared me to death!"

 ©Perfection Learning® • No Reproduction Permitted

20   He got off of me and I threw the blanket over to the side. "You don't know how lucky you are, I was just about fixing to stab you in the heart!"

    Bugs looked like he knew he'd just had a real close call. He said, "I'm sorry, Bud, I didn't mean to scare you, but everybody

25 knows how you like to sleep with that knife open so I figured I'd best grab holt of you so's you wouldn't wake up slicing nobody."

    Shucks, even though it was Bugs who'd come real close to getting his heart poked, I was the one who was still having

30 trouble catching my breath.

    I asked, "How come you aren't back at the Home?" But before he had a chance to answer I knew. "You're **on the lam**."

    Bugs said, "Yup, I'm going back to **riding the rails**. When

35 I heard about you beating that kid up so bad that you had to take off, I figured it was time for me to get going too. I thought you might be hanging around the library so I come down to see if you wanted to go with me."

    "Where you heading?"

40   "There's always fruits to be picked out west, I heard we can make enough money to get by out there. There's supposed to be a train leaving sometime tomorrow. Did you really beat that kid up in the **foster home**?"

    I said, "Uh-huh, we kind of had a fight. How long's it take

45 to get out west?"

    Bugs said, "Depends on how many trains you got to hop. Was he really two years older than you?"

    "Uh-huh, he was twelve. Is it fun to hop a train?"

---

on the lam: hastily escaped; on the run
riding the rails: hitching rides on freight trains to travel for free
foster home: a household in which an orphaned or neglected child is placed for care

©Perfection Learning® • No Reproduction Permitted

My Thoughts

"Some of the time it is, some of the time it's scary. We
50 heard he was kind of big too, was he?"

I said, "He was pretty big. I can't see how we can hop on a
train, they look like they're moving pretty doggone fast."

Bugs said, "Most times you don't hop them when they're
going fast, most times you try to climb on one when it's sitting
55 in the train yard. Did the guy cry after you whupped him?"

"Well, kind of, he looked real scared, then told his momma
to keep me away from him. They even said I was a hoodlum.
Will we be sleeping on the train and everything?"

"Sure we will. Some of the time the train don't stop for
60 two or three days. Man, I always try to tell people that just
because someone's skinny it don't mean they can't fight,
you're a hero now, Bud!"

"Naw, I didn't really do nothing much. Well, how 'bout the
toilet? How we going to use the toilet if the train doesn't stop?"

65 Bugs said, "You just kind of lean out of the door and go."

"When the train is still moving?"

"Yeah. You get a real nice breeze."

"Oh, man! That sounds great! Count me in, I can't wait!"

Bugs spit a big glob of slob in his hand and said, "I knew I
70 could depend on you, Bud."

I spit a big glob in my hand and said, "We're brothers
forever, Bugs!"

We slapped our hands together as hard as we could and
got our slobs mixed up real good, then waved them in the air
75 so they'd dry. Now it was official, I finally had a brother!

Bugs said, "We'll go down to the mission. There's bound
to be someone there that knows about where we can hop this
train, then we'll be on the lam together!"

©Perfection Learning® • No Reproduction Permitted

What inferences did you make about Bud and Bugs's relationship? If someone disagreed with your inference, what lines from the excerpt would you use to defend your answer? Write your answers to these questions in your response journal.

Focus on Citing Textual Evidence to Support Inferences

Good readers often have to make inferences about the setting and characters they read about in stories.

An *inference* is a conclusion based upon what the text states and your own background knowledge of life. It is an informed guess.

What can be inferred about Bud's emotions from these sentences?

> I held my breath and kept as still as I could. Whatever it was that was sneaking up on me knew I'd woked up 'cause it stopped moving and kept as still as it could too.

The text says that Bud held his breath and tried not to move. You know from your own experiences of playing hide and seek that if you don't want to be found, you stay extremely still and try not to breathe—even if your heart is pounding. Bud also says something was "sneaking up on me." Think about how you feel when people are sneaking up on you. Based on what the text says and what you know, you can infer that Bud is scared and doesn't want to be found by the person approaching him.

Use the following chart to make your own inferences about the excerpt. Use the annotations you made during the first read to help you. The first row has been filled in for you.

	My Inferences	Evidence from the Text	My Own Knowledge
Setting (time and place where the story is taking place)	The setting is Flint, Michigan, on the ground outside the library.	*Something stepped on a little stick. As soon as the twig cracked my eyes snapped open and I was wide awake.* *I had to suck all the air out of Flint.* *"I thought you might be hanging around the library."*	Sticks are found outside so Bud must be sleeping on the ground. I have relatives that live in Flint, Michigan.

continued on next page

	My Inferences	Evidence from the Text	My Own Knowledge
Bud's current situation— why he is sleeping outside by himself			
Bugs and Bud's relationship			
How Bugs and Bud know each other			
What it means to "ride the rails"			

As you write and discuss texts throughout this book, you will be asked to support your inferences by citing textual evidence. There are several ways to include evidence in your writing.

- Quote the text: Bud is scared of the person sneaking up on him <u>because</u> he says "these eyes made the hair on the back of my neck raise up."

- Paraphrase the text: Clearly Bud is scared <u>because</u> he holds his breath and tries not to move.

    ©Perfection Learning® • No Reproduction Permitted

Notice that both sentences use the word *because* to indicate that the information that follows is providing a reason why the inference is correct. Here are some other sentence frames to use when writing about inferences and evidence. Think about which blanks would contain the words and phrases used to introduce evidence and which ones would contain the inference or conclusion made about the text.

- One example of ___ is . . . .

- The text says ___ so . . . .

- According to line ___, the reader can infer . . . .

- For instance, ...

- The character says . . . . which shows . . . .

Write In your response journal, write five good sentences that contain inferences supported by textual evidence from the chart on pages 13 and 14. Use the sentence starters provided.

Second Read: Analyzing Characters

Follow along with the text as your teacher reads the excerpt aloud.

Objective: As you read, notice and underline dialogue and other details that explain what Bud and Bugs are like. In the My Thoughts column, write a word or phrase that explains the characteristic your underlined sentence reveals.

Focus on Analyzing Characters

Authors develop and reveal their characters in various ways. The process of developing characters is called *characterization.* The list below shows ways that authors use characterization to create characters so real that they come to life each time we open a book.

- what characters look like

- what characters say

- what the characters do

- what other characters say and think about them

- characters' private thoughts (not always directly known and may need to be inferred)

We care about characters that we can see and hear in our minds. Then we can't wait to read and find out more about them and what happens next in a story.

> **CONNECT TO ESSENTIAL QUESTION**
>
> Can you infer how the friendship between Bud and Bugs began? Can you predict whether it will be broken by choice or by circumstances?

continued on next page

Use the chart below to analyze the characterization of Bud and Bugs.

	Private Thoughts	What He Says	What He Does	What Others Say About Him
Bud				
Bugs	(infer)			

(**Speak and Listen** Based upon your answers to the chart above, how would you describe the personalities of Bud and Bugs? Use the following sentence frames to guide your discussion. Use specific traits and textual evidence.

Bud is _____ (character quality) because . . . . (evidence)

Bugs is _____ (character quality) because . . . . (evidence)

Write Write a one-paragraph description of Bud and a one-paragraph description of Bugs. Include specific evidence from the text to support your conclusions.

TECH-CONNECT

Research Christopher Paul Curtis to learn more about his life and his works. His website is nobodybutcurtis.com.

Third Read: Analyzing Dialogue

Listen as two of your classmates read the text aloud, taking the parts of the two main characters.

Objective: Listen for words and phrases that make the characters sound as if they are actually living in 1936 during the Great Depression. Draw a box around words that reflect a regional difference in vocabulary, grammar, and pronunciation.

©Perfection Learning® • No Reproduction Permitted

Focus on Analyzing Dialogue

The conversation between Bud and Bugs matches the time and place in which they live. If a character's speech is to sound realistic, it must reflect the dialect of the setting. *Dialect* refers to the spelling, sounds, grammar, and pronunciation used by a particular group of people. Dialect reflects the specific area in which a person lives and often their social and educational backgrounds.

Notice the use of dialect in this example from the book *To Kill a Mockingbird* by Harper Lee:

> Reckon I have. Almost died first year I come to school and et them pecans—folks say he pizened 'em and put 'em over on the school side of the fence.

Reckon—I think   **come**—came

et—ate   **pizened 'em**—poisoned them

Look over the words that you boxed during your second reading, and complete the following chart with examples of dialect for both characters.

Speaker	Dialect	Interpretation
Bud	'cause	because
Bugs	grab holt of	grab ahold of

> **REFLECT**
>
> Don't confuse slang with dialect. Slang words are informal words and phrases used primarily among peers in social situations, and they come and go quickly. Slang is not acceptable in formal academic writing.

Another interesting thing about the dialogue between the two boys is that they are carrying on two conversations at the same time. One asks a question and the other answers it and then immediately asks another question about something else.

1. What does Bud want to talk about?

2. What is Bugs more interested in hearing about?

3. What can you infer about the characters' relationship based on their rapid-fire conversation?

TECH-CONNECT

Do you drink pop or soda or Coke? The term you use for your carbonated soft drink reflects your regional dialect. Search online to find a map of which parts of the country use the terms *pop, soda,* or *Coke*. At popvssoda. com, you can participate in a web-based project to plot the regional variations in these terms.

▼**Write** In your response journal, write a few paragraphs in which you explain how the dialogue between Bugs and Bud reveals their personalities and their friendship.

Language: Standard English

In this chapter you read dialogue that captured the informal conversation of two characters. The dialogue included examples of dialect, informal register, and slang; this made the characters come to life and the writing realistic.

However, using dialect and slang is not always appropriate. For more formal writing and speaking in school and business settings, you should use standard English. Standard English conforms to established rules of spelling, grammar, pronunciation, and vocabulary.

©Perfection Learning® • No Reproduction Permitted

Standard English is used for journalism, publishing, and academics. You are learning standard English each time you study vocabulary and writing. When you take a test at school, it is written in standard English. Most of the informational books you read are written in standard English.

Here are some examples of when standard English is important for you to use. Can you think of more? Add two more ideas to this list.

- a paper or test written for school.

- an article for the school newsletter.

- an application to be a student leader.

Rewrite the following sentences in standard English

- I ain't got no homework tonight.

- We are posta get a storm perty soon.

- The teachers are fixin to learn us alot.

Project-Based Assessments

Comic Strip

Create a comic book strip of selected events from the excerpt of Christopher Paul Curtis's *Bud, Not Buddy.*

- You may use a comic book creator app, website, or hand-drawn storyboards. Search online to find a good selection of free storyboards.
- Use a minimum of four images, presented in order and with captions briefly explaining each scene.
- Use thought bubbles and speech bubbles to accurately reflect the thoughts and words of the characters.

Ideas to help you be a successful comic book author:

- Read the rubric that follows so you know what is expected of you from the beginning.
- Plan your images before you begin so you can search more effectively. Remember, that you may need to revise your plan depending on the images you find.
- Search for images using keywords such as *Great Depression*; *Bud, Not Buddy*; and *riding the rails.* (These words are only suggestions. You may use other keywords for your search.)
- Refine your search by clicking on Images along the top of your browser window.
- Save images or take screenshots. Paste them into your comic and crop them.

Use the following guidelines for your comic strip.	
To receive the highest score (4.0), the comic strip must meet all of these criteria.	Your comic strip • uses media and/or drawings in a professional and appealing way. • contains interesting images that tell the events in the order in which they happened. • reflects the personalities of the characters. • includes short, interesting captions that are free from spelling and grammar errors.

On Your Own: Integrating Ideas

1. Read *Bud, Not Buddy* by Christopher Paul Curtis. Bud is on a quest to find a place he can call home. Discover whether he meets other friends in his travels.
2. Read *The Watsons Go to Birmingham—1963*, another historical fiction novel by Christopher Paul Curtis. The book is built around the 1963 racially motivated bombing of the Sixteenth Street Baptist Church in Birmingham, Alabama, where four young girls were killed during Sunday morning worship.

    ©Perfection Learning® • No Reproduction Permitted

Connect to Testing

Questions on reading tests will require you to make inferences about situations and characters. Often a second part of the question will test your ability to identify strong evidence that supports the correct inference. Answer question 1 below. Then read the explanation. Answer the rest of the questions on your own.

1. **Part A:** At the beginning of the passage, Bud feels

    A. scared of who is creeping up on him.

    B. worried that the family from the foster home will find him.

    C. sad that he doesn't have any friends.

    D. uncertain about what will happen to him.

    Part B: Choose **two** details from the passage that best support the answer to Part A.

    A. *Something stepped on a little stick.*

    B. *I held my breath and kept as still as I could.*

    C. *these eyes made the hair on the back of my neck raise up the way only human bean eyes can do.*

    D. *Without wiggling or jiggling around too much under my blanket*

    E. *Right when I was ready to push the covers off of me*

EXPLANATION

- Read through the answer choices for Part A.

- From reading the passage, you can infer that Bud is afraid of the person sneaking up on him. There is no mention of choices B, C, and D.

- To answer Part B, read through the choices and think about which of these reactions indicate that Bud was afraid. The best answers are choices B and C because staying still and feeling the hair rise up on your neck are both responses to a threat.

continued on next page

2. **Part A:** Bugs's attitude toward Bud is **mainly**

   A. anger for almost getting them in trouble at the Home.

   B. anxious that they will be traveling alone on the train.

   C. fear that Bud will get upset and stab him with a knife.

   D. admiration for Bud's willingness to stand up for himself.

   Part B: Choose a detail from the text that best supports the answer to Part A.

   A. *I'm sorry, Bud, I didn't mean to scare you.*

   B. *When I heard about you beating that kid up so bad that you had to take off, I figured it was time for me to get going too.*

   C. *you're a hero now, Bud.*

   D. *There's bound to be someone there that knows about where we can hop this train, then we'll be on the lam together!*

3. Which of the following best supports the inference that Bud has needed to defend himself in the past?

   A. He has been called a hoodlum.

   B. He is excited to ride a train.

   C. He sleeps with a knife.

   D. He has run away from his foster home.

4. Do you think Bud and Bugs are resourceful? Support your answer with two examples from the passage.

©Perfection Learning® • No Reproduction Permitted

Chapter 2

Analyzing Plot and Theme in a Memoir

Preview Concepts

As a reader, it is important to choose a wide variety of books to read from different genres. *Genre* refers to a category or type of writing. Categorizing written works into genres helps us organize and compare texts. Here are some genres to consider when selecting your next great read.

- **Memoir**—This type of writing is more focused than an autobiography or biography. In a memoir, the writer narrates the details of a specific event or memorable, shorter period of time that occurred in his or her lifetime. Memoirs may contain multiple themes.

- **Biography**—This type of writing gives a detailed account about a large portion of—or the entire life of—a person, including facts about birth, childhood, education, career, personal life, and death. It is usually written in a chronological order. This life story is written by *another* person.

- **Autobiography**—This type of writing includes the same information as a biography but is written by the person himself or herself. It covers a longer period in the author's life.

continued on next page

CHAPTER GOALS

In this chapter, you will:

- write a summary of the plot of a narrative.
- analyze the theme of a memoir.
- identify how word choice reveals an author's point of view.

PREVIEW ACADEMIC VOCABULARY

central idea

connotation

genre

point of view

summary

theme

verb tenses

- **Narrative nonfiction** (literary nonfiction)—This genre uses literary styles and techniques to create a factually accurate narrative. Narrative nonfiction can be about a person or an event. Different from a memoir, it is written by someone who researched the events but did not actually experience them. Simply put, it is fact-based, engaging, and compelling storytelling.

Below each of the genres, list two or three books that would fit that category. (You may want to get some idea from your library website or an online book recommendation site, such as goodreads.com.) Based upon your research and your friends' recommendations, put a star by the book you would most like to read.

Making Connections

Identify each of the following titles as

Biography (B), Autobiography (A), Memoir (M), or Narrative Nonfiction (NN). Each label will be used once.

MAKING CONNECTIONS

In this chapter you will analyze a memoir to summarize the plot and determine the themes.

Title	Type of Book
1. *How Angel Peterson Got His Name* by Gary Paulsen: The story of Paulsen and his friends, who pull hilarious and dangerous stunts to entertain themselves and impress the girls.	
2. *Trapped: How the World Rescued 33 Miners from 2,000 Feet Below the Chilean Desert* by Marc Aronson: A true, miraculous survival story about the miners and the rest who collaborated to make it happen.	
3. *Knots in My Yo-Yo String* by Jerry Spinelli: The author tells his touching and humorous story spanning from his first memories through his high school years.	
4. *Some Writer!: The Story of E. B. White* by Melissa Sweet: The author mixes White's personal letters, photos, and stories to tell the story from his birth to his death.	

Discuss your answers with a partner.

©Perfection Learning® • No Reproduction Permitted

First Read: Summarizing Plot

Renowned author Gary Paulsen has written more than 175 books for young adults. As a child, he lived many places—with his grandmother, with his parents, and even on the streets. In his writing, he explores the importance of relationships with friends, family, nature, and also with his many pets.

Objective: As you read the following, picture in your mind the events that are taking place. Stop when you come to the sentence "And then I met Dirk." Make a prediction about who Dirk is and how he might change Paulsen's life. Write your predictions in the My Thoughts column.

from
My Life in Dog Years
"Dirk the Protector"

by Gary Paulsen

	My Thoughts

1   For a time in my life I became a street kid. It would be nice to put it another way but what with the drinking at home and the difficulties it caused with my parents I couldn't live in the house.

5   I made a place for myself in the basement by the furnace and hunted and fished in the woods around the small town. But I had other needs as well—clothes, food, school supplies— and they required money. . . . All the conventional jobs like working in the markets or at the drugstore were gone and all I

10   could find was setting pins in the small bowling alley over the Four Clover Bar. . . .

Unfortunately it also put me in the streets at a time when there was what might be called a rough element. There weren't gangs then, not exactly, but there were groups of boys

15   who more or less hung out together and got into trouble. . . .

These groups were predatory, and they hunted the streets at night.

I became their favorite target in this dark world. Had the town been larger I might have hidden from them, or found
20 different routes. But there was only a small uptown section and it was impossible for me to avoid them. They would catch me walking a dark street and surround me and with threats and blows steal what money I had earned that night.

I tried fighting back but there were usually several of them.
25 I couldn't win. Because I was from "the wrong side of the tracks" I didn't think I could go to the authorities. It all seemed hopeless.

And then I met Dirk.

The bowling alley was on a second floor and had a window
30 in back of the pit area. When all the lanes were going, the heat from the pin lights made the temperature close to a hundred degrees. Outside the window a ladder led to the roof. One fall evening, instead of leaving work through the front door, I made my way out the window and up the ladder onto
35 the roof. I hoped to find a new way home to escape the boys who waited for me. That night one of the league bowlers had bowled a perfect game—300—and in celebration had bought the pit boys hamburgers and Cokes. I had put the burger and Coke in a bag to take back to my basement. The bag had
40 grease stains and smelled of toasted buns, and my mouth watered as I moved from the roof of the bowling alley to the flat roof over the hardware store, then down a fire escape that led to a dark alcove off an alley.

There was a black space beneath the stairs and as I reached
45 the bottom and my foot hit the ground I heard a low growl. It was not loud, more a rumble that seemed to come from the

earth and so full of menace that it stopped me cold, my foot frozen in midair.

I raised my foot and the growl stopped.

50　　I lowered my foot and the growl came again. My foot went up and it stopped.

I stood there, trying to peer through the steps of the fire escape. For a time I couldn't see more than a dark shape crouched back in the gloom. There was a head and a back, and

55　as my eyes became accustomed to the dark I could see that it had scraggly, scruffy hair and two eyes that glowed yellow.

We were at an impasse. I didn't want to climb up the ladder again but if I stepped to the ground it seemed likely I would be bitten. I hung there for a full minute before I

60　thought of the hamburger. I could use it as a decoy and get away.

The problem was the hamburger smelled *so* good and I was *so* hungry.

I decided to give the beast under the stairs half a burger.

65　I opened the sack, unwrapped the tinfoil and threw half the sandwich under the steps, then jumped down and ran for the end of the alley. I was just getting my stride, legs and arms pumping, pulling air with a heaving chest, when I rounded the corner and ran smack into the latest group of boys who were

70　terrorizing me.

There were four of them, led by a thug—he and two of the others would ultimately land in prison—named, absurdly, "Happy" Santun.

Happy was built like an upright freezer and had just about

75　half the intelligence but this time it was easy. I'd run right into him.

"Well—lookit here. He came to *us* this time . . ."

Over the months I had developed a policy of flee or die—run as fast as I could to avoid the pain, and to hang on to my
80 hard-earned money. Sometimes it worked, but most often they caught me.

This time, they already had me. I could have handed over the money, taken a few hits and been done with it, but something in me snapped and I hit Happy in the face with
85 every ounce of strength in my puny body.

He brushed off the blow easily and I went down in a **welter** of blows and kicks from all four of them. I curled into a ball to protect what I could. I'd done this before, many times, and knew that they would stop sometime—although I
90 suspected that because I'd hit Happy it might take longer than usual for them to get bored hitting me.

Instead there was some commotion that I didn't understand and the kicks stopped coming. There was a snarling growl that seemed to come from the bowels of the
95 earth, followed by the sound of ripping cloth, screams, and then the fading slap of footsteps running away.

For another minute I remained curled up, then opened my eyes to find that I was alone.

But when I rolled over I saw the dog. It was the one that
100 had been beneath the stairs. **Brindled**, patches of hair gone, one ear folded over and the other standing straight and notched from fighting. He didn't seem to be any particular breed. Just big and **rangy**, right on the edge of ugly, though

---

welter: a chaotic mass or jumble
Brindled: having faint dark streaks or spots on a gray or light brown background
rangy: long-legged

I would come to think of him as beautiful. He was Airedale
105 crossed with hound crossed with alligator.

Alley dog. Big, tough, mean alley dog. As I watched he spit
cloth—it looked like blue jeans—out of his mouth.

"You bit Happy, and sent them running?" I asked.

He growled, and I wasn't sure if it was with menace, but
110 he didn't bare his teeth and didn't seem to want to attack me.
Indeed, he had saved me.

"Why?" I asked. "What did I do to deserve . . . oh, the
hamburger."

I swear, he pointedly looked at the bag with the second
115 half of hamburger in it.

"You want more?"

He kept staring at the bag and I thought, Well, he sure as
heck deserves it. I opened the sack and gave him the rest of
it, which disappeared down his throat as if a hole had opened
120 into the universe.

He looked at the bag.

"That's it," I said, brushing my hands together. "The whole
thing."

A low growl.

125 "You can rip my head off—there still isn't any more
hamburger." I removed the Coke and handed him the bag,
which he took, held on the ground with one foot and deftly
ripped open with his teeth.

"See? Nothing." I was up by this time and I started to walk
130 away. "Thanks for the help . . ."

He followed me. Not close, perhaps eight feet back, but
matching my speed. It was now nearly midnight and I was tired

and sore from setting pins and from the kicks that had landed on my back and sides.

135   "I don't have anything to eat at home but crackers and peanut butter and jelly," I told him. I kept some food in the basement of the apartment building, where I slept near the furnace.

    He kept following and, truth be known, I didn't mind. I
140 was still half scared of him but the memory of him spitting out bits of Happy's pants and the sound of the boys running off made me smile. When I arrived at the apartment house I held the main door open and he walked right in. I opened the basement door and he followed me down the steps into the
145 furnace room.

    I turned the light on and could see that my earlier judgment had been correct. He was scarred from fighting, skinny and flat sided with patches of hair gone. His nails were worn down from scratching concrete.

150   "Dirk," I said. "I'll call you Dirk." I had been trying to read a detective novel and there was a tough guy in it named Dirk. "You look like somebody named Dirk."

    And so we sat that first night. I had two boxes of Ritz crackers I'd hustled somewhere, a jar of peanut butter and
155 another one of grape jelly, and a knife from the kitchen upstairs. I would smear a cracker, hand it to him—he took each one with great care and gentleness—and then eat one myself. We did this, back and forth, until both boxes were empty and my stomach was bulging; then I fell asleep on the old outdoor
160 lounge I used for furniture.

My Thoughts

FIRST RESPONSE: KEY IDEAS AND DETAILS

In your response journal, write a summary of your predictions about Dirk after reading the line "And then I met Dirk." In your response, answer these questions: *Were your predictions correct? How does this line foreshadow what happens in the rest of the story?*

Focus on Summarizing Plot

In this excerpt, the narrator tells the story of a hopeless situation suddenly changed by a mutt named Dirk. The memoir follows the traditional structure of a narrative with a series of events or episodes. Use the chart below to organize key details of the events for each stage of the story.

Exposition—beginning events that set up the setting, situation, and characters
Key Details:

Rising Action—events that create conflict and build suspense
Key Details:

Climax—turning point of the story; moment of greatest conflict
Key Details:

Falling Action—events immediately after the climax; the direct effects of the climax
Key Details:

Resolution—ties up loose ends
Key Details:

▼Write Use your details from above to write a summary of Paulsen's story about Dirk. Here are a couple of tips for writing a good summary.

CONNECT TO ESSENTIAL QUESTION

How are friendships with pets similar to and different from human friendships?

- A good summary reflects the facts of the story. It does not include personal opinions and judgments about whether the story is interesting or boring.

- Use transitional phrases to indicate the order of events. Examples of transitional words include *at the beginning, first, next, later, after, finally, in the end.*

- Summaries focus on major events, not minor details. Do not include minor descriptions of setting or characters.

Second Read: Analyzing Theme

Paulsen's memoir about Dirk is an informational text. In most cases, we study informational texts to discover a central idea—a statement specific to the text that relates what the text is mostly about. Memoirs, however, have more in common with literature than they do with nonfiction, such as a textbook or a newspaper article. For that reason, we determine a theme of the text instead of a central idea.

Objective: The theme of a literary text is a universal truth that is developed and supported by the characters and conflicts. With a partner, read the excerpt aloud. As you read, underline details about characters and conflicts that provide insight into possible themes.

TECH-CONNECT

Research to learn about animal shelters in your area. Are there any immediate needs? Consider volunteering or donating items to a local animal shelter or humane society.

Focus on Analyzing Theme

The theme(s) of a narrative text
- can be stated as a sentence that expresses a general, universal truth explored by the author.

- can be applied to many situations and people.

- is reflected by the characters, conflict, and resolution of the conflicts.

- is usually inferred rather than directly stated.

- a single text can have multiple themes

The theme of narrative text **is not**
- a plot event.

- a topic (love, friendship, family).

- so specific that it cannot be applied to other texts.

©Perfection Learning® • No Reproduction Permitted

Authors use characters, conflicts, and plot to communicate themes. Understanding how the conflict is resolved is important to determining the theme. Fill in the following graphic organizer. Use the questions to guide you in determining the theme of the excerpt.

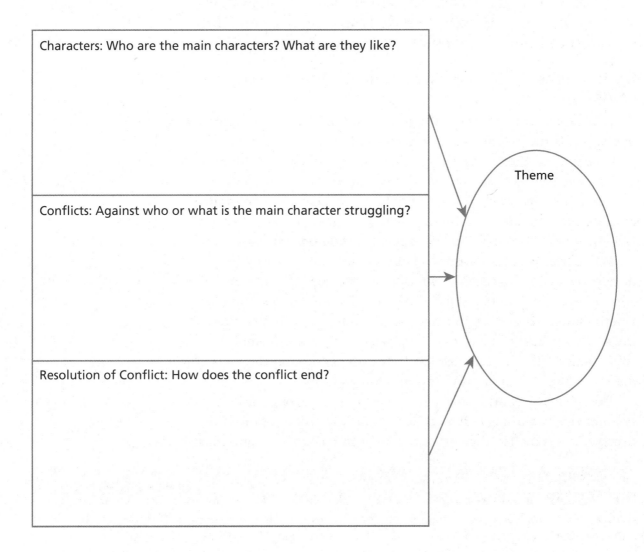

Characters: Who are the main characters? What are they like?

Conflicts: Against who or what is the main character struggling?

Resolution of Conflict: How does the conflict end?

Theme

Speak and Listen Share your answers to the organizer above with a partner. Use the following questions to evaluate your partner's theme.

- Is the theme supported throughout the story's beginning, middle, and end?

- Is the theme supported by the characters, conflicts, and resolution?

- Is the theme a complete sentence?

- Can you think of another work with a similar theme? (If you can, this means your theme is universal.)

Third Read: Identifying How Word Choice Reveals Point of View

Objective: Read the text a third time. As you read, underline words and phrases that help you infer the author's feelings toward Dirk and Happy. Next to the underlined words and phrases, draw an emoji that communicates the author's beliefs and feelings.

Focus on Identifying How Word Choice Reveals Point of View

Like most memoirs, this text is written in first-person point of view. This means the narrator is the main character in the story. However, the term *point of view* also means "a position or perspective from which something is considered or evaluated." The author's point of view is his or her opinion of the characters and events in the narrative. Authors reveal their perspective or point of view through their choice of words, details, and descriptions.

When evaluating an author's point of view by analyzing his or her word choices, consider what the words imply and their connotations, or emotional meaning. For example, notice the line where Paulsen describes the boys as "predatory . . . they hunted the streets at night" (lines 16–17). What do these words imply? What images do you think of? Paulsen is implying that the boys are more like wild animals than human teenagers.

Complete the chart below to gain a clearer sense of Paulsen's point of view regarding Dirk and Happy and the other boys in the excerpt. You may use any part of the excerpt to complete your chart.

Words that describe Happy and the other boys	What is Paulsen's point of view of Happy and the other boys?
These groups were predatory, and they hunted the streets at night. (lines 16–17)	They are like wild animals. They are less than human.
led by a thug—he and two of the others would ultimately land in prison (lines 71–72)	

©Perfection Learning® • No Reproduction Permitted

Words that describe Dirk	What is Paulsen's point of view of Dirk?
it had scraggly, scruffy hair and two eyes that glowed yellow (line 56)	

Speak and Listen With a partner, share your answers to the chart above. Then discuss these questions.

- How does Paulsen's point of view of Dirk change during the story?
- Which lines from the text are the strongest evidence for his changing point of view?

Write Write a paragraph analyzing Paulsen's points of view toward Dirk and Happy and the other boys. Use textual evidence to support your ideas. At the end, discuss your point of view toward the same topic. Is your point of view similar to or different from Paulsen's? Explain your answer.

Language: Consistent Verb Tenses

Memoir, biography, and autobiography describe events that happened in the past. Thus, writers mainly use past tense verbs. The underlined verbs in the following passage are in past tense.

The bowling alley <u>was</u> on a second floor and <u>had</u> a window in back of the pit area. When all the lanes were going, the heat from the pin lights <u>made</u> the temperature close to a hundred degrees. Outside the window a ladder <u>led</u> to the roof. One fall evening, instead of leaving work through the front door, I <u>made</u> my way out the window and up the ladder onto the roof. I <u>hoped</u> to find a new way home to escape the boys who <u>waited</u> for me.

continued on next page

When writing about events that happened before other events in the past, use the past perfect tense. Past perfect usually includes the verb "had" and a past tense verb.

> Example: I **had worked** at the bowling alley for a few months when the boys <u>started</u> harassing me.

The phrase *had worked* indicates that he started working at the bowling alley before the boys started picking on him.

When writing about life events, make sure you are consistently using past tense verbs. Avoid switching into the present tense.

- Incorrect: The problem <u>was</u> the hamburger smelled so good and I <u>am</u> so hungry. (mixing past tense and present tense)

- Correct: The problem <u>was</u> the hamburger smelled so good and I <u>was</u> so hungry. (both past tense)

The following paragraph describes events that happened in the past. Cross out any verbs that switch tenses and write the correct verb above it.

Sixth grade was an exciting year for me. I am very excited

to move up from elementary school to middle school. I loved

traveling from class to class instead of having every class in the

same room with the same teacher. However, some of my friends

from elementary are not in my classes. This turns out okay because

I made many new friends. I loved being able to participate in more

activities like sports and music.

Project-Based Assessments

Milestone Map

In Paulsen's memoir, *My Life in Dog Years,* each chapter is named to reflect the important role a dog has played in the author's life. Map some important milestones in your own life. A milestone is a life-changing event. Examples include changing schools, moving from one state to another, and gaining or losing an important person in your life.

Use technology to create a poster divided into sections for different milestones in your life. Make sure you have at least four sections describing four milestones. Each section must include:

1. A TITLE: A well-constructed theme statement that expresses a universal truth about life. This is what you learned from the milestone. Put this TITLE at the top of your section. You may wish to use a different font to make it stand out.
2. The WHEN: date
3. The WHERE: setting or location
4. A list of important subjects, events, and people that begin with a verb in the past tense.
5. An image, photo, or sketch that reflects the milestone of that section.

An example of one milestone:

"An Unwanted Change Brings Unexpected Connections" (Title)

September 2017 (When)

Elkhorn Ridge Middle School, Omaha, Nebraska, (Where)

- moved from Michigan (list of important events)

- played basketball with school team

- lived near aunts, uncles and cousins

continued on next page

Use the following guidelines for your milestone map.	
To receive the highest score (4.0), the milestone map must meet all of these criteria.	Your milestone map includes • four milestones in four different sections of the poster. • titles that express general, universal truths about people and events in the milestones. • the when, the where, and the list of important subjects, events, and people. • a graphic or picture that represents each milestone. • correct spelling, grammar, and punctuation.

Memoir

Write a memoir about something significant that has happened to you. You may want to write about a relationship with a special pet or you may want to focus on a person or an experience. Here are some qualities of a good memoir.

- It focuses and reflects on the relationship between the writer and a particular person, place, animal, or object.

- It explains the significance of the relationship.

- It is limited to a particular phase, time period, place, or recurring behavior in order to fully develop the focus.

- It makes the subject of the memoir come alive.

- It maintains a first person point of view.

Use the following steps:

1. Brainstorm for an event that shows an important relationship with a pet, a person, a place, or an object. Focus in on a small part of the relationship. For example, don't write about three years of events during a friendship; instead, focus on an event, such as the day you met your best friend.

2. Write. Tell what happened. Write freely without being worried about errors. You may not remember every detail, such as every word that was said. When writing dialogue between people in your memoir, use your memory and imagination to fill the words, but stay true to the main ideas of the conversation.

3. Revise. Reread and cross out details that distract from the central relationship and events. Add details and description in places where the writing seems to drag or becomes boring.

©Perfection Learning® • No Reproduction Permitted

Use the following guidelines for your memoir.	
To receive the highest score (4.0), the memoir must meet all of these criteria.	Your memoir • focuses on a small part of a relationship with a person, place, animal, or object. • is written in first person point of view. • includes interesting details and descriptions that keep the action moving. • includes correct spelling, grammar, and punctuation.

On Your Own: Integrating Ideas

1. Search for Gary Paulsen online to learn more about his life and books.

2. If you enjoyed reading about Dirk and want to find out what happened to him, read the rest of the story in the book *My Life in Dog Years.* You can also learn about the other dogs in Paulsen's life.

3. Paulsen has written other unforgettable memoirs worth reading, including *How Angel Peterson Got His Name, Woodsong, Winterdance: The Fine Madness of Running the Iditarod* and *Guts.* Choose and enjoy one that appeals to your interests.

4. One of Paulsen's many humorous books is entitled *The Schernoff Discoveries.* In this hilarious book, the narrator, who remains unnamed, navigates the perils of high school with the help of his only friend, the genius and supergeek Howard Schernoff. The reader is led to believe that the narrator is Paulsen himself. Read it for yourself to decide.

5. Conduct research to discover a true story about a dog making a difference in your local community. You may learn how dogs are being used for pet therapy in hospitals and nursing homes, how dogs are trained as support animals for children and adults with disabilities, or how dogs support soldiers and others experiencing post-traumatic stress disorder. Write a summary of the story and share it with your class.

Connect To Testing

Questions on reading tests will require you to write summaries, determine theme, and identify point of view. Often a second part of the question will test your ability to identify textual evidence that supports the answer to the first part.

1. **Part A**: Which of the following details would most likely be included in a condensed or short summary of the excerpt in this chapter? Select **three**.

   A. Paulsen was out on the streets when predatory groups were out.

   B. Paulsen worked at a small bowling alley over a bar.

   C. Paulsen gave half of the hamburger to the dog he met beneath the stairs.

   D. Dirk came to Paulsen's rescue and chased the bullies away.

   E. Happy was built like an upright freezer and had just about half the intelligence.

   F. Paulsen's parents had a drinking problem and did not provide for their son's basic needs.

   Part B: Explain why the other detail(s) would not be included in a short summary. Write your answer below.

EXPLANATION

- Remember that a summary contains important events and excludes minor details.

- Part A: Choices A, C, and D are all major events or important details.

- Part B: The other choices are supporting details and may not be included in a short summary. The three chosen details reflect important events.

©Perfection Learning® • No Reproduction Permitted

2. **Part A:** Which of the following details are part of the rising action in the narrative? Be sure to select **all** of the correct details.

   A. Paulsen hears a growl below the stairs and makes a plan to get away.

   B. Paulsen was unable to live in his parents' house.

   C. Paulsen names the dog "Dirk."

   D. Paulsen runs smack into the latest group of four boys who were terrorizing him, and Paulsen hits Happy in the face.

   E. Paulsen spends a night in the pits at the alley, then heads home with a Coke and a burger.

   F. The dog rips open the empty bag open with his teeth.

   Part B: Refer to the plot chart from your first read and label where the other details appear in the narrative—exposition, climax, falling action, or resolution.

3. **Part A:** Which *three* details include the strongest evidence for the theme: *A friendship with a pet can change your life.*

   A. Three of the four attackers end up in prison later in life.

   B. Paulsen and Dirk take turns eating crackers on that first night, and Paulsen falls asleep with Dirk athis side.

   C. Paulsen does not think he can talk to the authorities about the street gangs, and believes that his situation is impossible.

   D. Paulsen works a job as a pin setter in a bowling alley where the temperature can reach 100 degrees.

   E. Paulsen realizes that the dog bit the attackers, scaring them away.

   F. Paulsen hunts and fishes in the wood around his small town.

continued on next page

Part B: Write a constructed response to answer the following question:

How does Gary Paulsen reveal that *a friendship with a pet can change your life* in his story about Dirk? Use details about the events and characters to support your answer.

4. What does young Gary Paulsen have in common with Dirk, and how might this have impacted their relationship? Write a well-developed answer in paragraph form below.

©Perfection Learning® • No Reproduction Permitted

Chapter 3

Identifying an Argument

Preview Concepts

How would you define the word *argument*?

Think about a time when you disagreed with someone in your family. What did you claim? What did the other person claim? A claim is an opinion or point of view, such as *I need a new cell phone.*

My claim:

His/her claim:

What reasons did you give to support your side of the argument, or your claim? What reasons did the other side give? Write them below.

My reasons:

His/her reasons:

Why is it important to have reasons to support an argument?

CHAPTER GOALS

In this chapter you will:

- use context clues and a dictionary to determine the denotative and connotative meanings of words.
- identify the central claim, reasons, and evidence in an argument.
- use quotation marks in direct quotations.

PREVIEW ACADEMIC VOCABULARY

claim

connotative meaning

denotative meaning

evidence

reasons

Making Connections

Read the following quotation about social media. Think about the claim the author is making.

> It is widely accepted that technology allows us to communicate quickly and frequently with more people than ever in history. We can stay connected with friends who have moved away, across the state, country, or world.

Reseach how your classmates use social media. Form a small group with three other students. List the forms of social media your group members regularly use. Keep in mind that there may be a wide range of responses, as families may choose to allow their students limited access to some applications and sites. Show respect for differences in preferences about the use of social media.

©Perfection Learning® • No Reproduction Permitted

Discuss the following questions. Summarize your discussion below.

1. What are the advantages and disadvantages of connecting with friends through technology?

2. Do you predict that the number of people you connect with via social media will increase as you move on to high school? college? adulthood? Why do you think they will they increase or decrease?

MAKING CONNECTIONS

In this chapter you will analyze an argument, identifying claims, reasons, and evidence.

©Perfection Learning® • No Reproduction Permitted

First Read: Understanding Word Meanings

The text in this chapter is an informational article about friendship from an online magazine.

Objective: As you read this article, think about the main point or claim the author is making. When you see a word that is in **bold** print, write what you know or can infer about that word's meaning in the My Thoughts column.

©Perfection Learning® • No Reproduction Permitted

excerpt
Why We Need Friends Now More Than Ever
by Lori Chandler

1   In an age **obsessed** with popularity, where how many

friends you have on social media has become a bragging

right, one has to stop and wonder: What are the value of

friends, and can't we have too many? Many of us are familiar

5   with Dunbar's Number, which states that we can only maintain

150 relationships in our minds at any given time in our lives.

But many experts say we are better off with a quality-over-

quantity attitude, which may come as a relief to those of us

who, after the *gotta-collect-'em-all* approach of our 20s, have

10   entered a phase of wanting fewer, but closer friends.

As a recent *Quartz* piece explained via the work of Tim

Kasser, people have two **predominant** attitudes toward

friendships: one where popularity (being liked or admired

by many) is the goal, and another where affinity (or striving

15   for deeper relationships) was preferred. As it turns out, those

who longed for popularity were "less happy, less healthy,

more depressed, and used more drugs." And those who put

in the time for deeper, more meaningful relationships had

the opposite finding: They were happier, healthier, and less

20   depressed. In fact the Mayo Clinic suggests that having close

friends can increase your happiness, self-confidence, and sense

of purpose, while reducing stress. They can also help you cope

with **traumas** and illness: In a 2006 study, women with breast

cancer who were without close friends were four times more

25   likely to die as a result of breast cancer than women with 10 or

more close friends.

Whatever our carefully **curated** social media profiles would have you believe, we are actually growing more isolated as a culture. We have fewer close friends than we did 30 years

30 ago. In 1985, most people had three good friends they could confide in, and now the "number of discussion partners has gone from three to zero, with almost half of the population (43.6 percent) now reporting that they discuss important matters with either no one or with only one other person." So

35 we know having friends is important to our health, and that a vast number of us don't have anyone to call on—should we just start **hoarding** as many friends as possible?

It's been well-documented that as adults leave their 20s behind for their 30s, their social circles tend to shrink. Is this

40 because so many choose to get married and have kids in their 30s, or is it that we lose our tolerance for flakey fairweather friends in favor of the evergreen sort? Probably both. As we become more of ourselves, we become less dependent on our friends to tell us what we're like. Cutting the fat is

45 an important part of growing up—who needs **superfluous** relationships, where you spread yourself so thin that you don't spend enough quality time with the people who really matter? Social connection, one study said, is "a leading factor in the promotion of health, well-being, and longevity, [and] requires

50 social knowledge and the capacity to cultivate intimacy." The more sophisticated our social knowledge, then, the more meaningful our friendships. The older and wiser we become, the more value we place on people who we know will be there for us.

My Thoughts

©Perfection Learning® • No Reproduction Permitted

What central claim about friendship is the author making? In your response journal, finish this statement: I think the central claim of the article is _____ because _____.

TECH-CONNECT

Send your claim statement from the First Response activity to polleverywhere. com. Is your sentence similar to or different from your classmates' statements?

Focus on Understanding Word Meanings

Words have a dictionary meaning, or denotative meaning, and a connotative meaning. A word's connotative meaning includes the emotions and associations connected to the word. Depending on our experiences, words may have a positive, negative, or neutral connotation.

Take a closer look at the words the author chose. Work with a partner to fill in the chart below.

Word	Denotative Meaning (Dictionary definition of the word. Include the part of speech as used in the text.)	Connotative Meaning (Implied emotional meaning of the word. Note if the connotation is positive [+], negative [-]or neutral [=]
obsessed		
predominant		
traumas		
curated		
hoarding		
superfluous		

continued on next page

Study these phrases from the article. Based on the context, what does each phrase mean? Return to the excerpt to find context clues that hint at the meaning of the phrases.

Phrase	Context Clues	Meaning
gotta-collect-'em-all		
flakey fairweather friends		
the evergreen sort		
cutting the fat		

Speak and Listen Share your answers to the charts above with a partner. If you disagree with your partner's answers, explain the reason for your answers respectfully. Listen carefully to understand your partner's reasoning too.

Second Read: Identifying Claims

Listen as your teacher reads the article or read the article aloud with a partner.

Objective: As you listen, write the key idea of each paragraph in the My Thoughts sidebar.

> **REFLECT**
>
> Do you think that the word *argument* has a positive or a negative connotation? Why?

©Perfection Learning® • No Reproduction Permitted

Focus on Identifying Claims

In order to convince people of an opinion, a writer constructs an argument. Study the following visual representation of an argument and the definitions below.

An Argument

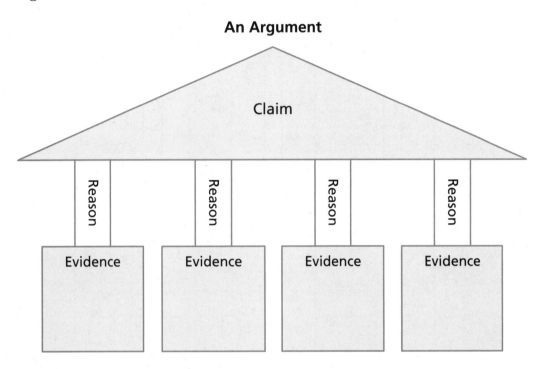

Claim	Opinion that the writer is trying to prove to the readers
Reasons	Statements that explain **why** the audience should agree with the claim
Evidence	Facts, data, testimony, expert opinion, and examples that support the reasons

Here is an example of an argument:

Claim: Sixth graders should have open and free access to technology.

Reason: Having access to technology will accelerate learning.

Evidence: According to the U.S. Department of Education, "Online learning opportunities and the use of open educational resources and other technologies can increase educational productivity by accelerating the rate of learning."

Here are some questions to help you determine the claim in the text you read.

1. Identify the topic of the article. Write it below.

continued on next page

2. Look at each paragraph and identify the key idea. Use the notes you took during the second read. Write the key ideas below.

Paragraph 1:

Paragraph 2:

Paragraph 3:

Paragraph 4:

    ©Perfection Learning® • No Reproduction Permitted

3. Looking at the key ideas, what do they have in common?

4. Putting all of this together, what is the author's central claim?

CONNECT TO ESSENTIAL QUESTION

According to this article, what are some reasons for breaking or ending friendships, and when are these breakups likely to occur?

Third Read: Identifying Reasons and Evidence

Objective: Read the article a third time. Focus on the first two paragraphs.

- In paragraph 1: Underline a sentence that expresses the central claim of the article.

- In paragraph 2: Identify the qualities related to being popular with a P and the qualities related to closer and deeper relationships with a D (deeper). Think about how this evidence supports the central claim.

Focus on Identifying Reasons and Evidence

The second paragraph provides support for the claim made in the first paragraph. How does the author support her claim with reasons and evidence?

1. Rewrite the central claim below.

continued on next page

2. In the second paragraph, the author provides evidence about people who want to be popular and those who prefer close, deep friendships.

   A. What evidence was given related to being popular, or having many friends?

   B. What evidence was given related to having a few close friends?

3. Based on this evidence, the reader can infer reasons why having a few close friends is better than having many friends. Write a reason that summarizes and explains the evidence explained in question 2.

©Perfection Learning® • No Reproduction Permitted

Write Write a paragraph explaining the claim, the reason, and the evidence the author explains in paragraphs 1 and 2 of the excerpt. Return to your answers to the questions on pages 53 and 54 to help you write. Use the following sentence stems to get started:

- In paragraph 1, the author claims that . . . .

- Paragraph 2 supports the claim with the reason . . . .

- Evidence that backs up this reason includes . . . .

REFLECT

Why is it important to learn about Internet safety when using social media? Consider what you have learned about the dangers of the Internet from your teachers and family. What can you do to encourage someone to seek help if an online friend makes him or her feel unsafe?

Language: Quotation Marks with Direct Quotations

The author of the article, Lori Chandler, uses several resources to build her argument. She had to make a decision about not only what details and facts to use to support her claim but also about *how* to use them. Writers have to choose between paraphrasing information in their own words or using direct quotations when including evidence as support for their claim. Using direct quotations correctly will help you avoid plagiarism, which is taking someone else's work and passing it off as your own.

Follow these guidelines when using direct quotations.

- Quotation marks always come in pairs. Use them at the beginning and at the end of the quote.

TECH-CONNECT

Go to ncpc.org to learn more about Internet safety.

Example: *As it turns out, those who longed for popularity were "less happy, less healthy, more depressed, and used more drugs."*

Capitalize the first letter of a quotation if the quote is a complete sentence. Do not capitalize the first letter when using only part of a sentence from the original source.

Social connection, one study said, is "a leading factor in the promotion of health, well-being, and longevity, [and] requires social knowledge and the capacity to cultivate intimacy."

- If a quotation is interrupted mid-sentence, do not begin the second part of the quote with a capital letter.

- Overall, quotations should be short and used only when the original source includes striking and memorable language. There should be a reason you are using the exact quote rather than summarizing and paraphrasing.

Finish the sentence starters on the next page with direct quotations from the text in this chapter. Use capitalization, punctuation, and quotation marks correctly.

continued on next page

1. The author says that

2. In the article, the author Lori Chandler writes,

3. The article explains Dunbar's Number as

Project-Based Assessments

Argument Analysis

Dig deeper into the third and fourth paragraphs of the excerpt. Identify the claims, evidence, and reasons in paragraphs 3 and 4. Remember that sometimes claims and reasons have to be inferred. Write several paragraphs explaining the argument developed in these two paragraphs and how they support the central claim of the entire article, which you identified during this chapter. Use at least two direct quotations to support your conclusions about the text.

Use the following guidelines for your analysis.	
To receive the highest score (4.0), the analysis must meet all of these criteria.	Your analysis • discusses the claims, reasons, and evidence in the third and fourth paragraphs of the article. • explains how the ideas in these paragraphs relate to the central claim of the first two paragraphs. • includes two correctly punctuated direct quotations. • uses correct spelling, grammar, and punctuation.

Ridiculous Arguments

Write an argument in support of a ridiculous claim. Here are some possible claims:

• The school mascot should be replaced with SpongeBob SquarePants.

• Each area of our school should be equipped with a napping station, with comfortable cots, pillows, and blankets for students to use upon request.

• The existing school cafeteria should be replaced with catering from Papa John's, Taco John's, Jimmy John's, McDonald's, and Panda Express.

©Perfection Learning® • No Reproduction Permitted

- Students should be allowed to bring their pets to school.

- Students should be allowed to bring their friends from other schools with them to school.

- Each school day should begin with a pledge of allegiance to junk food.

Your argument should include the following:
- a clearly worded claim

- three supporting reasons that tell why your audience should accept your claim

- two types of evidence such as facts, statistics, testimonials, or expert opinions

As much as possible, use actual facts to support your ridiculous argument. Your claim may be crazy, but the supporting evidence might be accurate. For example, studies supporting the health benefits of having a pet and of taking naps could be used to support the ridiculous claims above. Keep a record of your sources: title of the article or website, author's name, and date. Support your reasons with evidence that paraphrases and directly quotes sources.

Use the following guidelines for your ridiculous argument.	
To receive the highest score (4.0), the argument must meet all of these criteria.	Your argument • includes a clear but ridiculous claim. • contains three reasons supported by two pieces of evidence. • correctly paraphrases sources or uses direct quotations to avoid plagiarism. • uses transitional words and phrases to show relationships between ideas. • includes correct spelling, grammar, and punctuation.

On Your Own: Integrating Ideas

1. Read *The Truth About Truman School* by Dori Halsted Butler. This book features numerous narrators who create a school website where anyone can post anything. Of course, given the chance, some students will say anything to hurt someone else. Do you think this could ever happen at your school?

2. Read a book about bullying. Ideas include *Wonder* by R. J. Palacio, *The Bully Book* by Eric Kahn Gale, or *Goodbye Stranger* by Rebecca Stead. Write a review of the book and post it to your class website.

Connect to Testing

Questions on reading tests will require you to define terms based on context and analyze claims, reasons, and evidence in arguments. Often a second part of the question will test your ability to identify strong evidence that supports the answer to the first part.

1. **Part A:** Which of the following best explains the central claim of the article?

   A. Most people can't keep track of more than 150 friends.

   B. Younger people have time to develop stronger and deeper friendships.

   C. Having a few close friends is better than having many shallow relationships.

   D. People who value popularity have more mental health issues.

   Part B: Which **two** excerpts from the article are evidence that supports the answer to Part A?

   A. *And those who put in the time for deeper, more meaningful relationships had the opposite finding: They were happier, healthier, and less depressed.*

   B. *or is it that we lose our tolerance for flakey fairweather friends in favor of the evergreen sort?*

   C. *What are the value of friends, and can we have too many?*

   D. *But many experts say we are better off with a quality-over-quantity attitude,*

2. Which of the following quotes about friendship best supports the central claim of the article?

   A. "In the end, we will remember not the words of our enemies, but the silence of our friends." —Dr. Martin Luther King Jr.

   B. "Sometimes me think, 'What is friend?' Then me say, 'Friend is someone to share last cookie with.' " —Cookie Monster

   C. "How many slams in an old screen door? Depends how loud you shut it. How many slices in a bread? Depends how thin you cut it. How much good inside a day? Depends how good you live 'em. How much love inside a friend? Depends how much you give 'em." —Shel Silverstein

   D. "It doesn't matter if you have five friends or five-thousand friends. When it all comes down to it, popularity means nothing. All that matters is that you know those five will be there holding your hand, as the five-thousand walk by." —Unknown

©Perfection Learning® • No Reproduction Permitted

3. **Part A:** Based on the claim, circle all of the following actions the author would be likely to support.

   A. spending hours talking to strangers on the Internet

   B. prioritizing and spending time with your closest friends

   C. encouraging a relative with a serious illness to lean on her friends for support

   D. being there for a friend in need, even when it is awkward or inconvenient

   E. "friending" a friend of a friend of a friend.

   Part B. For each action above, find a detail from the text that either supports it or disproves it.

   A.

   B.

   C.

   D.

   E.

Chapter 4

Comparing and Contrasting Ideas from Multiple Texts

Preview Concepts

Imagine your mom and dad are trying to convince you to try out for the school play. The method each uses may be different.

> Mom: "Being in the school play is a great way to learn confidence. It's important to be able to speak in front of people. Sure, you'll probably get nervous, but by overcoming those nerves you'll learn to try things that are difficult and not give up. Another reason to try out is that you'll be able to get to know different kids and make new friends."
>
> Dad: "When I was in 6th grade I tried out for the school play. It was about mannequins that come to life when the store is closed. In one scene I got to jump out of a box and scare the audience. On the night my parents came to the play, I popped out and my mom screamed so loud! The audience laughed for five minutes. It was awesome!"

Think about the methods your parents are using to accomplish their purpose.

How is your mom trying to convince you?

How is your dad trying to convince you?

Which parent's method relies more on emotions? Which one relies on logic?

CHAPTER GOALS

In this chapter you will

- analyze how key ideas are developed.
- determine and explain an author's point of view.
- integrate information from multiple sources to understand a topic or issue.
- compare and contrast different authors' presentations of ideas.
- use intensive pronouns correctly.

PREVIEW ACADEMIC VOCABULARY

intensive pronouns

point of view

Making Connections

Writers have many tools in their writing tool boxes to develop key ideas. Here are just a few possibilities.

- provide examples
- tell a story or anecdote
- provide reasons
- relate personal experiences
- define key terms
- explain facts and data

Which tool above best describes Mom's dialogue on the previous page? Which one describes Dad's dialogue?

Discuss your answers to the questions with a partner. Which parent did you find more convincing? Why?

MAKING CONNECTIONS

As you read the excerpt in this chapter, you will examine how an author uses details to express his point of view about friendship.

What other ways can a writer develop key ideas? List two more below.

First Read: Analyzing How Key Ideas Are Developed

The following is a personal essay on the topic of friendship published in *The New York Times Magazine*.

Objective: Place a star by important questions the author asks. Think about how the author tries to answer these questions. Does he use facts, stories and anecdotes, or data? Use the My Thoughts column to list any questions you have about the article.

excerpt
Reflections on True Friendship
by Andrew O'Hagan

	My Thoughts

1   Is childhood the golden era of friendship? And can you get those relationships back? The other day . . . I realized . . . the unspoken bond, the constant availability, the relentless promise that friendship is when you are 12. My great friend at

5   that age was Mark MacDonald. In those early, rain-soaked days on Scotland's west coast, Mark was my constant companion and my secret weapon: Whatever happened at home, there would always be Mark to brighten the day and spit with style . . . . We would be up at the crack of dawn to wander

10   over the fields, scan the beaches for coins, climb the hills together and sit in the graveyard comparing our plans for world domination . . . .

When I recently tried to find Mark again, he didn't appear to exist. . . . he seemed like a figment, or a fragile piece of

15   memory that crumbles when you turn it in your hands. . . . When I went back to Scotland recently, I drove to the square where we once lived, and I looked up at the window of my old house, remembering how I used to shine a **torch** from there to Mark's bedroom. Two flashes meant good night. Three flashes

20   meant see you tomorrow.

---

torch: a flashlight

©Perfection Learning® • No Reproduction Permitted

I wonder if technology has changed the meaning of friendship. My daughter is 12 and most things that happen to her are photographed. She and her friends get together and spend hours trying out poses, making videos, retouching

25 them, setting them to music and posting them on this or that social media network. I'm sure the girls are bonded in many of the traditional ways, but I also wonder if they'll ever lose sight of each other, which was always one of the possibilities of friendship, an aspect of its mystery. I think we always knew

30 we would move on in life and that our great friendships would be a matter of memory. I don't have a single photograph of Mark MacDonald. I don't think we were ever photographed together, and that adds to the notion that our friendship was a fiction. Social media is a vehicle of self-promotion, a means of

35 fixing an idea of yourself in the social sphere, without people actually knowing you at all. And that's a change: The thing about friendship used to be that the ideal was shared entirely by the pair of you, or sometimes by a group, yet it remained local, and that was part of its power.

40 It's the mindfulness I miss. A pair of excellent youngsters in my wider family have over 1,000 Facebook "friends" between them. They say they don't know half of them, and that some of them are "frenemies." The social network gives them the option of corralling people into "close friends" or

45 "acquaintances," and, naturally, they always have the option of clicking "unfriend." But are the majority of these people friends or are they just names? You can know everything that's going on in people's lives without knowing a single thing going on in their hearts. But is that friendship? . . .

50   "Friendship is the hardest thing in the world to explain," the late Muhammad Ali is thought to have said. "It's not something you learn in school. But if you haven't learned the meaning of friendship, you really haven't learned anything." And that is why I miss my old friend Mark. There

55 was something there that stood outside of achievement or romance, money or technology, religion or reputation. As I say, I was never photographed with Mark MacDonald and I never hugged him or bought him lunch either. But sometimes in a dark hour I'll look up and imagine I see him, not far distant, a

60 living guarantee that there will always be someone in life who really knows who you are. When all the machines are off and when all the chips are down, I see his light. Three flashes.

FIRST RESPONSE: KEY IDEAS AND DETAILS

This article included details about middle school users of technology. Do you think the descriptions of the author's daughter and her friends and the two young relatives with more than 1,000 Facebook friends is typical for students at your middle school? Write an answer in your response journal. Explain your answer.

TECH-CONNECT

Research Scotland's west coast. Limit your search to images and videos to build an understanding of the country where the author grew up.

Focus on Analyzing How Key Ideas Are Developed

Writers often introduce ideas by asking a question. Return to the excerpt and notice the questions you starred. Write those questions in the chart on the next page. A question for paragraph 2 has been added for you. Then paraphrase the question and add some related questions. Then turn to page 66 for more directions on completing the chart.

Paragraph 1 questions:	My paraphrase of the questions and related questions:

The author develops these questions by _____ .

One sentence that supports this:

Paragraph 2 question: Has technology changed the meaning of friendship?	My paraphrase of the question and related questions:

The author develops these questions by _____ .

One sentence that supports this:

Paragraph 3 question:	My paraphrase of the question and related questions:

The author develops these questions by _____ .

One sentence that supports this:

continued on next page

Writers develop their key ideas in a text in various ways. Here is a list of a few:

- providing examples
- telling a story or anecdote
- providing reasons and evidence
- relating personal experiences
- defining key terms

Determine how the author develops answers to the questions you added to the chart on page 65. Use the list of techniques above to complete the blanks in the chart. Then quote a sentence that provides evidence to support your listed technique. (Some paragraphs may use more than one technique from the list.)

Write Which of the author's techniques do you think was the most effective in sharing his ideas about friendship? Write your answer in your response journal.

REFLECT

Why is it important to use a variety of methods to develop an idea in your writing?

REFLECT ON ESSENTIAL QUESTION

How was the friendship between Mark and Andrew built? What possibly caused the friendship to break?

Second Read: Understanding Author's Point of View

Read the article a second time. With a partner, take turns reading a paragraph aloud.

Objective: As you read, focus on the two friendships being compared in this text: the friendship between the author and Mark and the friendships among the author's daughter and those among his young relatives and their friends. Identify how the author describes each and label them with A (author) and D (daughter/young relatives). Notice how the friendships are alike and different.

Focus on Understanding Author's Point of View

An author's point of view is his opinion or perspective on a topic. How an author develops key ideas reveals his point of view. In the first read, you identified questions in the text and analyzed the author's development of ideas introduced by the questions. In the first two paragraphs of the article, the author compares and contrasts his childhood friendships with his daughter's friendships. Understanding the similarities and differences he explains will help you understand the author's point of view.

Fill in the Venn diagram below with details about the two friendships from the article. Think about how friends spend their time together, the goals of their friendship, and the role of technology.

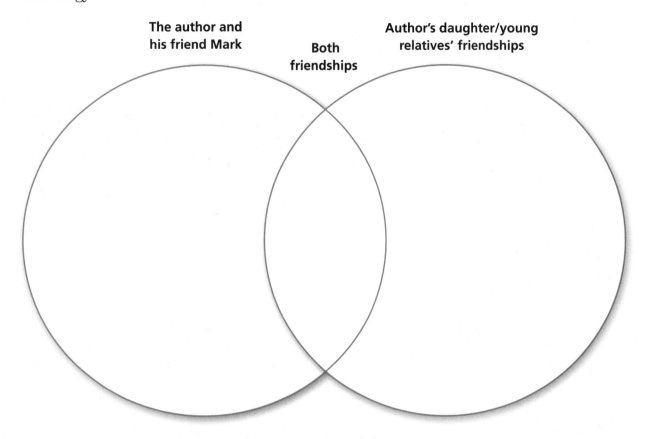

The author and his friend Mark

Both friendships

Author's daughter/young relatives' friendships

☾**Speak and Listen** Discuss your details in the Venn diagram above with a partner. If you change or add answers based on your discussion, use a different color pen. Discuss the following question: What is the author Andrew O'Hagan's point of view about friendship? What information on your Venn diagram supports your conclusion about the author's point of view?

▌Third Read: Comparing Ideas Presented in Multiple Texts

Read the article from this chapter a third time. Keep the key ideas in mind as you return to the text from Chapter 3, "Why We Need Friends Now More Than Ever," and read it.

Objective: Place a star by ideas in the text from Chapter 3 that relate to the author's point of view developed in the essay from this chapter, "Reflections on True Friendship."

©Perfection Learning® • No Reproduction Permitted

Focus on Comparing Ideas Presented in Multiple Texts

To *integrate* is "to bring together or incorporate parts into a whole." You have read two different articles about friendship in this unit. Now you will integrate ideas, combining them to build a deeper understanding of the impact of technology on friendship.

Complete the chart below using details from both articles. Use the last column to integrate the information from both sources. You may paraphrase or use direct quotations from the text.

Technology Topic	Chapter 3: "Why We Need Friends Now More Than Ever"	Chapter 4: "Reflections on True Friendship"	Integrating the Information
Social media's impact on friendship			
Having many friends vs. having a few close friends			
Qualities of a good friend			

The chart above helped you compare and contrast *what* the two texts said. The following exercise will help you analyze *how* the text says what it says.

Read the descriptions listed on the next page. Decide whether each one describes the text from Chapter 3, the text from Chapter 4, or both texts. On the line next to the description, write 3, 4 or both 3 and 4.

_____1. Contains a quotation

_____2. Relates a personal story

_____3. Includes information paraphrased from other resources

_____4. Shares opinion about social media

_____5. Author is emotionally close to the topic; text is written in first person

_____6. Includes evidence to show that social media has not brought people closer together

_____7. Contains statistical information and expert opinions about friendships

_____8. Explores childhood as an important time for developing close friends

_____9. Author is persuasive and controlled in regard to the topic; text develops an argument

(**Speak and Listen** Compare your answers to the chart and the list above. Then discuss these questions:

- Which article was easier to understand? Explain your answer.

- Which article was more opinionated? Explain your answer.

- If you were writing an argument on a contemporary topic for your social studies teacher, which article would your teacher be most likely to use as a model? Explain your answer.

Write Write a summary of what you have learned about how technology has impacted closeness and intimacy in friendship. Use direct quotations from both texts to support your conclusions.

Language: Intensive Pronouns

Writers use pronouns to avoid repetition of nouns. Pronouns replace nouns used earlier in a sentence or in a paragraph written about one person or topic. Without pronouns, sentences like this would be common: Mia ate Mia's sandwich for lunch and then Mia went back to class. Examples of pronouns include *I, he, she, they, him, her,* and *it.*

continued on next page

Intensive pronouns are a special kind of reflexive pronoun used to emphasize a noun or pronoun. While not essential to the overall meaning of a sentence, intensive pronouns usually come immediately after a "matching" noun or pronoun, emphasizing its importance. Do not use commas with intensive pronouns. Example: I myself would rather bring my lunch from home.

Personal Pronoun	Intensive Pronoun
I	myself
you	yourself/yourselves
he	himself
she	herself
it	itself
one	oneself
we	ourselves
they	themselves

Select five of the pairs above and write a sentence using an intensive pronoun. One example has been completed for you.

1. We are planning a school social by ourselves to raise money for a community garden.

2.

3.

4.

5.

6.

Project-Based Assessment

Interview and Presentation

Interview an adult in your life who has experienced a friendship that has continued for twenty years or more. Create a technology presentation, using an app or website approved by your teacher.

If possible, record parts of the interview to include in your presentation and include photos. Use questions such as the following. You may add questions of your own.

- How did you first meet?

- What are some activities you have enjoyed together in the past?

- What are some activities you have enjoyed together more recently?

- How do you stay in touch?

- In your opinion, why has this friendship continued for so many years?

- Is there anything else you would like to say about this friendship?

Use the following guidelines for your project.	
To receive the highest score (4.0), your project must meet all of these criteria.	Your project • uses the capabilities of the app or website effectively. • includes graphics to enhance the content of the presentation. • uses visually appealing text. • includes answers to all of the questions above. • includes a comparison and contrast section. • uses correct grammar, usage, punctuation, and spelling.

On Your Own: Integrating Ideas

1. Select one of the articles and create a technology project to showcase the most important ideas. You may use any technology available and approved by your teacher.

2. What would happen if Andrew O'Hagan and Mark McDonald were reunited? Would there be an awkward silence? Write the conversation they might have. Include a discussion of some of their adventures in the hills, beaches, or graveyard.

3. O'Hagan refers to his friend Mark as his, "constant companion and my secret weapon." Are there students in your school who may need a companion or a secret weapon because they are a victim of bullying? Learn how to help at www.stopbullying.gov.

Connect to Testing

Questions on reading assessments test your ability to identify key details in a text and to determine an author's point of view and how he or she introduces and develops ideas. Often a second part to the question will test your ability to identify strong evidence that supports the answer to the first part.

1. **Part A:** Both "Reflections on True Friendship" and "Why We Need Friends Now More Than Ever" share the point of view that friendship is

    A. built through sharing happy experiences.

    B. meaningful only when rooted in childhood.

    C. possible only with sophisticated social knowledge.

    D. important for our overall well-being.

    Part B: Find one piece of evidence from each of the texts that supports your answer to Part A. Write these sentences below.

2. **Part A:** The author develops the central idea of "Reflections on True Friendship" mainly by

    A. listing reasons why friendship is important to both him and his children.

    B. comparing and contrasting his childhood friendship with his daughter's friendships.

    C. explaining how his friendship with Mark has stayed active throughout the years.

    D. quotations from famous people.

©Perfection Learning® • No Reproduction Permitted

Part B: Which detail from "Reflections on True Friendship" best supports the answer to Part A?

A. *In those early, rain-soaked days on Scotland's west coast, Mark was my constant companion and my secret weapon.*

B. *You can know everything that's going on in people's lives without knowing a single thing going on in their hearts.*

C. *Friendship is the hardest thing in the world to explain.*

D. *I am sure the girls are bonded in many of the traditional ways, but I also wonder if they'll ever lose sight of each other, which was always one of the possibilities of friendship, an aspect of its mystery.*

3. **Part A:** Which of the following details from "Reflections on True Friendship" relates to the idea in the quote from Muhammad Ali: "Friendship is the hardest thing in the world to explain. It's not something you learn in school." Select **two**.

A. *The thing about friendship used to be that the ideal was shared entirely by the pair of you, or sometimes by a group, yet it remained local, and that was part of its power.*

B. *A pair of excellent youngsters in my wider family have over 1,000 Facebook "friends" between them.*

C. *The other day . . . I realized . . . the unspoken bond, the constant availability, the relentless promise that friendship is when you are 12.*

D. *Social media is a vehicle of self-promotion, a means of fixing an idea of yourself in the social sphere, without people actually knowing you at all.*

E. *My daughter is 12 and most things that happen to her are photographed.*

Part B: Using the answers from Part A, summarize the author's point of view about friendship.

Chapter 5

Understanding the Theme of a Play

Preview Concepts

Go on a human scavenger hunt. Fill in the chart below with the names of classmates who fit each category listed.

Find someone who:	Name of classmate	Title of play/podcast OR classmate comment about experience
Has performed in a Readers Theater		
Has seen a musical play		
Has seen a non-musical play		
Would like to study drama		
Has taken an acting class		
Has watched a live play on television		
Has read a play		
Has listened to a podcast of a radio play or story		

Now that you have talked with several classmates, work in a small group to discuss how reading a play is different from or the same as reading a story. Write your comments in your response journal.

CHAPTER GOALS

In this chapter you will:

- understand the theme of a play.
- analyze how characters change throughout a play.
- analyze the purpose of scenes from a play.

PREVIEW ACADEMIC VOCABULARY

act

brackets

colons

dashes

dynamic character

italics

scene

scripted dialogue

stage directions

static character

theme

topic

©Perfection Learning® • No Reproduction Permitted

Making Connections

Think of all the different programs you can watch on television—news, sports, reality, game shows, drama, comedy, and movies. Most shows are prerecorded, but some are shown live. Now imagine gathering around a radio instead of a television. Instead of hearing and seeing, you must listen and then visualize in your mind what is happening. In this chapter, you will read a radio play.

1920–1950 is known as the Golden Age of Radio in the United States. During this time, radio plays were popular. Some of the plays were recorded, but many were performed live and included sound effects and live music. Listening to the radio was replaced by watching television in the 1950s. However, with technology we are able to experience radio plays and stories once again. Today's listeners download podcasts from the Internet and enjoy stories and plays anywhere they go.

What types of podcasts would you be interested in listening to? Write your response below.

MAKING CONNECTIONS

In this chapter you will identify details that support a theme statement. You will also analyze how characters change and how scenes within a play contribute to the overall meaning.

First Read: Understanding Theme

This radio play is based on the ancient Greek story of close friends Damon and Pythias. Pythias has been sentenced to death for speaking out against the tyrannical king of Syracuse, Greece. When Damon visits Pythias in jail, Pythias expresses his wish to see his sister and mother one last time. Damon then goes to the King with a daring request.

Remember that the format of a play is different from other types of literature. Since it is meant to be performed, it is written in dialogue that is meant to be spoken aloud. Also included are instructions to the actors. Here are a few explanations of terms associated with plays:

- **scripted dialogue**—the lines the characters say; usually introduced by the character's name in all caps

- **stage directions**—directions on characterization, movement, setting, and music cues; usually set in brackets and sometime in italics

- **act**—a section of a play; longer plays have four or five acts with the earlier acts revealing the setting and introducing the characters and the final act revealing the conclusion of the conflict

- **scene**—smaller sections of dialogue that make up an act

Objective: As you read this play, underline the details that show the qualities of the friendship between Damon and Pythias. Be sure to read the stage directions and keep track of who is speaking.

excerpt
Damon and Pythias
by Fan Kissen

		My Thoughts
1	**DAMON:** [*Begging*] Your majesty! I beg of you! Let Pythias go home for a few days to bid farewell to his mother and sister. He gives his word that he will return at your appointed time. Everyone knows that his word can be trusted.	_____
5	**KING:** In ordinary business affairs—perhaps. But he is now a man under sentence of death. To free him even for a few days would strain his honesty—*any* man's honesty—too far.	_____

©Perfection Learning® • No Reproduction Permitted

Pythias would never return here! I consider him a traitor, but I'm certain he's no fool.

10   **DAMON:** Your Majesty! I will take his place in the prison until he comes back. If he does not return, then you may take *my* life in his place. . . .

    KING: You make me very curious, Damon, so curious that I'm willing to put you and Pythias to the test. This exchange of
15 prisoners will be made. But Pythias must be back two weeks from today, at noon.

    DAMON: Thank you, Your Majesty!

    KING: The order with my official seal shall go by your own hand, Damon. But I warn you, if your friend does not return on
20 time, you shall surely die in his place! I shall show no mercy!

    [*Music: In briefly and out*]

    NARRATOR: Pythias did not like the king's bargain with Damon. He did not like to leave his friend in prison with the chance that he might lose his life if something went wrong.
25 But at last Damon persuaded him to leave and Pythias set out for his home. More than a week went by. The day set for the death sentence drew near. Pythias did not return. Everyone in the city knew of the condition on which the king had permitted Pythias to go home. Everywhere people met, the
30 talk was sure to turn to the two friends.

    FIRST VOICE: Do you suppose Pythias will come back?

    SECOND VOICE: Why should he stick his head under the king's ax once he has escaped?

    THIRD VOICE: Still, would an honorable man like Pythias
35 let such a good friend die for him?

    FIRST VOICE: There's no telling what a man will do when

My Thoughts

it's a question of his own life against another's.

SECOND VOICE: But if Pythias doesn't come back before the time is up, he will be killing his friend.

40 **THIRD VOICE:** Well, there's still a few days' time. I, for one, am certain that Pythias *will* return in time.

SECOND VOICE: And *I am* just as certain that he will *not*. Friendship is friendship, but a man's own life is something stronger. I say! . . .

45 **NARRATOR:** Meanwhile, when Pythias reached the home of his family, he arranged his business affairs so that his mother and sister would be able to live comfortably for the rest of their years. Then he said a fast farewell to them before starting back to the city. . . . Pythias began his journey in plenty of time.

50 But bad luck struck him on the very first day. At twilight, as he walked along a lonely stretch of woodland, a rough voice called:

FIRST ROBBER: Not so fast there, young man! Stop!

PYTHIAS: [*Startled*] Oh! What is it? What do you want?

55 **SECOND ROBBER:** Your money bags.

PYTHIAS: My money bags? I have only this small bag of coins. I shall need them for some favors, perhaps, before I die.

FIRST ROBBER: What do you mean, before you die? We don't mean to kill you, only take your money.

60 **PYTHIAS:** I'll give you my money, only don't delay me any longer. I am to die by the king's order three days from now. If I don't return on time, my friend must die in my place.

FIRST ROBBER: A likely story! What man would be fool enough to go back to prison to die?

65 **SECOND ROBBER:** And what man would be fool enough to die *for* you?

©Perfection Learning® • No Reproduction Permitted

FIRST ROBBER: We'll take your money, all right. And we'll tie you up while we get away.

PYTHIAS: [*Begging*] No! No! I must get back to free my
70   friend! [*Fade*] I must go back!

NARRATOR: But the two robbers took Pythias's money, tied him to a tree, and went off as fast as they could. Pythias struggled to free himself. He cried out for a long time. But no one traveled through that lonesome woodland after dark. The
75   sun had been up for many hours before he finally managed to free himself from the ropes that had tied him to the tree. He lay on the ground, hardly able to breathe.

[*Music: In briefly and out*]

80   **NARRATOR:** After a while Pythias got to his feet. Weak and dizzy from hunger and thirst and his struggle to free himself, he set off again. Day and night he traveled without stopping, desperately trying to reach the city in time to save Damon's life.

85   **NARRATOR:** On the last day, half an hour before noon, Damon's hands were tied behind his back, and he was taken into the public square. The people muttered angrily as Damon was led in by the jailer. Then the king entered and seated himself on a high platform. . . .

90   **KING:** [*Loud, mocking*] Well, Damon, your lifetime is nearly up. Where is your good friend Pythias now?

DAMON: [*Firm*] I have faith in my friend. If he has not returned, I'm certain it is through no fault of his own.

KING: [*Mocking*] The sun is almost overhead. The shadow
95   is at the noon mark. And still your friend has not returned to give back your life!

My Thoughts

DAMON: [*Quiet*] I am ready and happy to die in his place.

KING: [*Harsh*] And you shall, Damon! Jailer, lead the prisoner to the—

100 [*Sound: Crowd voices up to a roar, then under.*]

FIRST VOICE: [*Over noise*] Look! It's Pythias!

SECOND VOICE: [*Over noise*] Pythias has come back!

PYTHIAS: [*Breathless*] Let me through! Damon!

DAMON: Pythias!

105 **PYTHIAS:** Thank the gods I'm not too late!

DAMON: [*Quiet, sincere*] I would have died for you gladly, my friend.

CROWD VOICES: [*Loud, demanding*] Set them free! Set them both free!

110 **KING:** [*Loud*] People of the city! [*Crowd voices out*] Never in all my life have I seen such faith and friendship, such loyalty between men. There are many among you who call me harsh and cruel. But I cannot kill *any* man who proves such strong and true friendship for another. Damon and Pythias, I set you

115 both free. [*Roar of approval from crowd*] I am king. I command a great army. I have stores of gold and precious jewels. But I would give all my money and power for one friend like Damon or Pythias.

[*Sound: Roar of approval from crowd up briefly and out*]

[*Music: Up and out*]

My Thoughts

_____
_____
_____
_____
_____
_____
_____
_____
_____
_____
_____
_____
_____
_____
_____
_____
_____
_____
_____
_____
_____
_____

FIRST RESPONSE: KEY IDEAS AND DETAILS

Look at the details about the characters you underlined as you read the radio play. Based on their actions, what do the friends value in life? Write your inferences in your response journal.

Focus on Understanding Theme

Do you think writers begin with a theme when they write a story? Most writers would say that themes emerge naturally as they tell a meaningful story about interesting characters.

What is the difference between a theme statement and a topic? A topic is an idea. Topics explored in literature include *family, jealousy, bravery, prejudice, perseverance, compassion, friendship, peace, fairness, growing up, hope,* and *war*. To discover a theme, ask the question: What *about* the topic? Themes are expressed as statements.

Fill out the chart below to discover a theme from the radio play.

CONNECT TO ESSENTIAL QUESTION

At what points in the story could the friendship have been broken?

List topics explored in the play. Circle the topic you believe to be most developed in the play.	
What conflict/obstacles did the characters face?	Damon: Pythias: King:
What was the outcome of the conflict/obstacles?	Damon: Pythias: King:
What did the characters learn? How did they grow or change?	Damon: Pythias: King:

Based on your answers from the chart on the previous page, write your theme statement below. There are several possibilities. Select the theme that has the strongest support in the text.

My theme statement is

Read the checklist below. Make sure your theme statement matches each of the characteristics in the checklist.

Theme Statement Checklist
My theme statement
☐ is written as a statement that expresses a general, universal truth about the topic or subject explored by the author.
☐ is not a plot event.
☐ is reflected by the characters, conflicts, and outcomes in the play.
☐ doesn't use a cliché or a "You should never…" statement.
☐ can be applied to many people and situations (universal).
☐ expresses a truth about people or human nature.

☾**Speak and Listen** Share your theme statement with a partner. Use the checklist to evaluate your partner's theme statement. If you disagree with his or her theme statement, respectfully explain your reasons, referring to evidence from the excerpt and checklist to support your opinion.

TECH-CONNECT

Search online for a video about how to identify theme statments in literature. Consider making your own video based upon what you've learned in this unit.

©Perfection Learning® • No Reproduction Permitted

Second Read: Analyzing Characters

Experience the radio play as it was intended—listen to a live or recorded performance. Under the guidance of your teacher, select one of the following options.

Option 1.   Cast the play and read it aloud as a class.
Option 2.   Read the play in groups of four. Assign roles.

Student 1:   Damon/Second Voice/Second Robber
Student 2:   Pythias
Student 3:   King/First Voice/First Robber
Student 4:   Narrator/Third Voice
All students: Crowd

Objective: Write the word *change* in the text where you recognize changes in a character or characters.

Focus on Analyzing Characters

Characters who stay the same in a story are called *static characters*. From a story's beginning to its end, static characters remain unchanged in the ways they speak, act, and think. Characters who change throughout the course of the story are *dynamic characters*.

Complete the graphic organizer below to determine whether the main characters in the radio play are static or dynamic. These changes may be positive or negative.

	Damon	King	Pythias
Characteristics at the beginning of the story			
Characteristics at the end of the story			

continued on next page

	Damon	King	Pythias
Static or dynamic?			
Other thoughts or observations			

Speak and Listen Discuss your analysis of the characters with a partner. Which character do you each think changes the most?

Write Write several paragraphs in which you describe the character in the play that changes the most. Include what causes the character to change and what can be inferred about how the character's thinking has changed.

REFLECT

Consider the book you are reading right now. Which characters are dynamic? static?

Third Read: Analyzing the Structure of a Play

Objective: Read the play again. Think about how your experience of reading this play is different from the experience of hearing it performed. Focus on the minor scenes with the three voices and the robbers. Think about how each of these is important to the events and the theme of the play.

Focus on Analyzing the Structure of a Play

Even minor scenes contribute to the overall plot and theme of a work. Use the following chart to analyze two short scenes in the play.

	Conversation with Three Voices (lines 31–44)	Scene with Robbers (lines 50–70)
Summary of what happens/ what is said		
Does this scene develop the theme? How?		
Does this scene build suspense? How?		

Write Write two paragraphs explaining how one of the scenes you analyzed in the graphic organizer on the previous page contributes to the overall plot and theme of the play. Include direct quotations from the play to support your conclusions.

REFLECT

Why are narrators often necessary in Readers Theater and radio plays?

Language: Punctuation in Plays

A play is written using a special format.

Text treatments:

- The speaker's name in bold capital letters makes it easier for actors to read their parts.

- Stage directions in italics separate directions from what is to be spoken.

Punctuation:

- Parentheses separate directions for actors, sound effects people, and the stage crew.

- Dashes indicate an interruption in thought or dialogue.

Study the following excerpt. Then answer the questions that follow.

NARRATOR: On the last day, half an hour before noon, Damon's hands were tied behind his back, and he was taken into the public square. The people muttered angrily as Damon was led in by the jailer. Then the king entered and seated himself on a high platform. . . .

KING: [*Loud, mocking*] Well, Damon, your lifetime is nearly up. Where is your good friend Pythias now?

DAMON: [*Firm*] I have faith in my friend. If he has not returned, I'm certain it is through no fault of his own.

KING: [*Mocking*] The sun is almost overhead. The shadow is at the noon mark. And still your friend has not returned to give back your life!

DAMON: [*Quiet*] I am ready and happy to die in his place.

KING: [*Harsh*] And you shall, Damon! Jailer, lead the prisoner to the—

[*Crowd voices up to a roar, then under.*]

FIRST VOICE: [*Over noise*] Look! It's Pythias!

1. Explain how each of the following are used in play format.

   colons:

   brackets:

   italics:

   dashes:

2. Write six lines of dialogue between Damon and Pythias which could have occurred after the play ends. Use colons, italics, brackets, and at least one dash correctly in your scene.

Project-Based Assessments

Friend or Foe of Humankind? Greek Gods and Goddesses Mini Poster

According to mythology, the Greek god Prometheus was considered a friend of humans. He stole fire from Hephaestus, the god of fire and patron of artisans and craftsmen, and gave it as a gift to humankind. Prometheus was punished severely for this generous act.

Use an app, an online design program, or a word processing program to create a page-sized poster about a Greek god or goddess. Research to determine if this god or goddess was considered a *friend* or a *foe* to the ancient Greek people.

1. Select a Greek god or goddess from an online list.

2. Find three sources to determine if the god was a friend or foe of humans.

3. Keep a list of your sources and take good notes. This list will be formatted as a Works Cited list and included with your poster.

4. Design your poster so that it includes the following information:
   - name and title of god/goddess (e.g., Prometheus, the Titan God of Fire)
   - sketch or other image
   - other art and design elements to reflect your research findings
   - use of font styles and sizes to make your poster readable and interesting
   - short summary of a key myth exlaining why the god or goddess is a friend or foe of humankind
   - Works Cited list correctly formatted. Follow your teacher's instructions for the requirements.

©Perfection Learning® • No Reproduction Permitted

Use the following guidelines for your mini poster.	
To receive the highest score (4.0), the project must meet all of these criteria.	**Your mini poster** • contains written elements: name, title, label of friend or foe. • includes visual elements: sketch or image, other art elements, variety of well-chosen font styles and sizes. • contains a summary of the myth and an explanation of why the god is a friend or foe. • is well organized, neat, and professional. • includes a Works Cited list. • uses correct grammar, punctuation, and spelling.

Podcast

Work with three other classmates and create a podcast of a host interviewing Damon, Pythias, and the King for the fictional show *Greece Today*. Include an introduction and summary of the events by the host, the host interviewing all three characters about the events, and a short wrap-up at the end.

Here are some tips for your project.

- Decide who will play the host of the podcast and the characters Damon, Pythias, and the King.

- Write the opening introduction and brief summary of the story.

- Write a script for the podcast. Include questions asked by the host and the characters' responses. Make inferences about how the characters think and feel about the events. Make sure the characters' answers are appropriate to the characteristics they showed in the play.

- Use clear, strong voices. Try to match the tone of your voices to the personalities of the host and the characters.

- Record your podcast using a recording app or software so that it sounds professional.

- Play your podcast for the class or post it on your class website.

continued on next page

	Use the following guidelines for your podcast.
To receive the highest score (4.0), the podcast must meet all of these criteria.	**Your podcast** • includes an introduction and interview with the three main characters from the radio play. • accurately reflects the characters and events from the story and also makes new inferences based on the text. • uses good vocal variety and tone to match the characters. • is recorded using an app or software so that it sounds professional. • includes appropriate grammar and usage according to the rules of standard English.

On Your Own: Integrating Ideas

1. In literature, the term *allusion* means a brief and indirect reference to a person, place, thing or idea with historical, cultural, literary or political significance. Conduct research to discover pieces of literature that contain an allusion to Damon and Pythias.

2. Find and watch a visual recording of *Damon and Pythias* online.

3. Research the life and philosophy of Pythagoras. Create a brochure about the man, his contributions, and his teachings about friendship.

4. Sources indicate that the tyrannical king in the play may be based on Dionysius I, also called Dionysius the Elder. Research the king to discover why his people may have been afraid to speak out against his policies.

©Perfection Learning® • No Reproduction Permitted

Connect to Testing

Questions on reading tests may ask you to determine theme statements, analyze characters, and focus on the structure of a text. Often a second part of the question will test your ability to identify strong evidence that supports the correct inference. Answer the following questions.

1. **Part A:** Which detail from the play most accurately connects to a central theme?

   A. *Everywhere people met, the talk was sure to turn to the two friends.*

   B. *But I would give all my money and power for one friend like Damon or Pythias.*

   C. *To free him for even a few days would strain his honesty—any man's honesty—too far.*

   D. *What man would be fool enough to go back to prison to die?*

   Part B: Explain how your response above supports a central theme of the play.

2. **Part A:** Which of the following characters is dynamic or shows the greatest change over the course of the play?

   A. Robber One

   B. Damon

   C. King

   D. Pythias

   Part B: Which of the following lines from the play provides the strongest evidence for the answer to Part A?

   A. *I consider him a traitor, but I'm certain he's no fool.*

   B. *No! No! I must get back to free my friend! [Fade] I must go back!*

   C. *I have faith in my friend. If he has not returned, I'm certain it is through no fault of his own.*

   D. *But I cannot kill any man who proves such strong and true friendship for another.*

continued on next page

Read the following scene from the play and answer the questions that follow.

FIRST ROBBER: Not so fast there, young man! Stop!

PYTHIAS: [*Startled*] Oh! What is it? What do you want?

SECOND ROBBER: Your money bags.

PYTHIAS: My money bags? I have only this small bag of coins. I shall need them for some favors, perhaps, before I die.

FIRST ROBBER: What do you mean, before you die? We don't mean to kill you, only take your money.

PYTHIAS: I'll give you my money, only don't delay me any longer. I am to die by the king's order three days from now. If I don't return on time, my friend must die in my place.

FIRST ROBBER: A likely story! What man would be fool enough to go back to prison to die?

SECOND ROBBER: And what man would be fool enough to die *for* you?

FIRST ROBBER: We'll take your money, all right. And we'll tie you up while we get away.

PYTHIAS: [*Begging*] No! No! I must get back to free my friend! [*Fade*] I must go back!

3. **Part A:** This scene is important to the overall events of the story because it— **(Choose two.)**

A. builds suspense by causing Pythias to be delayed.

B. highlights Pythias's intentions to return and save his friend.

C. introduces the conflict of greed vs. friendship.

D. shows that Pythias doesn't have much money left.

E. reveals how the setting affects the theme of friendship.

Part B: For each of the correct answers above, write a line from the text that supports your inference.

©Perfection Learning® • No Reproduction Permitted

Writing an Informative Essay

In poverty and other misfortunes of life,
true friends are a sure refuge.
—Aristotle

Think of all of the ideas about friendship that have been explored in this chapter.

- Novel excerpt from *Bud, Not Buddy*: Buddy and Bugs are two orphans on the run during the Great Depression.

- Memoir excerpt from *My Life in Dog Years*: Gary Paulsen tells a story about meeting Dirk, a mutt who protects him from roaming bullies.

- Nonfiction article excerpt from "Why We Need Friends Now More Than Ever." The author explores the benefits of having a few close friendships.

- Nonfiction essay excerpt from "Reflections on True Friendship." The author fondly remembers a childhood friend and wonders if technology has changed the nature of friendship.

- Radio play excerpt from *Damon and Pythias.* This ancient story contains a remarkable example of a loyal friendship.

WRITING PROMPT

You have seen that people of all ages, from the past to the present, have written about friendship. Friends are a source of comfort during tough times and a source of joy during good times. We grow as people when we have friends who can speak the truth when we need a reality check; a true friend will always bring out our best.

Write an informative/explanatory essay that answers the question, *What qualities make a good friendship?* In other words, what ingredients do lasting friendships have that allow them to endure, while other friendships fade? In your essay include three or four different qualities of a lasting friendship that you develop with definitions, anecdotes, and examples. Write a 2–3 page essay, typed and double-spaced in 12-point standard font.

Prepare to Write

Carefully read the prompt. Underline key words that explain the requirements of the task. Break it down based on purpose, audience, content, and additional requirements by filling in the chart below.

Purpose	
Audience	
Content Requirements	
Additional requirements	

▼ The Writing Process

Brainstorming for Ideas

Start by thinking about lasting friendships—both your own and those of your friends and family. How are they different from those that don't last? What qualities do they share? You may want to also consider the qualities of friendships that last only a short time. Finish the sentence starters below to give you some ideas.

> **CONNECT TO ESSENTIAL QUESTION**
>
> Do friendships last because of the way they are built? Or do friendships last because they withstand difficulties without breaking?

Strong friendships
Friendships become stronger when

If someone observed a strong friendship, they would notice

Good friends always

Unhealthy friends are

The people I choose to have as friends could be described as

One friendship that didn't last was

Our friendship ended because

I would end a friendship if a friend

Generate Ideas

After you brainstorm using the sentence starters, use your own ideas and/or research to begin examining three or more qualities that you feel are essential for a strong friendship.

Characteristic of good friend or a strong friendship	Definition of this characteristic (connotative, denotative or both)	Why is it important?	Examples or anecdotes

©Perfection Learning® • No Reproduction Permitted

Organize Ideas

Before you begin writing your paper, take some time to plan the order of your paragraphs. However, if you find that you don't have enough interesting details, revise your writing plan. Revisit the Generate Ideas step on page 96 and gather more ideas by talking to friends and family members or conducting further research.

As you organize your thoughts, consider the order of your three to four body paragraphs. Each will develop one of the qualities of a strong friendship. Which order would make the most sense? Usually writers save their most important point for last.

REFLECT

Think about the strong friendships you have read about in books or seen in movies. If you could ask the characters questions, what would they say is the secret to their friendship?

1. Write a thesis statement that explains the central idea of your paper. Your thesis statement should contain the qualities that you believe are necessary for a good friendship. A thesis sentence is your contract or agreement with the reader about your topic; you must stick to it! Since this is a personal informative essay, it is acceptable to write in first person and use the pronoun *I* in your thesis statement.

My thesis statement:

2. Create an outline based on your notes. Your paper should have an introduction, body, and conclusion. Study the following sample outline:

I Introduction

    A. Introduce the topic, capture your readers' interest, use a story or quotation about friendship.

    B. Give background on the topic.

    C. State your thesis.

II Body Paragraphs

    A. Quality or Characteristic #1

        1) Definition

        2) Explanation of why it's important

        3) Example(s)

continued on next page

B. Quality or Characteristic #2

    1) Definition

    2) Explanation of why it's important

    3) Example(s)

C. Quality or Characteristic #3

    1) Definition

    2) Explanation of why it's important

    3) Example(s)

III Conclusion

A. Summarize your main points and restate your thesis statement.

B. End with another story or quotation; Leave your readers something to think about.

First Draft

Use your outline to write a draft of your informative/ explanatory paper. Here are some hints.

- Remember that your thesis statement is a contract with the reader. You must write only about the thesis statement.

- Refer to your notes while drafting.

- Write quickly. You will revise and proofread later.

- Write on every other line or double space if working on a computer. This will make it easier to make revisions.

- If you take a break and then return to writing, reread what you have written. This will help you resume the flow of thought.

- Mark this paper Draft #1

Citing Sources

If you use outside sources, follow your teacher's instructions for citing them in your paper. Most often you will be required to place the name of the author and the page number in parentheses. For example: (Ramirez 24).

Revision

Ask other students and your teacher to read your essay. Listen carefully to their feedback. Applying their advice will improve your writing. Three ways to revise your paper begin on the next page.

First Peer Review

This review will evaluate whether your ideas are interesting and whether they flow together in a logical order. With a group of two to three people, complete the following steps for each group member.

Steps for Peer Review

1. Select a timekeeper. Each writer gets ten minutes. Stick to the time.
2. One person begins by reading aloud his or her introduction while the other members listen.
3. Pause. The same writer reads the introduction again.
4. Writer asks, "Does the beginning of my essay clearly explain my main idea?" Each member responds, as the writer takes notes on his or her draft.
5. Writer reads the entire essay, pauses, and then reads it again.
6. As writer reads, members take notes.
7. Writer asks, "What questions do you have about my topic? What else do you need to know about it?" Writer jots down replies.

As soon as possible after peer review, revise your draft based on your peers' questions and comments. Mark this paper Draft #2.

Second Peer Review (Self Review)

Ask yourself these questions to revise your own paper.

Think big. Look at the draft as a whole.

- Is my paper two to three pages long?
- Is the flow between paragraphs smooth?
- Is the overall essay focused on the thesis statement?

Think medium. Look at the draft paragraph by paragraph.

- Does the introduction hook my readers and make them want to read more?
- Do I provide enough background on my topic?
- Is my thesis statement clear and included in the introduction?
- Do I include a clear definition, explanation, and example(s) for each body paragraph?
- Are my body paragraphs in the best order for the strongest impact?

continued on next page

Think small. Look at the draft sentence by sentence.

- Which sentences are long and confusing? Short and choppy?
- Do I have variety in my sentence structures?
- Are there errors in spelling, grammar, or usage?
- Make changes as needed. Mark this draft #3.

Final Peer Review

Ask another student to read your essay and rate it using the rubric below.

Use the following guidelines for your informative/explanatory essay.	
To receive the highest score, the essay must meet all of these criteria.	Your essay • contains a thesis statement stating at least three characteristics that make a strong friendship. • gives background on strong friendships. • includes at least three different characteristics with a definition, an explanation, and examples for each. • is organized logically and includes good transitions to make the essay flow. • has a tone and style suitable for the topic of lasting friendships. • uses correct grammar, usage, punctuation, and spelling.

Proofread

Make sure you have included standard grammar and punctuation as you write your final draft. Proofread carefully for omitted words and punctuation marks. Use spell-check, but be aware of its limitations. Proofread again to detect the kinds of errors the computer can't catch. Read your essay aloud before submitting it.

Final Essay

Share your completed essay with audiences beyond your classroom. Read it to your family and friends. Share it with your school counselor. Upload your finished digital copy to your class website. If you have a school or personal blog or website, share it with your readers.

©Perfection Learning® • No Reproduction Permitted

Practice Performance Task

A performance task evaluates your ability to comprehend selections of literature or informational text and then demonstrate your knowledge in writing. The task often begins with several multiple-choice or short answer questions on key vocabulary and the central ideas of the passage(s). The task culminates with a writing assignment.

Complete the following performance task based on the selections from Unit 1.

Source #1

Read the following excerpt from *Bud, Not Buddy* from Chapter 1.

"Will we be sleeping on the train and everything?"

"Sure we will. Some of the time the train don't stop for two or three days. Man, I always try to tell people that just because someone's skinny it don't mean they can't fight, you're a hero now, Bud!"

"Naw, I didn't really do nothing much. Well, how 'bout the toilet? How we going to use the toilet if the train doesn't stop?"

Bugs said, "You just kind of lean out of the door and go."

"When the train is still moving?"

"Yeah. You get a real nice breeze."

"Oh, man! That sounds great! Count me in, I can't wait!"

Bugs spit a big glob of slob in his hand and said, "I knew I could depend on you, Bud."

I spit a big glob in my hand and said, "We're brothers forever, Bugs!"

We slapped our hands together as hard as we could and got our slobs mixed up real good, then waved them in the air so they'd dry. Now it was official, I finally had a brother!

Bugs said, "We'll go down to the mission. There's bound to be someone there that knows about where we can hop this train, then we'll be on the lam together!"

continued on next page

1. How does the author use details to create a humorous tone in the story? Even though the boys are on the run and on their own, which details allow us to smile alongside the author as we observe their struggles and adventures? Support your answer with details from the text.

Continue the performance task by reading a second source and answering the question.

Source #2

Read the following excerpt from *My Life in Dog Years* from Chapter 2.

It was not loud, more a rumble that seemed to come from the earth and

so full of menace that it stopped me cold, my foot frozen in midair.

I raised my foot and the growl stopped.

I lowered my foot and the growl came again. My foot went up and it

stopped.

I stood there, trying to peer through the steps of the fire escape. For a time I couldn't see more than a dark shape crouched back in the gloom. There was a head and a back, and as my eyes became accustomed to the dark I could see that it had scraggly, scruffy hair and two eyes that glowed yellow.

We were at an <u>impasse</u>. I didn't want to climb up the ladder again but if I stepped to the ground it seemed likely I would be bitten. I hung there for a full minute before I thought of the hamburger. I could use it as a decoy and get away.

The problem was the hamburger smelled *so* good and I was *so* hungry.

I decided to give the beast under the stairs half a burger. I opened the sack, unwrapped the tinfoil and threw half the sandwich under the steps, then jumped down and ran for the end of the alley. I was just getting my stride, legs and arms pumping, pulling air with a heaving chest, when I rounded the corner and ran smack into the latest group of boys who were terrorizing me.

2. **Part A**: Based on the context clues in the passage, what does the word *impasse* mean?

   A. a temporary situation that will pass, a phase

   B. a situation in which no progress is possible, a deadlock

   C. a situation of danger for a child, a crisis

   D. a passing trend, a fad

   Part B: Which of the following lines from the excerpt best supports the answer to Part A?

   A. *I was just getting my stride, legs and arms pumping, pulling air with a heaving chest, when I rounded the corner and ran smack into the latest group of boys who were terrorizing me.*

   B. *I couldn't see more than a dark shape crouched back in the gloom.*

   C. *The problem was that the hamburger smelled so good and I was so hungry.*

   D. *I didn't want to climb up the ladder again but if I stepped to the ground it seemed likely I would be bitten.*

Read the following excerpt from "Why We Need Friends Now More Than Ever" from Chapter 3.

    In an age obsessed with popularity, where how many friends you have on social media has become a bragging right, one has to stop and wonder: What are the value of friends, and can't we have too many? Many of us are familiar with Dunbar's Number, which states that we can only maintain 150 relationships in our minds at any given time in our lives. But many experts say we are better off with a quality-over-quantity attitude, which may come as a relief to those of us who, after the *gotta-collect-'em-all* approach of our 20s, have entered a phase of wanting fewer, but closer friends.

    As a recent *Quartz* piece explained via the work of Tim Kasser, people have two predominant attitudes toward friendships: one where popularity (being liked or admired by many) is the goal, and another where affinity (or striving for deeper relationships) was preferred. As it turns out, those who longed for popularity were "less happy, less healthy, more depressed, and used more drugs." And those who put in the time for deeper, more meaningful relationships had the opposite finding: They were happier, healthier, and less depressed. In fact the Mayo Clinic suggests that having close friends can increase your happiness, self-confidence, and sense of purpose, while reducing stress. They can also help you cope with traumas and illness: In a 2006 study, women with breast cancer who were without close friends were four times more likely to die as a result of breast cancer than women with 10 or more close friends.

3. Which of the following best supports the idea that having a large number of friends does not guarantee satisfying friendships?

   A. *how many friends you have on social media has become a bragging right*

   B. *those of us who, after the gotta-collect-'em-all approach of our 20s, have entered a phase of fewer, closer friends*

   C. *But many experts say we are better off with a quality-over-quantity attitude*

   D. *As a recent Quartz piece explained via the work of Tim Kasser, people have two predominant attitudes toward friendships.*

Reread this excerpt from, "Reflections on True Friendship," from Chapter 4.

When I recently tried to find Mark again, he didn't appear to exist. . . . he seemed like a figment, or a fragile piece of memory that crumbles when you turn it in your hands. . . . When I went back to Scotland recently, I drove to the square where we once lived, and I looked up at the window of my old house, remembering how I used to shine a torch from there to Mark's bedroom. Two flashes meant good night. Three flashes meant see you tomorrow.

I wonder if technology has changed the meaning of friendship. My daughter is 12 and most things that happen to her are photographed. She and her friends get together and spend hours trying out poses, making videos, retouching them, setting them to music and posting them on this or that social media network. I'm sure the girls are bonded in many of the traditional ways, but I also wonder if they'll ever lose sight of each other, which was always one of the possibilities of friendship, an aspect of its mystery. I think we always knew we would move on in life and that our great friendships would be a matter of memory. I don't have a single photograph of Mark MacDonald.

4. In the nonfiction article above, the writer uses examples and anecdotes from his own experiences. Write a paragraph that contrasts the friendship between the author and Mark with the one between the author's daughter and her friends.

continued on next page

5. Would the authors of Sources #3 and #4 agree or disagree with the claim that social media encourages deeper, longer lasting friendships? Use at least two pieces of evidence from the texts to support your answer.

Your Assignment

WRITING PROMPT

Based on the sources you read in this task and throughout the unit, write an informational/explanatory paper that answers the Essential Question: *How are friendships built and broken?* You are encouraged to return to the excerpts of the texts from each chapter to find ideas for your writing. Support your ideas with both quotations and paraphrased lines from the texts.

Read the prompt carefully. Underline words that indicate what and how to write your essay. Before you begin to write, study the qualities of Reading Comprehension, Writing Expression, and Writing Conventions shown on the next page. Your writing will be evaluated on these qualities.

Create a graphic organizer to help you plan your ideas. You may wish to create an organizer like the one below.

Text from Unit 1	Friendships *built* ideas	Friendships *broken* ideas

Your Assignment (continued)

Remember to infer ideas based on your evidence. Use at least five pieces of evidence from at least three different texts.

Once you have chosen your ideas, write a thesis sentence that contains your central idea about how friendships are built and broken. Draw conclusions from the experiences of the characters and authors from this unit. Consider the information you read about the value of close friendships. Explain your conclusion in one sentence.

Write your essay. Use good transitional phrases between ideas and between paragraphs. Useful transitional words and phrases include *first/second/third, next, in addition, by comparison, for the same reason, finally, summing up, in brief.*

Take time to edit and proofread your essay before turning it in.

Your essay will be graded on the following:

Reading Comprehension:

- How well did you understand the texts?

- Does your writing reflect your understanding of the sources?

Writing Expression:

- Does your writing answer the Essential Question?
- Does your essay contain information about both how friendships are built and how they are broken?
- Does your essay include at least five pieces of quoted (used sparingly) or paraphrased text evidence? Have you explained your evidence so that it answers the question?
- Does your essay flow logically, using transitional words and phrases?
- Does the writing style contain precise, accurate language and content appropriate to the purpose, task, and audience?

Writing Conventions:

- Does your writing follow the rules of standard English with few errors in grammar, usage, and spelling?

Unit 2

Essential Question
How do people deal with difficulties?

Think back to a time when you experienced a challenge in your life, something that caused you to feel discomfort, distress, or fear. It may have lasted a moment or years. Perhaps you had to move multiple times or you experienced a heartbreaking loss. Maybe you struggled to learn something that seemed to come easily to others. What allowed you to keep going and not quit? Did you find strength in something else, like nature, music, a sport, or a hobby? Or did the support of others help you cope?

All people face difficulties at some point in their lives, so what allows a person to get through such hardship? Some believe it's natural grit or a kind of inborn toughness. Perhaps certain people are braver than others. Some face misfortune again and again and never seem to get a break. They show resolve and determination that never seem to end.

Fiction and nonfiction both feature stories of human struggle. The story is what draws you in and keeps you wanting to find out more. In reading another's story, you seek to understand yourself and others better. You develop empathy. You feel encouragement. You broaden your beliefs. Even if you can't identify with the story itself, you can usually understand the emotions behind the story, or the human condition.

Unit 2 will explore stories of people rising above difficulty in their lives. You will read excerpts from an autobiography, a drama, a speech, and a poem, and you will watch a scene from a film. As you work through this unit, you will connect with the spirit, grace, and toughness of the people you read about.

GOALS
• To determine the central idea of informational text
• To uncover a poem's message and recognize tonal shifts
• To understand the character development and determine author's point of view in nonfiction
• To explore a speaker's rhetoric and determine a speaker's purpose
• To understand plot and characters in drama
• To compare a text with a film
• To write a personal narrative

Chapter 6

Analyzing the Power and Purpose of Nonfiction

Preview Concepts

Nature has the ability to create and to destroy, to calm and to terrify, to inspire and to discourage. Think of a blue sky over a quiet lake or a wild windstorm on a mountaintop. Make a list of the negative and positive impacts of nature.

Share your list with a partner, and then discuss the negative and positive impacts of *human* nature (the distinguishing characteristics of feeling, thinking, and acting that make one human). Talk about the ways people affect one another and their surroundings. Write a brief summary of your conversation.

CHAPTER GOALS

In this chapter you will:

- determine the central idea of an essay.
- identify examples of repetition and understand their purpose in a text.
- explore the effects of certain literary devices within a nonfiction text.

PREVIEW ACADEMIC VOCABULARY

anaphora

hyperbole

personification

redundant

repetition

sensory details

simile

topic

©Perfection Learning® • No Reproduction Permitted

Making Connections

Read the following poem.

> Rain on the face of the sea,
>   Rain on the sodden land,
> And the window-pane is blurred with rain
>   As I watch it, pen in hand.
> Mist on the face of the sea,
>   Mist on the sodden land,
> Filling the vales as daylight fails,
>   And blotting the desolate sand.
> Voices from out of the mist,
>   Calling to one another:
> "Hath love an end, thou more than friend,
>   Thou dearer than ever brother?"
> Voices from out of the mist,
>   Calling and passing away;
> But I cannot speak, for my voice is weak,
>   And . . . this is the end of my lay.

—"Commonplaces" by Rudyard Kipling

How do the images of nature reflect the speaker's mood in this poem? Underline lines from the text that support your answer and explain your thoughts below.

MAKING CONNECTIONS

As you read the essay in this chapter, you will observe how an author conveys a central idea about nature and human nature using repetition and other literary devices.

First Read: Determining the Central Idea

Read the essay "Sometimes, the Earth Is Cruel" by newspaper columnist Leonard Pitts. Pitts wrote this essay after Haiti, a nation of ten million in the Caribbean Sea, was struck by hurricanes and earthquakes in 2010. The disasters left this country and its people in a state of emergency.

Objective: As you read, think about the central idea of the text. Underline key sentences that help convey this idea. Write questions you have about the author's ideas or anything you find confusing in the My Thoughts column. If you answer your own question as you read on, record the answer as well.

Sometimes, the Earth Is Cruel
by Leonard Pitts Jr.

My Thoughts

1   Sometimes, the earth is cruel.

That is ultimately the fundamental lesson here, as children wail, families sleep out of doors, and the dead lie unclaimed in the rubble that once was Port-au-Prince, Haiti.

5   Sometimes the rains fall and will not stop. Sometimes the skies turn barren and will not rain. Sometimes the seas rise and smack the shoreline like a fist. Sometimes the wind bullies the land. And sometimes, the land rattles and heaves and splits itself in two.

10   Sometimes, the earth is cruel. And always, when it is, we do the same thing. We dig ourselves out. We weep and mourn, we recover and memorialize the dead, we rebuild our homes. And we go on. This is the price of being human. And also, arguably, the noblest expression.

15   Sometimes, the earth is cruel, and you have no choice but to accept that as part of the bargain called life. And when it is your turn to deal with it, you do.

    ©Perfection Learning® • No Reproduction Permitted

But what if it's always your turn?

Surely some homeless, dust-streaked Haitian can be
20 forgiven for thinking it is always Haiti's turn, just days after
the poorest nation in the Western Hemisphere saw its capital
city smashed by the strongest earthquake it has ever known,
a 7.0-magnitude monster. Surely, the rest of us watching from
afar, experiencing tragedy and **devastation** from the comfort
25 of desk chairs and living room couches, are tempted to believe
the same thing.

Bad enough, Haiti is wretchedly poor. Bad enough it has a
history of political instability and colonialism, of being ignored
by the major powers when it is not being exploited by them.
30 Bad enough, all that, yet at the end of the day, those are
disasters authored by human hands, by human greed, human
corruption, human economic **predation**.

Sometimes, though, you have to wonder if the planet itself
is not conspiring against this humble little nation.
35   After 1994, when Tropical Storm Gordon killed several
hundred people, after 1998, when Hurricane Georges swept
away more than 500 lives, after 2004, when the rains of
Tropical Storm Jeanne claimed more than 2,000 souls, after
2005, when Hurricane Dennis took 25 lives in July and Tropical
40 Storm Alpha snatched 17 in October, followed by Hurricane
Wilma, which stole 11 more, after the double whammy of
Hurricanes Fay and Gustav in 2008 killed more than 130 people
and destroyed 3,100 homes, after all that, comes this latest
insult—and a death toll officials cannot begin to even imagine.
45 Perhaps as many as 100,000, they were saying on Wednesday.

My Thoughts

---

devastation: destruction
predation: theft

Sometimes, the earth is cruel. To crawl the planet's skin, scanning for tornadoes in Oklahoma, charting storm tracks in Florida, running from wildfires in California, is to understand this in a primal, personal way. It is to breathe a prayer that

50 begins, "There, but for the grace of God . . ." It is to write relief checks, donate blood, volunteer material and time and to fear, even in the doing, that these gestures are small against the need, **inconsequential** against the ache of a people whose turn seems never to end.

55 But what else are you going to do? As the playwright put it, your arms too short to box with God. Even less have we the ability to answer the question that burns the moment: Why are the most **vulnerable** repeatedly assessed the highest price?

We are hamstrung by our own limitations, so we can only

60 do what we always do, only send prayers and help. And watch, staggered by the courage it takes, as Haitians do what human beings always do, the thing at which they have become so terribly practiced.

Dig out. Weep and mourn. Memorialize the dead. Rebuild.

65 Go on. And show the world once again a stubborn insistence on living, despite all the cruelties of the earth.

_____

inconsequential: having no effect
vulnerable: easily harmed

FIRST RESPONSE: KEY IDEAS AND DETAILS

Refer to the sentences you underlined, and consider the central idea of the text. What are you left thinking about? Is the essay about Haiti, human nature, nature, or all three? Be prepared to share your answers with the class.

My Thoughts

REFLECT

How many tropical storms hit Haiti between 1994 and 2010? About how many people were killed?

Focus on Determining the Central Idea

To determine the central idea of a text, look for a repeated topic. Then determine how the details in the passage are related to this topic. The central idea should be the main point of the text, which all the key ideas and details support.

In this short essay, the author weaves together several ideas to make a point. In order to identify the central idea, break down the essay into paragraphs and determine the topic of each. Then decide what is the central idea of the text as a whole.

Fill in the graphic organizer below with a short summary of what is being described in each paragraph. Note: Even if one sentence stands on its own, it is considered a paragraph. Paragraphs with similar topics have been listed together.

REFLECT

Did you know that the fight-or-flight response is a physical response to fear? The body releases hormones and activates its nervous system, preparing you to fight off a threat or flee from it.

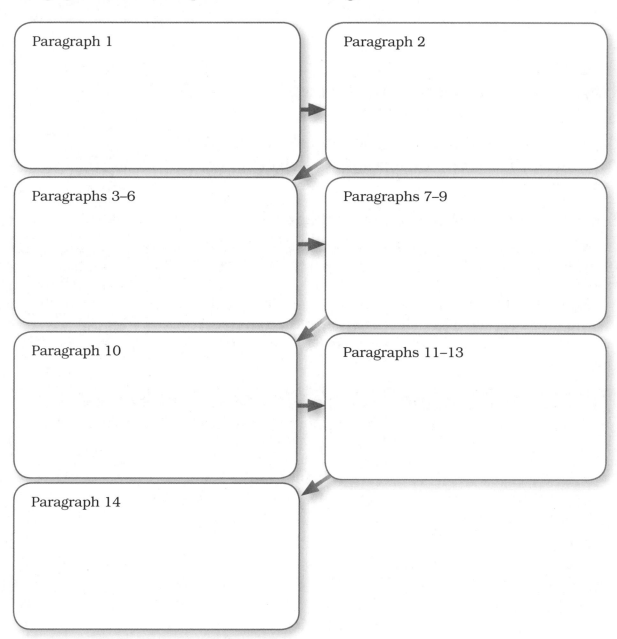

Paragraph 1

Paragraph 2

Paragraphs 3–6

Paragraphs 7–9

Paragraph 10

Paragraphs 11–13

Paragraph 14

(Speak and Listen With a partner, discuss the development of ideas in the essay. What is the central idea, and how is it developed over the course of the essay? Use specific examples from the graphic organizer on the previous page to support your answer. Be prepared to share your discussion with the class.

▼ Write After your discussion, write the central idea of the essay in one clear sentence in your response journal. To do this accurately, determine what the essay says about Haiti or Haitians. Think about the purpose of the text as a whole.

Helpful sentence starters may include the following:

- The essay reveals that . . . .

- The essay suggests that . . . .

- The essay highlights how . . . .

CONNECT TO ESSENTIAL QUESTION

What does it mean to be persistent in the face of misfortune?

REFLECT

How are nature and human nature alike? How are they different?

⌐ Second Read: Recognizing the Purpose of Repetition

Objective: Take turns reading paragraphs aloud with a partner. Circle words, phrases, or whole sentences the author uses more than once.

Focus on Recognizing the Purpose of Repetition

Writers use repetition, or the repeated use of a word or phrase, to add to the meaning of a text or to create a response in the reader.

Use the chart below to identify examples of repetition, locate them in the essay, and then comment on the effect. The first one has been completed for you, and others have been partially completed.

TECH-CONNECT

What is the difference between repetition and redundancy? Look up an online definition of each word. Write a sentence that explains the difference, and send it to your teacher.

Example	Location	Effect
sometimes	title; paragraphs 1, 3-5, 9, and 11	The word suggests that there is no exact time or place or pattern to disasters, that nature is unpredictable.
the earth is cruel		

Example	Location	Effect
	paragraph 8	
after	paragraph 10	
	Paragraph 11	
weep and mourn		

(**Speak and Listen** In groups of three or four, discuss your responses in the chart. How does the repetition of the words and phrases support the central idea you identified? What would be lost if the repetition were not there?

Third Read: Interpreting Literary Devices

Listen as your teacher reads the essay aloud a third time. Notice how the essay begins like a story. Nature itself is introduced as a character, making the Haitians' struggle against the elements more personal. Visualize the images in the text as you read along.

> Objective: Draw a box around details that create visual images.

CONNECT TO ESSENTIAL QUESTION

Think of a time when you went through something difficult. How were you able to manage the situation? In what ways could you have handled it better?

Focus on Interpreting Literary Devices

The author introduces the setting before describing the hardships Haiti has experienced. Look at the first three paragraphs (lines 1–9). What literary devices can you identify in this section? Four literary devices are listed and defined in the chart below. Fill in the last column with examples from the text.

Literary Device	Definition	Example	Example from "Sometimes, the Earth Is Cruel"
sensory detail	details about how something looks, sounds, smells, tastes, or feels	The trees sagged with snow.	1. 2.
personification	a human trait that is given to something nonhuman	The tea pot spoke in its loud voice, waking the house.	1. 2.
simile	a comparison between two dissimilar things using *like* or *as*	For the first time, the baby stood, rising like the sun.	1.

©Perfection Learning® • No Reproduction Permitted

Literary Device	Definition	Example	Example from "Sometimes, the Earth Is Cruel"
hyperbole	an exaggerated statement not meant to be taken literally	It was the six-hundredth time he had told her to get dressed.	1

▼**Write** How do the images of nature affect the overall meaning of the text? Explain your thoughts in a well-written paragraph in your response journal. Begin with a topic sentence and use details from the text to support your answer.

Think about these questions as you write:
- Why does the writer begin the essay with these paragraphs?
- What qualities of nature and human nature are emphasized by the literary devices?
- What are we made to notice about nature?
- What are we made to notice about human nature?

> **RULES FOR PEER REVIEW**
>
> 1. Be confident. Don't apologize for your writing.
> 2. Be open to advice.
> 3. Be polite.

Speak and Listen In groups of three or four, conduct a peer review of your paragraph. Follow these steps for your peer review.

Steps for Peer Review

1. Select a timekeeper. Stick to the time. Each writer gets five minutes.

2. One person begins by reading aloud his or her paragraph while the other members listen.

3. Pause. The same reader reads that paragraph aloud a second time. (Don't skip this step.) The group members listen and write comments or notes.

4. The writer asks, "What part was clearest to you?" Each member responds. The writer jots notes on the draft.

5. The writer asks, "Was there any part that confused you?" Each member responds. The writer jots notes on the draft.

6. The next member in the group becomes the writer. Repeat the steps until each member of the group has read their paragraph and been a timekeeper.

Revise your draft based on your peers' questions and comments. Then type it using a word processing program. Be sure to double-space and use 12-point font.

Language: Anaphora

Anaphora is the repetition of a word or phrase at the beginning of several sentences or clauses in a row. Read the example below.

> Bad enough, Haiti is wretchedly poor. Bad enough it has a history of political instability and colonialism, of being ignored by the major powers when it is not being exploited by them. Bad enough, all that, yet at the end of the day, those are disasters authored by human hands, by human greed, human corruption, human economic predation.

Notice how the expression *bad enough* begins three successive sentences. This repetition emphasizes the author's point that Haiti is a country that has experienced so much suffering. Also, the comma used to set off the phrase makes the point even stronger.

Write a paragraph in your response journal using anaphora to describe the people of Haiti working together to recover from the disaster. The paragraph should be at least three sentences long.

Project-Based Assessment

Digital Presentation

Conduct research and create a digital presentation about the 2010 Haiti earthquake. First, search online for articles that explain in greater detail the events that took place and the effects of the disaster. Look for information about both the short- and long-term effects and how people have responded. Be sure to find photos to show what occurred at the time and what has happened since.

Use reliable sources for your information. Websites that end in *.edu, .gov,* or *.org* usually have more reliable information than sites with many contributors such as Wikipedia. News organizations such as newspapers or magazines may also provide credible details about the earthquake and its aftermath.

Gather the following information for your presentation:

- a description of the conditions in Haiti just before the quake

- a list of the immediate effects of the quake on people and communities

- details about the recovery efforts made by individuals, governments, and organizations

- photographs showing the extent of the destruction and the success or failure of rebuilding

- three or more sources used for the project, including the name of the article, the website, and the date

TECH-CONNECT

Describe an interaction you have had with nature—positive or negative—and post it online using a site chosen by your teacher. Focus on describing aspects of nature rather than how you felt.

TECH-CONNECT

Save your presentation to a flash drive so you can bring it to school. Be sure to open your file before your presentation to make sure it will work on the school computer.

©Perfection Learning® • No Reproduction Permitted

Finally, create an interesting and well-organized computer presentation. Each slide should have both an image or video and text. Read the rubric carefully so you know what is expected of you. Practice your presentation. If working with a partner, decide in advance who will share which slides.

Use the following guidelines for your presentation.	
To receive the highest score (4.0), the project must meet all of these criteria.	Your presentation • uses multimedia (images, audio, video) in a professional way and is appealing both visually and aurally. • contains images or videos that clearly demonstrate understanding of the events and their effects. • contains images or videos that are appropriate for the intended audience and are not overly graphic or disturbing. • demonstrates that you clearly understand the events. • demonstrates confidence, eye contact, and proper volume. • uses correct grammar, usage, punctuation, and spelling.

On Your Own: Integrating Ideas

1. Research an organization that helps with disaster relief such as USAID, American Red Cross, or Oxfam. What is their mission? Where have they given aid in the last year? How did they help? How do they raise money for disaster relief? How do you know where the donated money goes?

2. Learn more about Haiti. Research its people, its history, its politics, its economy, and/or its ecology. What challenges have affected Haiti in the past and today? What are its strengths as a nation? Share your findings with a friend, your class, or an adult.

3. Read a book about a natural disaster, either fiction or nonfiction. Which aspect do you find more intriguing—the science behind the disaster or the human will needed to survive it? Consider asking a friend to read the same book so you can share your thoughts. Here are a few books to consider:
   • *Life as We Knew It* by Susan Beth Pfeffer
   • *Three Rivers Rising* by Jame Richards
   • *Out of the Dust* by Karen Hesse

Connect to Testing

In this chapter, you identified the central idea of an essay. You also identified and interpreted literary devices within a text. When you take assessments, you will be tested on your ability to understand the ideas expressed in a passage. Here are some examples of these types of questions.

1. According to the author, why aren't donations and other forms of aid enough to repair the lives of those who have experienced a disaster?

    A. It is difficult for foreigners to get to Haiti.

    B. Not enough money was donated to cover the expense.

    C. No amount of aid can repair the constant damage.

    D. Aid does not always reach the people who need it.

2. The author writes, "Why are the most vulnerable repeatedly assessed the highest price?" What does the author most likely mean?

    A. Why do those who get hurt again and again have to pay so much to get better?

    B. Why must those who are already challenged keep enduring more challenges?

    C. Why are the people at risk never given enough money to recover?

    D. Why do the people who are most hurt turn around and hurt others?

3. **Part A:** The author quotes a play that says "your arms too short to box with God." What is the meaning of this expression?

    A. A person cannot fight with God because people are smaller.

    B. If you try hard enough, you will be able to control your life.

    C. God is too far away to be reached, even in times of need.

    D. Human beings can't control the forces of nature.

    Part B: Which sentence from the text best supports the answer to Part A?

    A. *We are hamstrung by our own limitations, so we can only do what we always do, only send prayers and help.*

    B. *But what else are you going to do?*

    C. *It is to breathe a prayer that begins, "There, but for the grace of God . . ."*

    D. *Even less have we the ability to answer the question that burns the moment: Why are the most vulnerable repeatedly assessed the highest price?*

©Perfection Learning® • No Reproduction Permitted

4. How does the passage characterize the Haitian people?

   A. depressed and defeated

   B. strong and hardy

   C. limited and powerless

   D. lively and excited

5. Read this excerpt and answer the question that follows.

   > Sometimes, the earth is cruel. And always, when it is, we do the same thing. We dig ourselves out. We weep and mourn, we recover and memorialize the dead, we rebuild our homes. And we go on. This is the price of being human. And also, arguably, the noblest expression.

   Whom does the word *we* refer to in the excerpt?

   A. the Haitians and those who help them

   B. the writer and his family

   C. victims of natural disasters the world over

   D. all of humanity

6. Which of the following best states the central idea of the essay?

   A. Humans are limited by their abilities and can only do so much.

   B. Humans are able to thrive despite nature's merciless power.

   C. The earth is only as kind to humanity as humanity is to it.

   D. People are often too sad to push through difficult times in life.

Chapter 7

Understanding Poetry

Preview Concepts

When life hands you challenges, the words of your mentors can help you. Mentors are older, more experienced people who give you advice about all areas of your life. Mentors include parents, teachers, coaches, or other adults in your life. Make a list of the mentors who have helped you in difficult times.

With a partner, discuss why mentors are important for a young person to have. Summarize the main points from your discussion below.

CHAPTER GOALS

In this chapter you will:

- identify the unstated ideas of a poem.
- analyze the effect of concrete images in a poem.
- locate the tonal shift in a poem.

PREVIEW ACADEMIC VOCABULARY

concrete image

dialect

infer

shift

speaker

tonal

Making Connections

Read the following excerpt from a poem.

> Reg wished me to go with him to the field,
>
> I paused because I did not want to go;
>
> But in her quiet way she made me yield
>
> Reluctantly, for she was breathing low.
>
> Her hand she slowly lifted from her lap
>
> And, smiling sadly in the old sweet way,
>
> She pointed to the nail where hung my cap.
>
> Her eyes said: I shall last another day.
>
> But scarcely had we reached the distant place,
>
> When o'er the hills we heard a faint bell ringing;
>
> A boy came running up with frightened face;
>
> We knew the fatal news that he was bringing.
>
> I heard him listlessly, without a moan,
>
> Although the only one I loved was gone.

—"My Mother" by Claude McKay

What does the speaker suggest at the beginning of the poem, without coming right out and saying it? Underline details that help you understand the situation in the poem. In the space below, explain what is going on in the first eight lines.

MAKING CONNECTIONS

As you read the poem in this chapter, you will uncover the poet's message by exploring the details and the changing tone of the text.

First Read: Uncovering a Poem's Message

The Harlem Renaissance was a period of literary and artistic growth in the African American community of 1920s New York. One of the movement's most celebrated writers was Langston Hughes, who wrote the poem "Mother to Son" in 1922. Hughes uses words such as *I'se* in this poem to depict how some African Americans spoke at that time.

Objective: As you read, think about what the speaker's message is. Remember that the speaker is the person who is saying the words of the poem; it is not always the same as the writer. Underline two lines that suggest the message. Then write your response in the My Thoughts column.

Mother to Son
by Langston Hughes

		My Thoughts
1	Well, son, I'll tell you:	
	Life for me ain't been no crystal stair.	
	It's had tacks in it,	
	And splinters,	
5	And boards torn up,	
	And places with no carpet on the floor—	
	Bare.	
	But all the time	
	I'se been a-climbin' on,	
10	And reachin' landin's,	
	And turnin' corners,	
	And sometimes goin' in the dark	
	Where there ain't been no light.	
	So, boy, don't you turn back.	
15	Don't you set down on the steps	
	'Cause you finds it's kinder hard.	
	Don't you fall now—	
	For I'se still goin', honey,	
	I'se still climbin',	
20	And life for me ain't been no crystal stair.	

©Perfection Learning® • No Reproduction Permitted

TECH-CONNECT

Make up your own metaphor to connect your life to an object, as Hughes does with the image of the "crystal stair." Tweet your version of the line below, or post it to your class website.

Life for me hasn't been _____.

What is the mother trying to tell her son? Write your answer in your response journal and be prepared to share.

Focus on Uncovering a Poem's Message

SOAPSTone is a technique used to break down a text into its main parts. It helps the reader separate what is explicit (clearly stated) from what is implicit (indirectly stated).

Fill in the chart below to uncover the poem's message.

Element	Explanation	"Mother to Son"
Speaker	Who is the speaker of the poem? It is not the same as the poet.	
Occasion	What was going on outside the poem when it was written? What is the event or a situation inside the poem?	
Audience	To whom is the poem directed? It is not the same as the person the speaker is addressing.	

continued on next page

Element	Explanation	"Mother to Son"
Purpose	What does the poet want the audience to think about?	
Subject	What is the poem about?	
Tone	What is the speaker's attitude? Look at the language, imagery, and word choice.	

Speak and Listen *Two-four-eight, get it straight!* Compare your chart with a partner's. Discuss and adjust your responses so they are the same or similar. Once you agree on your responses, meet with another pair and share. Then, once the four of you agree on your responses, join another foursome and share again. Can all eight of you come to agreement on the answers for the chart above?

Second Read: Understanding Images in Poetry

Poets use words to create images in their readers' minds.

Objective: Listen as the poem is read aloud. Circle the concrete images that you can picture in your mind. Think about how these details help to tell the speaker's story.

Focus on Understanding Images in Poetry

Writers use concrete images to convey a message without having to directly explain it. The images represent a message. You, as the reader, must *infer* the message being expressed by the image. For example, the poet Langston Hughes uses a crystal stair to represent a rich or comfortable life, which his mother has not had.

Look at the chart below. How does each description of the stairs reveal an aspect of the speaker's journey? The first one has been done for you.

Concrete image	What it says about the speaker's life
no crystal stair	Her path in life has not been easy, rich, or comfortable.
tacks	
splinters	
boards torn up	
no carpet	
climbin' on	
reachin'	
turnin'	

Write On a separate piece of paper, write a clear and concise paragraph explaining how the concrete images in the poem contribute to the message of the poem. Type your paragraph and revise it carefully. Be prepared to share your paragraph with your class.

Third Read: Recognizing a Tonal Shift

Tone is the author's or speaker's attitude toward the subject he or she is writing about. Unpleasant or ugly images communicate a dark tone. Bright, uplifting words indicate the author's tone is happy and content.

Objective: As you read the poem a third time, notice where there is a change in the tone from negative to positive. Mark this line with a checkmark.

Focus on Recognizing a Tonal Shift

The point at which the speaker switches direction or introduces a change in understanding is called the *shift* or *turn*. The shift often begins with a word of contradiction, such as *but, although, yet, however, nevertheless, still,* or *even though.*

In many classic poems, the shift occurs in the same place each time, such as in the last two lines of a Shakespearean sonnet. However, a free verse poem—one that has no set form—can have a shift anywhere. Langston Hughes's poem is an example of free verse because it does not follow any specific structure or rhyme scheme.

Look back at the poem and note the place where you put a check mark. Write the line number below and then answer the questions that follow.

The shift occurs in line _____ and begins with the word _____.

1. What is the focus of the text that comes before the shift?

2. What is the focus of the text that comes after the shift?

3. How does the change in tone develop the speaker's point of view?

⌒Speak and Listen Share your answers with a partner. If you did not mark the same spot, try to agree on where the shift is. Then discuss the difference between what comes before the shift and what comes after. What new understanding does the speaker reveal after the shift?

CONNECT TO ESSENTIAL QUESTION

Think of a time when someone told you something was going to be difficult. Did this help you? Explain.

Language: Dialect

Dialect is a form of language that has its own grammar rules and vocabulary. It is particular to a specific region or social group. It may include not only a spoken accent but common expressions that may differ from standard English grammar or usage.

Writers often use dialect to help illustrate their characters' background, education, or social class.

Circle Langston Hughes's use of dialect in the following lines from the poem:

> Life for me ain't been no crystal stair . . . .
>
> I'se been a-climbin' on . . . .
>
> For I'se still goin', honey . . . .
>
> 'Cause you finds it's kinder hard.

These words and phrases reflect the voices of African Americans in the 1920s. Why do you think Hughes would find this important to show in his poem?

Project-Based Assessments

Poetry Explication

An explication is a short essay about the careful study of a poem. The reader determines the basic design of a poem and analyzes the details to explain the possible meanings. Answer the following questions to write an explication of "Mother to Son." The first six questions form the SOAPSTone technique, so you may use your answers to those questions from page 127–128.

- Who is the speaker?
- What is the occasion?
- Who is the audience?
- What is the purpose?
- What is the subject?
- What is the tone?
- What images are there? How do they affect the poem's meaning?
- What patterns do you notice? (statements, language, rhythm, rhyme, meter)
- What is the structure of the poem? (How does it look on the page? Look at the stanzas, punctuation, capital letters, number of lines, and line length.)
- Is there a tonal shift? How is it significant?
- How might the poem be important to the world outside of it?

Once you have gathered all your answers, write a draft of your essay. Walk your reader through the poem like you are a guide in a museum. Point out key aspects of the poem and then smaller details, going line by line. Use transitions and vary your sentence structure to keep it interesting.

Use the following guidelines for your poetry explication.	
To receive the highest score (4.0), the explication must meet all of these criteria.	Your explication • accurately identifies the speaker, occasion, audience, subject, and tone. • performs a line-by-line analysis, explaining what the details reveal about the speaker's life. • identifies any patterns or shifts in the poem. • explains the structure of the poem. • varies sentence structure and uses appropriate transition words. • is free from typos and uses correct grammar and punctuation.

©Perfection Learning® • No Reproduction Permitted

Pop-Up Poetry Presentation

In a pop-up poetry presentation, the presenter reveals observations about the poem that "pop up" on-screen. You can use a slideshow program or, If you do not have access to a computer, construction paper, scissors, and glue for your pop-up presentation.

Read another Langston Hughes poem, such as "Dream Deferred" or "Let America Be America Again." Then use Google Slides, PowerPoint, Prezi, Keynote, or a similar program to create a pop-up presentation for your class. Copy the poem onto a slide or a sheet of poster board. Then add pop-ups or speech bubbles to label different elements of the poem. This will make the elements "pop out" and also add an artistic component to your presentation.

Label the following in the poem:

- speaker

- occasion

- audience

- purpose

- tone

- figurative language (metaphor, simile, symbol)

- meter and rhyme, structure (line length/stanzas)

- language (dialect, repetition, word choice)

- theme

To keep the poem from looking too cluttered, use colors, shapes, and symbols to label the elements of the poetry. For example, make all words that relate to theme blue or place all words that support the tone in triangular bubbles. Then create a legend for your viewers to follow.

Use the following guidelines for your pop-up poetry presentation.	
To receive the highest score (4.0), the presentation must meet all of these criteria.	Your presentation • accurately identifies the speaker, occasion, audience, purpose, and tone of a poem. • correctly labels figurative language. • points out details that support the poem's theme or purpose. • has a legend at the bottom that defines the bubbles. • is neat, colorful, and edited for correct spelling and usage.

On Your Own: Integrating Ideas

1. Learn about the Harlem Renaissance. When and where was it? Who were some of the major writers, scholars, artists, musicians, and photographers? How did this important movement shape American culture?

2. Try writing a poem of your own. Use a dialect that is specific to your region, your background, or a relevant social group, such as teenagers. Write on any topic that is important to your group. Write with an informal voice and informal language in order to capture the essence of that group. Use "Mother to Son" as a model.

3. Read more about Langston Hughes. Who was he and how did he begin writing? Why did he become so famous? Create a presentation with multiple slides and share it with others.

©Perfection Learning® • No Reproduction Permitted

Connect to Testing

In this chapter, you gained an understanding of a poem by uncovering its message, analyzing the images, and recognizing the tonal shift. When you take reading assessments, you may be asked to make inferences about poetry and support them with evidence from the text. Here are some examples of these types of questions.

1. Which line suggests that the speaker continues trying to improve her life despite the difficulties?

    A. *And sometimes goin' in the dark*

    B. *Life for me ain't been no crystal stair.*

    C. *And places with no carpet on the floor—*

    D. *I'se still climbin',*

2. The speaker uses dialect throughout the poem "Mother to Son." Which of the following best describes the effect of this device?

    A. It suggests the meaning of the poem goes beyond advice to a single child.

    B. It helps readers picture the speaker and understand her as a character.

    C. It shows that the speaker has had a difficult life because of her speech.

    D. It reveals that the poet looks down on the character of the speaker.

3. **Part A:** Which of the following best describes the advice the speaker gives to her son?

    A. You should never give up working for a better life, even if you have setbacks.

    B. Life is never easy because there are constant challenges and sources of pain.

    C. We can only travel forward in our lives, not backward, so be cautious.

    D. Parents try to make a good life for children, who must then strive for a better life.

    Part B: Which excerpt from the text best supports the answer to Part A?

    A. *But all the time / I'se been a-climbin' on,*

    B. *It's had tacks in it, / And splinters, / And boards torn up,*

    C. *And sometimes goin' in the dark / Where there ain't been no light.*

    D. *Don't you fall now— / For I'se still goin', honey,*

continued on next page

4. **Part A:** Which of these best describes the poem's tone before it shifts?

   A. hopeful

   B. weary

   C. bitter

   D. proud

   Part B: What is the speaker's tone after the shift?

   A. amused

   B. desperate

   C. angry

   D. determined

5. The speaker repeatedly begins lines with the word *and*. What is the effect of the repetition in the poem? Write a paragraph that describes the effect, using evidence from the text to support your answer.

©Perfection Learning® • No Reproduction Permitted

Chapter 8

Exploring Character Development in Nonfiction

Preview Concepts

The world is full of people who struggled before rising to great success. They include artists and inventors, political leaders and athletes. Think about the traits that are typically associated with a person who rises after a struggle. Write a list of these characteristics below.

Are some people born with these characteristics, or do they learn them? How do we know that successful people possess these qualities? Share your thoughts with a partner. Summarize your discussion in the space below.

CHAPTER GOALS

In this chapter you will:

• observe the ways characters are developed in a text.

• consider the relationship between chapters in a book.

• analyze the author's point of view.

PREVIEW ACADEMIC VOCABULARY

character development

point of view

protagonist

Making Connections

Read the following excerpt.

I know I'm not an ordinary ten-year-old kid. I mean, sure, I do ordinary things. I eat ice cream. I ride my bike. I play ball. I have an XBox. Stuff like that makes me ordinary. I guess. And I feel ordinary. Inside. But I know ordinary kids don't make other ordinary kids run away screaming in playgrounds. I know ordinary kids don't get stared at wherever they go.

If I found a magic lamp and I could have one wish, I would wish that I had a normal face that no one ever noticed at all. I would wish that I could walk down the street without people seeing me and then doing that look-away thing. Here's what I think: the only reason I'm not ordinary is that no one else sees me that way.

But I'm kind of used to how I look by now. I know how to pretend I don't see the faces people make. We've all gotten pretty good at that sort of thing: me, Mom and Dad, Via. Actually, I take that back: Via's not so good at it. She can get really annoyed when people do something rude. Like, for instance, one time in the playground some older kids made some noises. I don't even know what the noises were exactly because I didn't hear them myself, but Via heard and she just started yelling at the kids. That's the way she is. I'm not that way.

Via doesn't see me as ordinary. She says she does, but if I were ordinary, she wouldn't feel like she needs to protect me as much. And Mom and Dad don't see me as ordinary, either. They see me as extraordinary. I think the only person in the world who realizes how ordinary I am is me.

—*Wonder* by R. J. Palacio

Describe the character from the excerpt in the space below. Underline the lines that support your response.

> **MAKING CONNECTIONS**
>
> As you read the excerpts in this chapter, you will study how authors of nonfiction, just like authors of fiction, develop real people as characters and what each part of a text adds to the whole.

©Perfection Learning® • No Reproduction Permitted

First Read: Understanding Character Development

Frederick Douglass was an African American who taught himself to read and write and then successfully escaped from slavery. He became well known as a leader of the antislavery movement and as a speaker and writer. His autobiography tells the story of his path to freedom. In this excerpt, Douglass relates experiences from when he was around ten years old.

Objective: As you read, consider how Frederick Douglass responds to his life as a slave. How does he feel at first? What inspires a change in him? What does he resolve to do? Underline key sentences that help you understand his character and his story. Record any questions you have in the My Thoughts column.

Narrative of the Life of Frederick Douglass, an American Slave
from Chapter 7

by Frederick Douglass

My Thoughts

1   I often found myself regretting my own existence, and wishing myself dead; and but for the hope of being free, I have no doubt but that I should have killed myself, or done something for which I should have been killed. While in this

5 state of mind, I was eager to hear any one speak of slavery. I was a ready listener. Every little while, I could hear something about the **abolitionists**. It was some time before I found what the word meant. It was always used in such connections as to make it an interesting word to me. If a slave ran away

10 and succeeded in getting clear, or if a slave killed his master, set fire to a barn, or did anything very wrong in the mind of a slaveholder, it was spoken of as the fruit of abolition. Hearing the word in this connection very often, I set about learning what it meant. The dictionary afforded me little or no help.

15 I found it was "the act of abolishing;" but then I did not

---

abolitionists: people working to end slavery

know what was to be abolished. Here I was perplexed. I did not dare to ask anyone about its meaning, for I was satisfied that it was something they wanted me to know very little about. After a patient waiting, I got one of our city papers,

20 containing an account of the number of **petitions** from the north, praying for the abolition of slavery in the District of Columbia, and of the slave trade between the States. From this time I understood the words *abolition* and *abolitionist*, and always drew near when that word was spoken, expecting to

25 hear something of importance to myself and fellow-slaves. The light broke in upon me by degrees. I went one day down on the wharf of Mr. Waters; and seeing two Irishmen unloading a **scow** of stone, I went, unasked, and helped them. When we had finished, one of them came to me and asked me if I were

30 a slave. I told him I was. He asked, "Are ye a slave for life?" I told him that I was. The good Irishman seemed to be deeply affected by the statement. He said to the other that it was a pity so fine a little fellow as myself should be a slave for life. He said it was a shame to hold me. They both advised me to

35 run away to the north; that I should find friends there, and that I should be free. I pretended not to be interested in what they said, and treated them as if I did not understand them; for I feared they might be **treacherous**. White men have been known to encourage slaves to escape, and then, to get the

40 reward, catch them and return them to their masters. I was afraid that these seemingly good men might use me so; but I nevertheless remembered their advice, and from that time I

My Thoughts

----

petitions: written statements, signed by many people, urging a certain action
scow: flat-bottomed boat
treacherous: untrustworthy

    ©Perfection Learning® • No Reproduction Permitted

45 resolved to run away. I looked forward to a time at which it would be safe for me to escape. I was too young to think of doing so immediately; besides, I wished to learn how to write, as I might have occasion to write my own pass. I consoled myself with the hope that I should one day find a good chance. Meanwhile, I would learn to write.

My Thoughts

_____

_____

_____

_____

_____

FIRST RESPONSE: KEY IDEAS AND DETAILS

Look back at the lines you underlined. What are your first impressions of Frederick Douglass? Share your thoughts with a partner.

TECH-CONNECT

What skill or hobby have you taught yourself? Or what would you like to teach yourself to do? Tweet your response to your teacher, or post your response on a website your teacher has chosen.

Focus on Understanding Character Development

This text is a work of nonfiction, but like fiction, it includes details and descriptions that develop character. Though Frederick Douglass was a real person writing a true story, he still was an author who developed his own character using techniques like the ones fiction writers use.

In the beginning of Chapter 7, the reader feels sympathy for Mr. Douglass and becomes invested in his desire for freedom. Fill in the map on the next page to help you analyze his character.

Portrait of Frederick Douglass

continued on next page

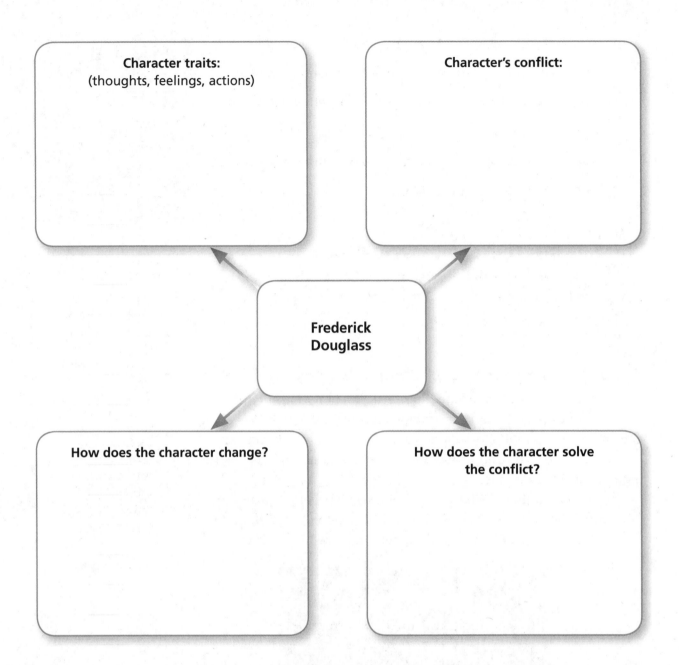

Character traits:
(thoughts, feelings, actions)

Character's conflict:

Frederick Douglass

How does the character change?

How does the character solve the conflict?

Second Read: Analyzing How Chapters Develop the Author's Ideas

Now read an excerpt from Chapter 10 of the same book, and consider how this chapter builds on ideas introduced in Chapter 7. Douglass is a teenager in this excerpt, and he has been sent to work for William Freeland, who treats him less cruelly than Douglass's previous masters.

Objective: As you read, look for the ways Douglass's desire to educate himself is reflected here and how that interest has changed over time. Write your thoughts in the My Thoughts column.

> **CONNECT TO ESSENTIAL QUESTION**
>
> Can a person learn to have grit?

Narrative of the Life of Frederick Douglass, an American Slave
from Chapter 10

by Frederick Douglass

1   Mr. Freeland was himself the owner of but two slaves. Their names were Henry Harris and John Harris. The rest of his hands he hired. These consisted of myself, Sandy Jenkins, and Handy Caldwell. Henry and John were quite intelligent, and

5 in a very little while after I went there, I succeeded in creating in them a strong desire to learn how to read. This desire soon sprang up in the others also. They very soon mustered up some old spelling-books, and nothing would do but that I must keep a **Sabbath** school. I agreed to do so, and accordingly devoted

10 my Sundays to teaching these my loved fellow-slaves how to read. Neither of them knew his letters when I went there. Some of the slaves of the neighboring farms found what was going on, and also availed themselves of this little opportunity to learn to read. . . .

15   I had at one time over forty scholars, and those of the right sort, **ardently** desiring to learn. They were of all ages, though mostly men and women. I look back to those Sundays with an amount of pleasure not to be expressed. They were great days to my soul. The work of instructing my dear fellow-

20 slaves was the sweetest engagement with which I was ever blessed. We loved each other, and to leave them at the close of the Sabbath was a severe cross indeed. When I think that these precious souls are to-day shut up in the prison-house of slavery, my feelings overcome me, and I am almost ready

My Thoughts

Sabbath: a day of religious observance; Sunday, for most Christians

ardently: deeply

25   to ask, "Does a **righteous** God govern the universe? and for

what does he hold the thunders in his right hand, if not to

smite the oppressor, and deliver the spoiled out of the hand

of the spoiler?" These dear souls came not to Sabbath school

because it was popular to do so, nor did I teach them because

30   it was reputable to be thus engaged. Every moment they spent

in that school, they were liable to be taken up, and given

thirty-nine lashes. They came because they wished to learn.

Their minds had been starved by their cruel masters. They had

been shut up in mental darkness. I taught them, because it

35   was the delight of my soul to be doing something that looked

like bettering the condition of my race. I kept up my school

nearly the whole year I lived with Mr. Freeland; and, beside my

Sabbath school, I devoted three evenings in the week, during

the winter, to teaching the slaves at home. And I have the

40   happiness to know, that several of those who came to Sabbath

school learned how to read; and that one, at least, is now free

through my **agency**.

My Thoughts

_____

righteous: morally good
smite the oppressor: strike the cruel
agency: action or intervention

Focus on How Chapters Develop the Author's Ideas

Narrative of the Life of Frederick Douglass is the true story of a real person. The author still had to consider the structure of his story as he told it. He had to decide which details to include and which to leave out. In a well-written story, all of the details relate to the main character, or protagonist, and the central idea. Consider how this chapter builds on Chapter 7.

Answer the questions on the next page. Remember to return to the text to find evidence. Include a quotation in your response. Be prepared to share your responses with the class.

1. Part A: Why does Frederick Douglass devote himself to teaching other slaves to read and write?

Part B: Provide a quotation from the text that supports your answer above.

2. Part A: Why do the other slaves come to his class? What does this detail help prove about the lives of Frederick Douglass and other slaves?

Part B: Provide a quotation from the text that supports your answer above.

continued on next page

3. Part A: How does the writer's tone change from Chapter 7 to Chapter 10?

Part B: Provide a quotation from the text that supports your answer above.

4. Part A: What character traits introduced in Chapter 7 allow Douglass to lead others in the pursuit of freedom in Chapter 10?

Part B: Provide a quotation from the text that supports your answer above.

©Perfection Learning® • No Reproduction Permitted

☾ **Speak and Listen** In small groups of four to six people, discuss the answers to the questions on pages 145–146. Take turns speaking, and focus on listening to others' responses. Try to build on each other's comments and find a new or deeper understanding of the text together.

Steps for a Group Discussion

1. Select one person to begin the conversation.

2. Without raising hands, allow the discussion to be free-form, speaking one at a time. Try not to interrupt one another.

3. Relate your comments to another person's by using his or her name and a phrase such as the following: *As _____ said . . .; I agree that _____ because . . .;* or *An example of what _____ said is . . . .*

Third Read: Determining the Author's Point of View

Objective: As you reread both excerpts, pay attention to how the author reveals his point of view about the events in his life. Draw a box around short sentences he uses to communicate big ideas.

Focus on the Determining the Author's Point of View

Writers often include a moment of reflection within the narration. Frederick Douglass offers these reflections in the form of brief statements, or asides. Don't skim over these short sentences. They may seem unimportant, but they add meaning to the text. For Douglass, these are moments when he recalls the person he was before he found freedom. The sentences are short, but powerful.

Look at the following chart. Rewrite the quotations from the text into your own words. Then determine what they add to the meaning of the chapter(s) overall.

Quotation	In my own words	What it reveals about Douglass's point of view
I was a ready listener.		

continued on next page

Quotation	In my own words	What it reveals about Douglass's point of view
The light broke in upon me by degrees.		
I consoled myself with the hope that I should one day find a good chance.		
They were great days to my soul.		
They have been shut up in mental darkness.		

▼**Write** Make a personal connection with Frederick Douglass. Which quotation do you relate to most? Copy the quote into your response journal, and do a freewrite in which you connect your experience to the quotation. Try writing for 15 minutes without stopping to edit. If you feel comfortable, share your response with a friend.

CONNECT TO ESSENTIAL QUESTION

How can suffering inspire strength?

©Perfection Learning® • No Reproduction Permitted

Language: Comma with an Introductory Phrase

One of the uses of a comma is to separate introductory prepositional phrases from an independent clause (one that can stand on its own). Consider this example adapted from *Narrative of the Life of Frederick Douglass*. The introductory prepositional phrases are underlined.

> <u>In this state of mind</u>, I was eager to hear any one speak of slavery.

Introductory phrases begin with prepositions such as *in, of, after, on, because of,* and *without* and end with a noun. Review the sentences below and then rewrite them by moving the prepositional phrase(s) to the beginning of the sentence. Be sure to include a comma.

1. Emily reached into the fireplace to rescue the kitten without a second thought.

2. The gym teacher gave each player three strikes due to the rules of baseball.

3. Mountain snow remains frozen year round because of the thin air at high altitudes.

continued on next page

Write two sentences of your own using introductory prepositional phrases.

4.

5.

REFLECT

What makes *Narrative of the Life of Frederick Douglass, an American Slave* more intriguing than a history book on slavery?

Project-Based Assessments

Digital Presentation

Conduct research on slavery in the United States. First, search online by using relevant terms and consulting reliable sources.

Remember, websites that end in *.org, .edu., or .gov.* usually have more reliable information than sites with many contributors such as Wikipedia. Check the website's About tab to find out if it is maintained by a reputable source, such as a college, a historical society, or a government agency.

Gather the following information for your presentation:

- dates of slavery in North America
- how and why it began, including the role of the cotton gin
- states where slavery was allowed
- condition and treatment of slaves
- laws around the purchase and sale of slaves
- how slavery ended

Create an interesting and well-organized computer presentation. Each slide should have both an image or video and text. Read the rubric carefully so you know what is expected of you from the beginning. Practice your presentation. If you are working with a partner, decide in advance who will share which slides.

Use the following guidelines for your presentation.	
To receive the highest score (4.0), the presentation must meet all of these criteria.	**Your presentation** • uses multimedia (images, audio, video) in a professional way and is appealing both to see and to hear. • contains information that clearly demonstrates understanding of American slavery. • contains images or videos that are appropriate for the intended audience and are not overly graphic or offensive. • demonstrates confidence, eye contact, and proper volume. • uses correct grammar, punctuation, and spelling.

Staged Interview

Work with a partner and stage an interview with Frederick Douglass. Decide who will be the interviewer and who will play Frederick Douglass. Read transcripts of interviews with a musician, artist, athlete, or another author to use as a model. Then together compose relevant, appropriate, and interesting questions on topics such as the following:

- Douglass's birth and family life
- a story about growing up in slavery
- the major turning point in his life
- the beginning of his career as a writer
- other life achievements

Research the answers using reliable sources, including other chapters from *Narrative of the Life of Frederick Douglass*. Then practice your interview and take on the personality of the role you are playing. Remember that your audience will be more interested in questions that begin with *how* or *why* than in *yes/no* questions.

Use the following guidelines for your interview.	
To receive the highest score (4.0), the interview must meet all of these criteria.	**Your interview** • is clear, practiced, and appropriate. • communicates important information about the life of Frederick Douglass. • reveals specific details about his life. • includes questions that are not yes or no answers. • appropriately portrays the character of Frederick Douglass and of an interviewer.

On Your Own: Integrating Ideas

1. Read the rest of the *Narrative of the Life of Frederick Douglass, an American Slave.* Discuss the book with someone else who has read it. Think about how and why Douglass became so famous.

2. Learn more about Frederick Douglass by watching a movie or TV program about his life. For example, the A & E series *Biography* featured an episode on Douglass, which is available to watch on www.biography.com.

3. Read *Incidents in the Life of a Slave Girl* by Harriet Jacobs. Discover how this courageous, spirited young woman escaped from her master in North Carolina and eventually found freedom—and her children—in the North. How was her experience different from that of Frederick Douglass? How was it similar?

    ©Perfection Learning® • No Reproduction Permitted

Connect to Testing

Questions on reading tests often require you to make inferences. In this chapter, you spent time analyzing character development and point of view. Answer the following questions based on the excerpts in this chapter. Return to the texts as needed.

1. **Part A:** Which word best describes Frederick Douglass's state of mind before he met the Irishmen in Chapter 7?

   A. hopeful

   B. depressed

   C. angry

   D. thoughtful

   Part B: Which statement from the text best supports the answer to Part A?

   A. *I often found myself regretting my own existence, and wishing myself dead . . .*

   B. *I was a ready listener.*

   C. *. . . I was satisfied that it was something they wanted me to know very little about.*

   D. *The light broke in upon me by degrees.*

2. Which of the following best describes Douglass's emotional reaction after meeting the Irishmen?

   A. guilt

   B. hopelessness

   C. resolve

   D. jealousy

3. How did learning to read and write affect Frederick Douglass?

   A. It kept him inspired until he was old enough to escape.

   B. It made the Irishmen think more highly of him.

   C. It got him a well-paid job working for Mr. Freeland.

   D. It offered him a way to please his master.

continued on next page

4. Explain whether Frederick Douglass enjoyed teaching. Why or why not? Support your answer with details from the text.

5. **Part A:** Paraphrase, or write in your own words, the following quotation from the text: "*Does a righteous God govern the universe? and for what does he hold the thunders in his right hand, if not to smite the oppressor, and deliver the spoiled out of the hand of the spoiler?*"

   Part B: Explain what the quotation reveals about the author's point of view.

    ©Perfection Learning® • No Reproduction Permitted

Chapter 9

Determining Speaker's Purpose

Preview Concepts

A good speech can change minds. A great speech can change the world. Politicians deliver speeches hoping to persuade voters to support them. Coaches give speeches to lead their teams to victory. Leaders give speeches to inform and inspire citizens.

Have you ever changed your mind (or made up your mind) because of a speech? How did the speaker convince you? If you haven't had this experience, think about how someone's words, even on a personal level, caused you to change or make up your mind. Explain below.

Discuss your responses with a partner. Then share your discussion with another pair.

CHAPTER GOALS

In this chapter you will:

- determine the points made by a speaker.
- explore a speaker's rhetoric.
- determine a speaker's purpose.

PREVIEW ACADEMIC VOCABULARY

occasion

purpose

repetition

rhetoric

rhetorical question

tone

Making Connections

Read the following excerpt from an interview with Steve Jobs, cofounder of Apple, Inc.

CONNECT TO ESSENTIAL QUESTION

Have you ever had to fail in order to succeed? What allowed you to turn your failure into a success?

Now, I've actually always found something to be very true, which is most people don't get those experiences because they never ask. I've never found anybody that didn't want to help me if I asked them for help. I always call them up. . . .

I called up Bill Hewlett when I was 12 years old, and he lived in Palo Alto. His number was still in the phone book, and he answered the phone himself. He said, "Yes?" I said, "Hi, I'm Steve Jobs, I'm 12 years old. I'm a student in high school, and I want to build a frequency counter. And I was wondering if you had any spare parts I could have." And he laughed, [but] he gave me the spare parts to build this frequency counter, and he gave me a job that summer at Hewlett-Packard . . . .

I've never found anyone who's said no or hung up the phone when I called—I just asked. And when people ask me, I try to be as responsive, to pay that debt of gratitude back. Most people never pick up the phone and call, most people never ask. And that's what separates, sometimes, the people that do things from the people that just dream about them. You gotta act. And you've got to be willing to fail, you gotta be willing to crash and burn, with people on the phone, with starting a company, with whatever. If you're afraid of failing, you won't get very far.

How does Jobs support the idea that most people do not succeed, because they are afraid to ask for help? Explain your answer below.

MAKING CONNECTIONS

In the excerpt in this chapter, you'll be reading a speech by a famous leader who had no choice but to act without fear of failure in the face of adversity.

First Read: What the Speech Says

Winston Churchill, having just become prime minister of Britain three days earlier, gave this—his first speech before the House of Commons. World War II had just started, and in this speech, he offers his bold plans for Britain's resistance against Germany.

Objective: As you read, underline sentences that show his resolve in making the hard decisions in the face of adversity.

Blood, Toil, Tears and Sweat
Winston Churchill
13 May 1940, House of Commons

1   Mr. Speaker:

On Friday evening last I received **His Majesty's** commission to form a new Administration. It was the evident wish and will of **Parliament** and the nation that this should be conceived

5   on the broadest possible basis and that it should include all parties, both those who supported the late Government and also the parties of the Opposition.

I have completed the most important part of this task. A **War Cabinet** has been formed of five Members, representing,

10   with the Liberal Opposition, the unity of the nation. The three party Leaders have agreed to serve, either in the War Cabinet or in high executive office. The three Fighting Services have been filled. It was necessary that this should be done in one single day, on account of the extreme urgency and rigour of

15   events. A number of other key positions were filled yesterday, and I am submitting a further list to His Majesty tonight. I hope to complete the appointment of the principal **Ministers** during tomorrow. The appointment of the other Ministers usually

---

His Majesty: King George VI, Queen Elizabeth's father

Parliament: legislature in Britain; similar to Congress in the United States

War Cabinet: committee formed by a government in a time of war

Ministers: chosen by the prime minister to lead on specific policy issues; known as *secretaries* in American government, such as secretary of state

takes a little longer, but I trust that, when Parliament meets

20 again, this part of my task will be completed, and that the Administration will be complete in all respects.

Sir, I considered it in the public interest to suggest that the House should be summoned to meet today. Mr. Speaker agreed and took the necessary steps, in accordance with the

25 powers conferred upon him by the Resolution of the House. At the end of the proceedings today, the Adjournment of the House will be proposed until Tuesday, the 21st May, with, of course, provision for earlier meeting, if need be. The business to be considered during that week will be notified to Members

30 at the earliest opportunity. I now invite the House, by the Resolution which stands in my name, to record its approval of the steps taken and to declare its confidence in the new Government.

Sir, to form an Administration of this scale and complexity

35 is a serious undertaking in itself, but it must be remembered that we are in the preliminary stage of one of the greatest battles in history, that we are in action at many points in Norway and in Holland, that we have to be prepared in the Mediterranean, that the air battle is continuous and

40 that many preparations have to be made here at home. In this crisis I hope I may be pardoned if I do not address the House at any length today. I hope that any of my friends and colleagues, or former colleagues, who are affected by the political reconstruction, will make all allowances for any lack of

45 ceremony with which it has been necessary to act. I would say to the House, as I said to those who've joined this government: "I have nothing to offer but blood, toil, tears and sweat."

We have before us an ordeal of the most grievous kind.

My Thoughts

©Perfection Learning® • No Reproduction Permitted

We have before us many, many long months of struggle
50   and of suffering. You ask, what is our policy? I will say: It is
to wage war, by sea, land and air, with all our might and
with all the strength that God can give us; to wage war
against a monstrous tyranny, never surpassed in the dark and
55   lamentable catalogue of human crime. That is our policy. You
ask, what is our aim? I can answer in one word: victory. Victory
at all costs, victory in spite of all terror, victory, however long
and hard the road may be; for without victory, there is no
survival. Let that be realised; no survival for the British Empire,
60   no survival for all that the British Empire has stood for, no
survival for the urge and impulse of the ages, that mankind
will move forward towards its goal.

But I take up my task with buoyancy and hope. I feel sure
that our cause will not be suffered to fail among men. At this
65   time I feel entitled to claim the aid of all, and I say, "Come
then, let us go forward together with our united strength."

FIRST RESPONSE: KEY IDEAS AND DETAILS

How would you feel as a member of the House of Commons
or a citizen of England after hearing this speech? Share your
thoughts with a partner.

TECH-CONNECT

Post your favorite sentence from the speech to Twitter, Facebook, or a website your teacher has chosen. Be sure to read your classmates' favorite lines and "like" at least two of them. Be prepared to explain why the sentence is your favorite.

REFLECT

Think of a time when you stood by a friend who had failed or when a friend stood by you. What was it like sharing that kind of embarrassment or disappointment?

Focus on What the Speech Says

This speech by Winston Churchill is considered one of the best speeches in history. He had just been appointed prime minister, and his country was on the brink of war with Germany. His speech lasted only five minutes. In just a few words, he informed and assured the people of Britain.

Each paragraph was written and delivered to make a point. What does each paragraph say? What point is he making? Analyze each paragraph to determine what it says and how it contributes to Mr. Churchill's message of strength and hope. Complete the chart that begins on the next page. The first row has been completed for you.

Paragraph	What's his point?
1 (lines 2–7)	Mr. Churchill opens by explaining that just three days prior the king of England had appointed him prime minister of England.
2 (lines 8–21)	
3 (lines 22–33)	
4 (lines 34–47)	
5 (lines 48–61)	
6 (lines 62–65)	

©Perfection Learning® • No Reproduction Permitted

Second Read: Exploring Rhetoric

Audio of Winston Churchill delivering his first speech as prime minister of England is available online. Find an audio recording and listen to the speech as it was delivered while you follow along.

Objective: This time as you listen to the speech, evaluate the prime minister's delivery. Does he sound strong? Does he sound confident?

REFLECT

How is listening to the speech different from reading it? Do you think you understood it better because you read it first?

Focus on Exploring Rhetoric

Rhetoric is defined as "the art of effective or persuasive speaking." It comes from a Greek word meaning "speaker." Rhetorical techniques are methods that speakers use to persuade or convince their audience. Winston Churchill wrote his own speeches, and he had his own style that changed little over time.

One technique that Mr. Churchill used effectively in the speech featured in this chapter is the *rhetorical question*. A rhetorical question is asked to make a point, not to get an answer. Analyze the rhetorical questions from the speech as shown in the chart below. Return to the speech and read the rhetorical question in context to gain a better understanding of its purpose and effect.

Rhetorical Question	Purpose	Effect
You ask, what is our policy?		
You ask, what is our aim?		

Speak and Listen Work with a partner and discuss this famous quote from Winston Churchill:

> "Success consists of going from failure to failure without loss of enthusiasm."

Consider the following questions in your discussion.

CONNECT TO ESSENTIAL QUESTION

Have you ever had to act strong in front of others when you were worried and afraid?

- What does this say about Mr. Churchill's attitude in the face of adversity?

- How is this attitude reflected in his speech included in this chapter?

Third Read: Determining a Speaker's Purpose

Objective: Read the speech again. Underline one sentence that you think captures the tone of the speech. Remember, the tone is the attitude of the speaker.

Focus on Determining a Speaker's Purpose

Once you understand *what* a speech says, it is important to determine *why* it was written. This means considering the occasion and the tone. Was the speech written to persuade, inform, or entertain the audience?

The occasion for which a speech is written often determines its purpose. A speech written for a high school graduation would have a different purpose than one written to deliver as closing arguments to a jury in a murder trial.

Another way of determining the purpose of a speech is to look at the reaction of the audience. Is the audience made to feel a certain emotion, react in a particular way, or believe in something? In other words, what kind of a reaction is the speaker expecting from his audience?

Complete the chart below to determine how Winston Churchill's purpose is conveyed in the text of his speech. Refer to your answers to the chart on page 160. Transfer these to the first column of this chart to explain what each paragraph says. In the next column, explain what the speaker was most likely hoping to provoke in listeners, such as a particular emotion. The first row has been completed for you.

What does the paragraph say?	Why does the speaker include this paragraph?
Mr. Churchill opens by explaining that just three days prior, the king of England had appointed him prime minister of England.	to inform his audience who is speaking and why he has made the decisions that he is about to share

What does the paragraph say?	Why does the speaker include this paragraph?

©Perfection Learning® • No Reproduction Permitted

▼ Write On a separate sheet of paper, use your answers from the chart to write an explanation of the author's purpose. Overall, does he seek to persuade, inform, entertain, or do something else? What is his tone and how does it fit the purpose?

Language: Repetition in Rhetoric

Repetition of a word, phrase, or complete sentence is a common rhetorical technique used in writing. Repetition adds emphasis, unity, and power to the text. When speakers use repetition, the audience takes notice of what's being said. It adds a sort of rhythm to prose. Notice the use of repetition in these examples from the speech.

> We have before us an ordeal of the most grievous kind. We have before us many, many long months of struggle and of suffering.

> I can answer in one word: victory. Victory at all costs, victory in spite of all terror, victory, however long and hard the road may be; for without victory, there is no survival.

> Let that be realised; no survival for the British Empire, no survival for all that the British Empire has stood for, no survival for the urge and impulse of the ages, that mankind will move forward towards its goal.

Practice the use of repetition as a rhetorical technique to add emphasis to your own writing. Imagine that you are trying to persuade your teacher to let you take a test over. Write a few sentences below using repetition to add emphasis to your plea.

©Perfection Learning® • No Reproduction Permitted

Project-Based Assessments

Graduation Speech

Imagine that you have been invited to your elementary school to give a graduation speech. Write a 200- to 300-word speech to inform and inspire the fifth-graders to make the most of middle school. If your school includes grades K through 6, then imagine your speech is for your fellow sixth-graders at a graduation ceremony.

Think about the following as you plan:

- What mistakes have you made in sixth grade? What did you learn from them? Would you go back and change those if you could?

- What successes have you had in sixth grade? What allowed these to occur?

- What have you learned about yourself, your studies, friendship, and leadership?

- What advice would you give a student who is nervous or even afraid to go to middle school?

Use the following guidelines for your speech.	
To receive the highest score (4.0), the speech must meet all of these criteria.	Your speech • is clearly focused around one central idea or claim. • supports the claim with evidence from your own experiences. • avoids blaming or judging others. • is structured so it moves from specific to general. • uses appropriate tone and language for the intended audience and purpose. • is presented with appropriate speaking rate, volume, enunciation, and gestures. • follows the conventions of grammar and usage to communicate effectively.

Speedy Speeches

Gather three objects that hold meaning to you, and place them in a box or a bag so they cannot be seen. Choose a different purpose for each object and plan a speech for each. With one object, your purpose will be to inform; with another, to entertain; and finally, with the third, to persuade.

Walk around the room and take turns choosing objects out of people's bags and listening to their speeches. Then invite your classmate to select an object from your bag and give your speech. Your speech should only take a minute or two. After each speech, determine the speaker's intended purpose.

continued on next page

Use the chart below to determine which object you will use for each purpose, and add it to the chart in the first column. Then make notes for your speech. If your purpose is to inform, explain why you chose the object or its history. If your purpose is to persuade, offer an opinion and evidence to support your opinion. If your purpose is to entertain, tell an interesting or humorous story.

Object and Purpose	Notes
Persuade	
Inform	
Entertain	

©Perfection Learning® • No Reproduction Permitted

Face the wall and practice at least one time with each object. When everyone is ready, begin walking around the room and exchanging speeches.

Use the following guidelines for your speech.	
To receive the highest score (4.0), your speech must meet all of these criteria.	Your speech • introduces the audience to an object. • gives a clear description of an object. • engages the audience with a clear purpose. • uses eye contact, adequate volume, and clear pronunciation. • is presented with appropriate speaking rate, volume, enunciation, and gestures. • follows the conventions of grammar and usage to communicate effectively.

On Your Own: Integrating Ideas

1. Research Winston Churchill's "We Shall Fight on the Beaches" speech delivered to the House of Commons on June 4, 1940. What was the purpose of this speech? Are there famous quotes from the speech? How is it similar to his speech featured in this chapter?

2. Search for a TED Talks playlist on the benefits of failure, and choose one to watch. What ideas can you connect to? What can you learn about failure and success? Write down an inspirational comment from the talk, and post it online for others to see.

3. Research another famous speech. Consider the following:

   • surrender speech by Chief Joseph, October 5, 1877.

   • "Farewell to Baseball" address by Lou Gehrig, July 4, 1939

   • "Day of Infamy" speech by President Franklin D. Roosevelt, December 8, 1941

   • inauguration address by President John F. Kennedy, January 20, 1961

   • "I Have a Dream Speech" by Martin Luther King Jr, August 28, 1963

   • Stanford commencement speech by Steve Jobs, June 12, 2005

Connect to Testing

Questions on reading tests often require you to identify the author's purpose. In this chapter, you spent time analyzing the purpose of a speech. Answer the following questions based on the reading in this chapter.

1. **Part A:** What is the purpose of the first and second paragraphs of the speech?

   A. to inform the audience of his failure as the new prime minister

   B. to announce that World War II has started

   C. to explain his progress in forming his new administration

   D. to plead with the House of Commons to forgive his lack of progress

   Part B: Which quotation from the speech best supports the answer to Part A?

   A. *On Friday evening last I received His Majesty's commission to form a new Administration. . . . I have completed the most important part of this task.*

   B. *It was the evident wish and will of Parliament and the nation that this should be conceived on the broadest possible basis*

   C. *The three party Leaders have agreed to serve, either in the War Cabinet or in high executive office. The three Fighting Services have been filled.*

   D. *The appointment of the other Ministers usually takes a little longer*

2. Which of the following best describes the tone of this speech?

   A. entertaining and humorous

   B. frustrated and honest

   C. disheartening and depressing

   D. confident and determined

3. **Part A:** Which of the following best states the purpose of the speech?

   A. Rough times are ahead for Britain, but Churchill is up to the challenge.

   B. Churchill wants people to know that he has just been appointed and will need some time to make decisions.

   C. Churchill will be forming his government over the next few months.

   D. Churchill is not hopeful about the future of Britain.

   Part B: Write the sentence from the speech that you think best captures Churchill's purpose.

    ©Perfection Learning® • No Reproduction Permitted

Chapter 10

Reading and Comprehending Drama

Preview Concepts

Think about two movie characters in the same film who are opposites. Perhaps one is lazy and the other hardworking, or one looks on the bright side of things and the other is dark. What makes these two characters so different? Is it their attitudes and beliefs? Is it their behavior? Describe their differences in the space below.

CHAPTER GOALS

In this chapter you will:

- understand how the plot and characters of a drama are developed.
- determine the theme of a scene in a play.
- compare a film with the play it is based on.

PREVIEW ACADEMIC VOCABULARY

character

compare

contrast

plot

setting

theme

Over the course of the story, is one character shown to be right and the other wrong? Or are their different approaches equally useful? How do the events of the story show this? With a partner, talk about the characters you have chosen and answer the questions above.

Making Connections

Read the following poem by Emily Dickinson.

"Hope" is the thing with feathers—
That perches in the soul—
And sings the tune without the words—
And never stops—at all—

And sweetest—in the Gale—is heard—
And sore must be the storm—
That could abash the little Bird
That kept so many warm—

I've heard it in the chillest land—
And on the strangest Sea—
Yet—never—in Extremity,
It asked a crumb—of me.

How would you describe the speaker's attitude towards having hope? Share your thoughts with a peer or with the class. Cite evidence from the poem to support your answers.

MAKING CONNECTIONS

In the excerpt in this chapter, you'll be reading a play written for radio where one character never gives up hope.

©Perfection Learning® • No Reproduction Permitted

First Read: Understanding Plot and Characters in Drama

The play *The Diary of Anne Frank* is an adaptation of the famous book that records the thoughts of a young girl. The Frank family were Jews living in Germany when the Nazi Party came to power. The family moved to Amsterdam, the Netherlands, to avoid the Nazis' anti-Jewish policies. But during World War II, Germany invaded the Netherlands, and the Franks went into hiding for two years. They lived in hidden rooms in the building where Anne's father had worked. Anne kept a diary throughout this time, until her family was discovered and arrested in 1944.

After the war, Anne's father published her diary, which became widely read. It was later adapted into a prize-winning play. In this scene, the characters include fourteen-year-old Anne; her parents, Otto and Edith; and her older sister, Margot. Another family is also in hiding: Mr. and Mrs. Van Daan and their sixteen-year-old son, Peter. Mr. Dussel is a dentist who has taken refuge there, as well. The characters also mention Mr. Kraler and Miep, who helped the Franks and the others by bringing them food and news of the outside world.

Objective: As you read, notice Anne Frank's character in contrast to the others around her. How is she different? Write your observations in the My Thoughts column.

> **CONNECT TO ESSENTIAL QUESTION**
>
> Do you tend to think things will go well? Or do you expect the worst? Explain.

excerpt
The Diary of Anne Frank
Act 2, Scene 4
by Frances Goodrich and Albert Hackett

My Thoughts

1   [. . . *Everyone but* MARGOT *is in the main room. There is a sense of great tension.*

Both MRS. FRANK *and* MR. VAN DAAN *are nervously pacing back and forth.* DUSSEL *is standing at the window, looking down fixedly*

5   *at the street below.* PETER *is at the center table, trying to do his lessons.* ANNE *sits opposite him, writing in her diary.* MRS. VAN DAAN *is seated on the couch, her eyes on* MR. FRANK *as he sits reading.*

The sound of a telephone ringing comes from the office below. They all are rigid, listening tensely. DUSSEL *rushes over to*

10   MR. FRANK.]

Dussel. There it goes again, the telephone! Mr. Frank, do you hear?

Mr. Frank. [*quietly*] Yes. I hear.

Dussel. [*pleading, insistent*] But this is the third time, Mr.

15   Frank! The third time in quick succession! It's a signal! I tell you it's Miep, trying to get us! For some reason she can't come to us and she's trying to warn us of something!

Mr. Frank. Please. Please.

Mr. Van Daan. [*to* Dussel] You're wasting your breath.

20   **Dussel.** Something has happened, Mr. Frank. For three days now Miep hasn't been to see us! And today not a man has come to work. There hasn't been a sound in the building!

Mrs. Frank. Perhaps it's Sunday. We may have lost track of the days.

25   **Mr. Van Daan.** [*to* Anne] You with the diary there. What day is it?

Dussel. [*going to* Mrs. Frank] I don't lose track of the days! I know exactly what day it is! It's Friday, the fourth of August. Friday, and not a man at work. [*He rushes back to* Mr. Frank,

30   *pleading with him, almost in tears.*] I tell you Mr. Kraler's dead. That's the only explanation. He's dead and they've closed down the building, and Miep's trying to tell us!

Mr. Frank. She'd never telephone us.

Dussel. [*frantic*] Mr. Frank, answer that! I beg you, answer

35   it!

Mr. Frank. No.

Mr. Van Daan. Just pick it up and listen. You don't have to speak. Just listen and see if it's Miep.

Dussel. [*speaking at the same time*] For God's sake . . . I ask

40   you.

Mr. Frank. No. I've told you, no. I'll do nothing that might let anyone know we're in the building.

Peter. Mr. Frank's right.

Mr. Van Daan. There's no need to tell us what side you're on.

45 **Mr. Frank.** If we wait patiently, quietly, I believe that help will come.

[*There is silence for a minute as they all listen to the telephone ringing.*]

Dussel. I'm going down. [*He rushes down the steps.* Mr. 50 Frank *tries* **ineffectually** *to hold him.* Dussel *runs to the lower door, unbolting it. The telephone stops ringing.* Dussel *bolts the door and comes slowly back up the steps.*] Too late.

[Mr. Frank *goes to* Margot *in* Anne's *bedroom.*]

Mr. Van Daan. So we just wait here until we die.

55 **Mrs. Van Daan.** [*hysterically*] I can't stand it! I'll kill myself! I'll kill myself!

Mr. Van Daan. For God's sake, stop it!

[*In the distance, a German military band is heard playing a Viennese waltz.*]

60 **Mrs. Van Daan.** I think you'd be glad if I did! I think you want me to die!

Mr. Van Daan. Whose fault is it we're here? [Mrs. Van Daan *starts for her room. He follows, talking at her.*] We could've been safe somewhere . . . in America or Switzerland. But no! 65 No! You wouldn't leave when I wanted to. You couldn't leave your things. You couldn't leave your precious furniture.

Mrs. Van Daan. Don't touch me!

[*She hurries up the stairs, followed by* Mr. Van Daan. Peter, *unable to bear it, goes to his room.* Anne *looks after him,*

---

ineffectually: without any effect

70 *deeply concerned.* DUSSEL *returns to his post at the window.* MR. FRANK *comes back into the main room and takes a book, trying to read.* MRS. FRANK *sits near the sink, starting to peel some potatoes.* ANNE *quietly goes to* PETER'S *room, closing the door after her.* PETER *is lying face down on the cot.* ANNE *leans over*

75 *him, holding him in her arms, trying to bring him out of his despair.*]

ANNE. Look, Peter, the sky. [*She looks up through the skylight.*] What a lovely, lovely day! Aren't the clouds beautiful? You know what I do when it seems as if I couldn't

80 stand being cooped up for one more minute? I think myself out. I think myself on a walk in the park where I used to go with Pim. Where the jonquils and the crocuses and the violets grow down the slopes. You know the most wonderful part about thinking yourself out? You can have it any way you

85 like. You can have roses and violets and chrysanthemums all blooming at the same time. . . . It's funny . . . I used to take it all for granted . . . and now I've gone crazy about everything to do with nature. Haven't you?

PETER. I've just gone crazy. I think if something doesn't

90 happen soon . . . if we don't get out of here . . . I can't stand much more of it!

ANNE. [*softly*] I wish you had a religion, Peter.

PETER. No, thanks! Not me!

ANNE. Oh, I don't mean you have to be **Orthodox** . . . or

95 believe in Heaven and Hell and Purgatory and things . . . I just mean some religion . . . it doesn't matter what. Just to believe in something! When I think of all that's out there . . . the trees . . . and flowers . . . and sea gulls . . . When I think

Orthodox: strictly traditional

of the dearness of you, Peter . . . and the goodness of the

100 people we know . . . Mr. Kraler, Miep, Dirk, the vegetable

man, all risking their lives for us every day . . . When I think

of these good things, I'm not afraid anymore . . . I find

myself, and God,

and I . . .

105   [PETER *interrupts, getting up and walking away.*]

   PETER. That's fine! But when I begin to think, I get mad!

Look at us, hiding out for two years. Not able to move!

Caught here like . . . waiting for them to come and get us .

. . and all for what?

110   **ANNE.** We're not the only people that've had to suffer.

There've always been people that've had to . . . sometimes

one race . . . sometimes another . . . and yet . . .

   PETER. That doesn't make me feel any better!

   ANNE. [*going to him*] I know it's terrible, trying to

115 have any faith . . . when people are doing such horrible

. . . But you know what I sometimes think? I think the

world may be going through a phase, the way I was with

Mother. It'll pass, maybe not for hundreds of years, but

someday . . . I still believe, in spite of everything, that

120 people are really good at heart.

   PETER. I want to see something now . . . not a thousand

years from now! [*He goes over, sitting down again on the

cot.*]

   ANNE. But, Peter, if you'd only look at it as part of a

125 great pattern . . . that we're just a little minute in the life

. . . [*She breaks off.*] Listen to us, going at each other like

a couple of stupid grown-ups! Look at the sky now. Isn't

it lovely? [*She holds out her hand to him.* PETER *takes it

and rises, standing with her at the window looking out,*

My Thoughts

_____

_____

_____

_____

_____

_____

_____

_____

_____

_____

_____

_____

_____

_____

_____

_____

_____

_____

_____

_____

_____

_____

_____

_____

130 *his arms around her.*] Someday, when we're outside again, I'm

going to . . .

[*She breaks off as she hears the sound of a car, its brakes*

squealing as it comes to a sudden stop. The people in the other

rooms also become aware of the sound. They listen tensely.

135 *Another car roars up to a screeching stop.* ANNE *and* PETER *come*

from PETER's *room.* MR. *and* MRS. VAN DAAN *creep down the*

stairs. DUSSEL *comes out from his room. Everyone is listening,*

hardly breathing. A doorbell clangs again and again in the

building below. MR. FRANK *starts quietly down the steps to*

140 *the door.* DUSSEL *and* PETER *follow him. The others stand rigid,*

waiting, terrified.

In a few seconds DUSSEL *comes stumbling back up the steps.*

He shakes off PETER's *help and goes to his room.* MR. FRANK *bolts*

the door below and comes slowly back up the steps. Their eyes

145 *are all on him as he stands there for a minute. They realize*

that what they feared has happened. MRS. VAN DAAN *starts to*

whimper. Mr. Van Daan *puts her gently in a chair and then*

hurries off up the stairs to their room to collect their things.

PETER *goes to comfort his mother. There is a sound of violent*

150 *pounding on a door below.*]

MR. FRANK. [*quietly*] For the past two years we have lived in

fear. Now we can live in hope.

[*The pounding below becomes more insistent. There are*

muffled sounds of voices, shouting commands.]

155 **MEN'S VOICES.** Aufmachen! Da drinnen! Aufmachen!

Schnell! Schnell! Schnell! [*Etc., etc.*] [*"Open up! You in there!*

Open up! Quickly! Quickly! Quickly!"]

[*The street door below is forced open. We hear the heavy*

tread of footsteps coming up. MR. FRANK *gets two school bags*

My Thoughts

©Perfection Learning® • No Reproduction Permitted

160 *from the shelves and gives one to* Anne *and the other to*
Margot. *He goes to get a bag for* Mrs. Frank. *The sound of
feet coming up grows louder.* Peter *comes to* Anne, *kissing her
goodbye; then he goes to his room to collect his things. The
buzzer of their door starts to ring.* Mr. Frank *brings* Mrs. Frank

165 *a bag. They stand together, waiting. We hear the thud of gun
butts on the door, trying to break it down.*

Anne *stands, holding her school satchel, looking over at
her father and mother with a soft, reassuring smile. She is no
longer a child, but a woman with courage to meet whatever*

170 *lies ahead.*

*The lights dim out. The curtain falls on the scene. We hear
a mighty crash as the door is shattered. After a second* Anne's
voice *is heard.*]

Anne's Voice. And so it seems our stay here is over. They are

175 waiting for us now. They've allowed us five minutes to get our
things. We can each take a bag and whatever it will hold of
clothing. Nothing else. So, dear Diary, that means I must leave
you behind. Goodbye for a while. P.S. Please, please, Miep, or
Mr. Kraler, or anyone else. If you should find this diary, will you

180 please keep it safe for me, because someday I hope . . .

[*Her voice stops abruptly. There is silence. . . .*]

FIRST RESPONSE: KEY IDEAS AND DETAILS
What do the stage directions tell us about the mood and the
atmosphere? Share your thoughts with a partner.

Focus on Understanding Plot and Characters in Drama

In a drama, the dialogue and stage directions are the main
ways in which a playwright reveals information about the
characters and plot. Because there is no narration, the reader
must rely solely on these clues in order to comprehend the play.
Use the chart on the next page to uncover important information
about the scene you just read.

continued on next page

©Perfection Learning® • No Reproduction Permitted

My Thoughts

Element	Details from the Play
Characters Give basic descriptions of the characters based on the dialogue and stage directions. What are they like? How do they respond to events?	Anne: Peter: Mr. Frank: Dussel: Mrs. Frank: Mr. Van Daan: Mrs. Van Daan:
Plot What is going on during this scene? Why won't Mr. Frank answer the phone? What happens at the end? How does the historical setting influence the plot?	
Conflict Describe one external and one internal conflict in this scene.	External (person vs. person or society): Internal (person vs. self):

Review your chart with a partner.

©Perfection Learning® • No Reproduction Permitted

▼Write What questions can you ask about the play? On a separate piece of paper, write two questions for each of the three levels of questioning described below. When you are finished, trade questions with a partner and answer each other's questions.

1. **Level One:** These are questions that recall information in the text. The answer can be found in the text. Questions begin with phrases like these: *List the . . . , Name the . . . , Where did . . . , What was . . . ,* and *Who was . . . .*

2. **Level Two:** These are questions about the meaning of the text. They ask the reader to infer. Questions begin with words and phrases like these: *Explain . . . , Give an example of . . . , What caused . . . , What led to . . . ,* and *Describe how . . . .*

3. **Level Three:** These are questions that ask you to think about the effect of the text. They ask the reader to analyze the text as a whole and consider what the author intended. Questions begin with phrases like these: *What is the purpose of . . . , Why did the author . . . ,* and *What does the character show us about . . . .*

Second Read: Determining the Theme

Assign parts and read the play aloud as a class. As you read the script a second time, focus on the theme. What are the major ideas conveyed by the text?

Objective: Underline at least two lines of dialogue that help express the theme.

Focus on Determining the Theme

Theme is the underlying message of a literary work. Rather than a description of what happens in the text, a theme is more general and universal. It is a message about what it means to be human.

To identify the theme, first think about what major topics are introduced. Topics may be described in simple terms, such as *competition, ambition,* or *loyalty.* List three topics in the space below.

continued on next page

Decide which topic is the most relevant to the scene as a whole. Circle your choice.

Next, identify what the text says about this topic in the form of a short statement about human nature. Avoid phrasing this idea as a lesson or a moral. Think, instead, of what truth the text reveals about humanity. For this text, consider the following

- the way Anne and the others treat each other during a time of great uncertainty

- how the characters feel about their situation and how they act on their feelings

- Anne's faith and Peter's doubt; their different points of view about human nature

Remember not to use names of characters in your theme statement. Also, avoid clichés or generic statements like "Life is like a box of chocolates—you never know what you are going to get." Write your theme statement in the space below.

Speak and Listen Share your theme statement with a partner. Help each other refine your statements so they meet the requirements below.

The theme statement
- captures a truth about humans that is reflected by the text.

- is phrased in a statement with a subject and a verb.

- is not a cliché or an overused saying.

- is not so broad that it could describe any text.

- is not so narrow that it fails to address something significant in the text.

- does not include the names of characters or places.

Third Read: Comparing the Play with the Film

The play *The Diary of Anne Frank* has been adapted for film and television several times. The first film was made in 1959, written by the playwrights and featuring some of the original stage actors, and won three Academy Awards.

   ©Perfection Learning® • No Reproduction Permitted

Objective: Follow along with the script as you watch this scene in the film. As you watch, note the similarities and differences, and write your observations in the My Thoughts column. It may be helpful to pause the film as you watch it or to replay as necessary.

Focus on Comparing the Play with the Film

A comparison discusses both similarities and differences. Each relies on your ability to think critically and to dig deeply into a text. The first step in a comparison activity is to merely note the similarities and differences.

Focus on how the following elements are conveyed in both the play and the film, and record the similarities and differences in the Venn diagram below.

- the overall mood of the scene
- the setting, including the use of light and space and the positioning of the actors
- the appearance, behavior, and voices of the characters, especially Anne
- the portrayal of Anne and Peter together
- the significance of images such as the diary or the window
- the endings (the film has an additional brief scene)

The Diary of Anne Frank

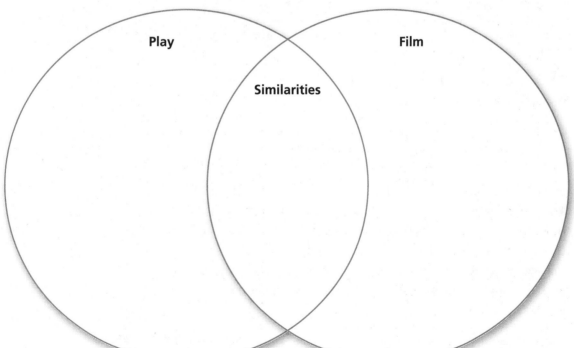

Play

Film

Similarities

Write Now that you have noted the similarities and differences, think about how they impact your understanding of the scene as a whole. On a separate sheet of paper, write two clear and concise paragraphs, one highlighting the comparisons and one the contrasts. What new insights about *The Diary of Anne Frank* and/or the Nazi invasion of the Netherlands do you have after comparing the film and the text? Do both the film and the play achieve the same ends? How do they differ as a whole? Use relevant facts and evidence to support your claims.

TECH-CONNECT

Type your paragraphs and post them to a website your teacher has chosen. Comment on the paragraphs of two other classmates.

Revise your writing to make sure that it

- uses appropriate transitions.
- varies sentence structure.
- uses precise language.
- maintains a formal style with appropriate tone.

Language: Ellipsis

An ellipsis is a set of three evenly spaced dots. (The plural of *ellipsis* is *ellipses*.) An ellipsis has three distinct uses.

1. To indicate that the speaker is trailing off in thought. Notice this use of an ellipsis in Anne's dialogue. In this example, the reader or listener can fill in the last few words and imagine that she hopes her diary will be found. Notice that there is no additional end punctuation when an ellipsis is used for this purpose.

> "If you should find this diary, will you please keep it safe for me, because someday I hope . . ."

2. To indicate a pause or a moment of hesitation. Notice Anne's use of ellipses for hesitation.

> "Oh, I don't mean you have to be Orthodox . . . or believe in Heaven and Hell and Purgatory and things . . . I just mean some religion . . . it doesn't matter what. Just to believe in something! When I think of all that's out there . . . the trees . . . and flowers . . . and sea gulls . . ."

3. To indicate the omission, or leaving out, of words that are not necessary to understand the meaning of a sentence. This is used mainly to shorten a quotation from a text. In the following quote from the play, Anne explains how she deals with her problems. The ellipsis takes the place of the omitted words "where I used to go with Pim."

> "You know what I do when it seems as if I couldn't stand being cooped up for one more minute? I think myself out. I think myself on a walk in the park . . . ."

In the space below, write two lines of dialogue between two characters. Use ellipses to show the characters trailing off or hesitating as they speak.

REFLECT

What do you think allowed Anne Frank to respond to her situation with such a positive attitude?

Project-Based Assessments

Readers Theater

In groups of six or seven, stage a readers theater version of the scene you read in this chapter. Readers theater is a way of performing a scene without costumes or a set. The performers read their parts from the script and may act out the stage directions using chairs or tables in the room.

CONNECT TO ESSENTIAL QUESTION

Think of a time when you felt trapped. What was the situation, and how did you react?

First, have a group reading with readers sitting in a circle. Read the script all the way through, taking turns rather than assigning parts. This allows everyone to have a chance to try on different roles. Then sign up for the role you are interested in. If two people want to play the same part, consider holding auditions. The group can vote to decide who best fits each role. Students can play two roles if working in smaller groups.

Now you are ready to study the script as a group. Discuss the following.

- What do you know about each character and their relationships to each other?

- What do you already know about World War II? What do you need to know so that the story makes more sense?

- Determine what the purpose of your production will be. What message would you like your production to convey to the audience?

continued on next page

Focus on the following as you plan for your character:

- voice (tone, volume, and pace)

- speech (understand what he or she says and why)

- mannerisms (how he or she stands, walks, and behaves toward others)

Practice your performance as a group. Separate the script into sections, and study one section at a time. Stop as needed, and give each other time to ask questions and provide feedback. Keep your purpose in mind as you practice. Remember that you are working as a team toward the same end goal.

Set a performance date for your class, your parents, members of the staff at your school, or all of the above.

Use the following guidelines for your readers theater performance.	
To receive the highest score (4.0), your role must meet all of these criteria.	Your role in the performance • helps to present an interpretation of *The Diary of Anne Frank*, Act 2, Scene 4. • accurately depicts a character (or characters). • is practiced and professional. • adds to the success of the group and is consistent with the group's intended purpose.

Write a New Ending

Imagine a different ending for *The Diary of Anne Frank*. For instance, what might have happened if Mr. Frank had answered the phone? What events would show that Anne was right about people's goodness? Write a scene that could replace the scene you studied in this chapter. It must begin with the same characters in the same situation, hiding in the secret rooms in Amsterdam.

First, decide what is different in this version of the scene. You could have a character reveal something important. You could introduce a new character to provide information or take an action that affects the others. What could happen differently? What would be the same? How would the characters respond to these events? Be sure you create some conflict or resolution that connects with the rest of the play.

Next, begin writing. Make sure the dialogue accurately reflects the tone and language of the characters presented and that any new character speaks and acts appropriately to the time and place.

Remember to include stage directions. Where are the characters during the scene? What are they doing? What objects or props are in the room? What is the mood of the scene? Follow the format of the script in the chapter. Use brackets, capital letters, italics and boldface print, or ellipses where necessary.

©Perfection Learning® • No Reproduction Permitted

Use the following guidelines for your script.	
To receive the highest score (4.0), the script must meet all of these criteria.	**Your script** • provides a new ending to the play *The Diary of Anne Frank*. • adds to a theme, plot, or character development from the original play. • follows the format for a script, using punctuation and print styles for dialogue and stage directions. • is free of errors in spelling, punctuation, and grammar.

On Your Own: Integrating Ideas

1. Watch the movie *Life Is Beautiful* and compare it to *The Diary of Anne Frank.* How are the two stories different? How are they similar? What did you learn more about? What are you left wondering about?

2. Read the book *Anne Frank: The Diary of a Young Girl,* and discuss it with a parent or friend. How is reading the book different from reading the play or watching the film?

3. Learn more about Anne Frank and her family. What else is known about her and her family? Who found her diary and how did it get published? Why do you think her diary is read so widely today?

4. Read the novel *Making Bombs for Hitler* by Marsha Forchuk Skrypuch. Though it is fiction, the story is based on real events because it tells about a girl who is forced to make bombs in Nazi Germany. Read the book to find out why she does it.

TECH-CONNECT

What did Anne Frank name her diary? Search for the answer and learn more about how her diary played an important role in her life while she was in hiding.

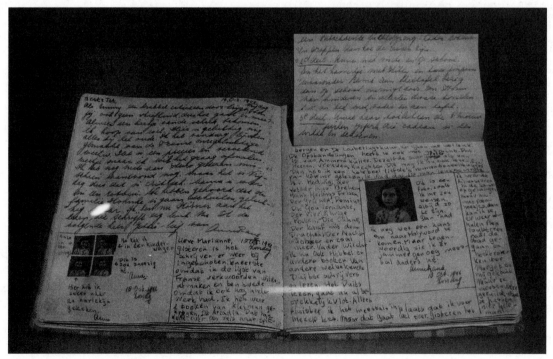

Source: www.heatheronhertravels.com

Connect to Testing

Reading tests often require you to read a section of a play. In this chapter, you spent time analyzing plot, character, and theme in a drama. Answer the following questions based on the reading.

1. **Part A:** Which of the following best describes Anne as a character?

   A. ignorant

   B. annoyed

   C. reassuring

   D. shy

   Part B: Which line of dialogue best supports the answer to Part A?

   A. *I wish you had a religion, Peter.*

   B. *When I think of these good things, I'm not afraid anymore . . .*

   C. *I know it's terrible, trying to have any faith . . . when people are doing such horrible . . .*

   D. *Listen to us, going at each other like a couple of stupid grown-ups!*

2. In this scene, what do Peter and Anne mostly discuss?

   A. their plan to escape

   B. whether to answer the phone

   C. their religious beliefs

   D. ways of coping with stress

3. **Part A:** Which of these statements best describes the difference between the ways in which Peter and Anne respond to their situation?

   A. Peter has lost all hope, but Anne refuses to give up.

   B. Peter wants to take action, but Anne is content to wait.

   C. Peter is realistic about the future, but Anne is foolish.

   D. Peter tries not to think about things, but Anne faces them.

   ©Perfection Learning® • No Reproduction Permitted

Part B: Which lines of dialogue best support the answer to Part A? Choose one line from Peter and one line from Anne.

A. **PETER.** *I've just gone crazy. I think if something doesn't happen soon . . . if we don't get out of here . . . I can't stand much more of it!*

B. **PETER.** *. . . . Look at us, hiding out for two years. Not able to move!*

C. **PETER.** *I want to see something now . . . not a thousand years from now!*

D. **ANNE.** *What a lovely, lovely day! Aren't the clouds beautiful?*

E. **ANNE.** *We're not the only people that've had to suffer. There've always been people that've had to . . . sometimes one race . . . sometimes another . . . and yet . . .*

F. **ANNE.** *. . . . I still believe, in spite of everything, that people are really good at heart.*

4. Read this line from the scene.

> **ANNE.** . . . It's funny . . . I used to take it all for granted . . . and now I've gone crazy about everything to do with nature.

What does Anne mean by this statement? Explain why Anne has "gone crazy about . . . nature." Refer to details from the text to support your ideas.

Writing a Personal Narrative

I have learned that success is to be measured not so much by the position that one has reached in life as by the obstacles which he has overcome while trying to succeed.
—Booker T. Washington

CONNECT TO ESSENTIAL QUESTION

How do you feel when things go wrong? Do you become angry, sad, or something else?

In Chapters 6–10, you read the true stories of people who faced misfortune in their lives. In this chapter, you will write a personal narrative about a challenge that you have faced in your own life.

WRITING PROMPT

Everyone endures hardships, from simple failure to heartbreaking loss. Think about a time when you faced a challenging situation. What did you experience? Think about how you reacted and why. What gave you the strength to get through this difficult time? Try to remember when, where, and who was involved. Write a personal narrative (a story from your own life) in which you explain what you learned. Use thoughtful description and realistic dialogue so that your reader will understand what happened and how you felt. Make a connection to at least one of the readings from this unit. Compare your response to a challenge with the challenge faced by one of the people you read about. Your personal narrative should be between 400 and 500 words.

Prepare to Write

Read the prompt carefully. Underline key words that explain the requirements of the task.

To write a personal narrative, you must do more than recount an event. Though you are telling a story about something that happened in your life, you also need to reveal something about who you are as a person and how that affected the situation. Think about Anne Frank's upbeat outlook, Winston Churchill's message of strength, or the Haitians' refusal to give up. You are the storyteller, and you are also the main character.

Include information that is relevant to the difficulty you faced or the way in which you dealt with it.

The Writing Process

Brainstorming

Think about two or three difficulties you have faced in your own life. These could be moments, events, or even years of struggle. What was it that made the time challenging? How did you feel during the experience? How did you deal with it? Write what feels comfortable and appropriate for the task and the audience.

Use the chart below to help you brainstorm.

Experience	Why it was hard	What you did to get through it	What you learned about yourself

Now circle the experience from the list above that you feel most clear about. This will be the story you tell.

Next, connect your story to other people you read about in this unit. Refer to the readings to support an insight you have about yourself or about human nature. Use the chart below to review the texts from this unit and find ones that support your ideas about how people act during difficult times. You may need to reread the texts.

Text	What it says about responding to misfortune	How this connects to me
"Sometimes, the Earth Is Cruel"		
"Mother to Son"		
Narrative of the Life of Frederick Douglass, an American Slave		
"Blood, Toil, Tears and Sweat" speech		
The Diary of Anne Frank		

Choose one or two texts that will best support your personal narrative and your understanding of how people handle difficulties in general. Circle your choices in the chart.

   ©Perfection Learning® • No Reproduction Permitted

Citing Authors

When you cite evidence from one of the texts in the chapter, remember to include the title and the author's full name the first time you mention each text. After that, you may refer to the author by his or her last name.

Purpose

Before you begin organizing, be sure you know the purpose of your narrative. What are you trying to show about yourself? Write your purpose in one sentence below. This sentence will not be in your essay but should be in the back of your mind as you write.

REFLECT

What three qualities best define you? Do these qualities help or hurt you in difficult times?

Organize ideas

Most narratives present events in exactly the order in which they occurred, moving from beginning to end. On a separate sheet of paper, create an outline based on your brainstorming notes to organize your ideas. The sequence of events should be in chronological order, and the outline should show multiple paragraphs.

Follow the outline below to help you organize your ideas.

I. Introduction: Begin your paragraph with a description, a quotation, or a general statement related to the prompt. Then make a connection between that sentence and your own experience. Your introduction should be between two to five sentences.

Examples:
- A gentle rain was falling and the sky was grey the morning we lost Bo. He was my dog, my best friend, my buddy.
- Sigmund Freud stated that "one day, in retrospect, the years of struggle will strike you as the most beautiful." I understand this after moving eight times in the last three years.
- Many people find strength during difficult times. I have found this to be true. When I was twelve . . .

(Review "Sometimes the Earth Is Cruel" as an example.)

continued on next page

II. Body paragraphs: Follow your own timeline of events and write in chronological order. Be sure to *show* your experience rather than tell about it. To do this, use sensory imagery and explain what you saw, heard, tasted, touched, or smelled. Instead of saying, "I was nervous," you might say, "I chewed on my fingernails and stared down at my feet." Focus on your actions and reactions more than those of others because this is a story about you.

Make connections with one or two readings from this chapter. Use transitions to show the relationship between ideas. For example, you could begin a sentence like this: "Just like Anne Frank, I . . . ."

Start a new body paragraph
- when the story changes direction or something different happens.
- when the setting changes in time or place.
- each time there is a different speaker in dialogue.

(Review *Narrative of the Life of Frederick Douglass* as an example.)

III. Conclusion: This is where you will reveal what you learned about yourself from the experience. How did the experience change you or affect the way you see the world? This is also another place to make connections with readings from this unit. Comment on human nature and make a statement about how people tend to react during struggles. What has this unit taught you about human strength or the human spirit? What have you noticed about people's responses to tragedy and despair? Choose a strong image to show who you are after your own struggle.

(Review *The Diary of Anne Frank* or "Mother to Son" as an example.)

Develop Character

You are the author, the narrator, and the main character, so this means you have to consciously develop yourself as a character.

Like other types of writing, narratives need rich, specific detail to be convincing. Each detail should dramatize your experience. This doesn't mean you need to exaggerate but rather that you emphasize the ideas you would like the reader to understand (i.e., your feelings or the size of the fire you saw).

©Perfection Learning® • No Reproduction Permitted

Consider the following questions as you build yourself as a character.

- How did you experience the event?

- How did you adapt to the situation?

- How did you change or refine your actions?

- How did you grow as a result of the experience?

- What did you learn about your own strengths or flaws?

Add Style

Because personal narratives are often told from your perspective and usually present a series of events, all the sentences can begin to sound alike: "I made . . . . I helped . . . . I went . . . ." Avoid this repetition by playing with your sentence structures. For instance, differ your sentence openings, combine simple sentences, vary sentence length, and experiment with figurative language.

Notice Frederick Douglass's variation in sentence length.

> I often found myself regretting my own existence, and wishing myself dead; and but for the hope of being free, I have no doubt but that I should have killed myself, or done something for which I should have been killed. While in this state of mind, I was eager to hear any one speak of slavery. I was a ready listener.

Notice Leonard Pitts's use of repetition and simile.

> Sometimes the rains fall and will not stop. Sometimes the skies turn barren and will not rain. Sometimes the seas rise and smack the shoreline like a fist. Sometimes the wind bullies the land. And sometimes, the land rattles and heaves and splits itself in two.

First Draft

Use your outline to write a draft of your personal narrative. The purpose of the first draft is to get your ideas down on paper in an organized way. Here are some helpful hints:

- Refer to your outline as well as the notes you wrote in the brainstorming activity.

- Write quickly so you don't lose your train of thought. You will revise and proofread later. Try to write as much as you can in one sitting. Set a timer if that helps you.

- Write on every other line, or double-space if working on a computer. This will make it easier to make revisions.

> **REFLECT**
>
> Which part of the writing process do you struggle with the most? Which part do you enjoy the most?

continued on next page

- If you take a break and then return to drafting, reread what you have written before continuing. This will help you resume the flow of thought.

- Mark this paper Draft #1.

Revision

There is great benefit to having other people read your writing. Below are three ways to revise your paper. Choose at least one way and then mark the revision as Draft #2.

First Peer Review

This review will judge whether your ideas are clear and compelling and whether they flow together in a logical order. With a group of two or three people, complete the following steps.

Steps for Peer Review

1. Select a timekeeper. Each writer gets five minutes. Stick to the time.
2. One person begins by reading aloud his or her first paragraph while other members listen.
3. Pause. The same writer reads the first paragraph aloud a second time.
4. The writer asks, "Does the opening grab my reader? Is it original?" Each member responds as the writer takes notes on the draft.
5. The writer reads the rest of the essay, pauses, and then reads it again.
6. As the writer reads, the other members take notes.
7. The writer asks, "Do I tell a story of an experience in my life? Do I reveal something about myself? Do I support my points with details from the readings?"
8. Peers offer helpful comments, and the writer makes note of their suggestions.
9. Repeat steps 1–8 with the next writer.

   ©Perfection Learning® • No Reproduction Permitted

Self Review

Ask yourself these questions to revise your own paper.

Think big. Look at the draft as a whole.

- Do I show, rather than tell, a story about myself?

- Have I focused the essay on me and not on someone or something else?

- Have I shown what qualities allow me to get through something hard?

- Have I shown how I have changed, adapted, or overcome something?

- Have I connected my experience to one I read about in this unit?

Think medium. Look at the draft paragraph by paragraph.

- Does my introduction hook the readers?

- Do I have details to engage the readers and keep them interested?

- Does each paragraph support the purpose statement that I made at the beginning?

- Do I use transitions to connect paragraphs?

Think small. Look at the draft sentence by sentence.

- Have I varied my sentence length so some are short and some are long?

- Have I varied my sentence beginnings and verb choices?

- Have I used transitions to show the relationship between ideas?

- Have I edited for errors in spelling, grammar, and usage?

- Have I stayed within the word limit (400-500)?

REFLECT

Which aspect of yourself do you most want others to know about when they meet you?

REFLECT

Have you chosen a formal tone and word choice to fit your audience? Avoid slang words, addressing your reader, and contractions.

Final Peer Review

Ask another student to read your essay and rate it using the rubric below.

Use the following guidelines for your personal narrative.	
To receive the highest score (4.0), the narrative must meet all of these criteria.	Your narrative • tells a story that shows a challenge you faced. • includes details and descriptions to engage the reader. • shows how you handled a difficult situation. • reveals something you have learned about human nature. • includes at least one line of dialogue to develop character. • organizes events chronologically and with multiple paragraphs. • refers to at least one reading in the unit. • stays within the word count. • contains correct grammar, usage, punctuation, and spelling.

Proofread

As you prepare a final draft, make sure you have included correct grammar and punctuation. Proofread carefully for missing words and punctuation marks, especially when using a direct quotation. If you used a computer, run a spell-check, but be aware of its limitations. Proofread your essay again, reading it from the last sentence to the first in order to catch errors in fluency. By reading the sentences out of context, you are more likely to find mistakes. Mark this Draft #3.

Final Essay

Make all the necessary changes from Draft #3 to complete your final essay. If your teacher uses an online turn-in site, be sure to upload your essay before the due date in case you have any problems.

If you are comfortable, share your completed essay with audiences beyond your classroom. Read it to your family and friends, or share your ideas in a conversation. Upload your finished digital copy to your class website or personal blog. Remember that when others read your essay, they will be inspired to be strong in difficult times.

> **FLUENCY CHECK**
>
> Before submitting your paper, check for the following:
>
> 1. Count the words in four consecutive sentences. Do they vary?
>
> 2. List the main verbs in four consecutive sentences. Do they vary?
>
> 3. Underline the first five words of four consecutive sentences. Do they vary?

©Perfection Learning® • No Reproduction Permitted

Practice Performance Task

A performance task evaluates your ability to comprehend selections of literature and informational texts and then demonstrate your knowledge in writing. The task often begins with several multiple-choice or short-answer questions on key vocabulary and the central ideas of the passage(s). The last step of the task is a writing assignment.

Complete the following performance task based upon selections from Unit 2.

Source #1

Read the following excerpt from "Sometimes, the Earth is Cruel" by Leonard Pitts Jr., which you read in Chapter 6.

Sometimes, the earth is cruel. To crawl the planet's skin, scanning for tornadoes in Oklahoma, charting storm tracks in Florida, running from wildfires in California, is to understand this in a primal, personal way. It is to breathe a prayer that begins, "There, but for the grace of God . . ." It is to write relief checks, donate blood, volunteer material and time and to fear, even in the doing, that these gestures are small against the need, inconsequential against the ache of a people whose turn seems never to end.

But what else are you going to do? As the playwright put it, your arms too short to box with God. Even less have we the ability to answer the question that burns the moment: Why are the most vulnerable repeatedly assessed the highest price?

We are hamstrung by our own limitations, so we can only do what we always do, only send prayers and help. And watch, staggered by the courage it takes, as Haitians do what human beings always do, the thing at which they have become so terribly practiced.

1. What is the central idea of this excerpt?

    A. Nature's power is dangerous and unavoidable.

    B. Many storms and other disasters have hit Haiti.

    C. People have always had to face terrible troubles.

    D. Disaster recovery efforts feel too small to help.

continued on next page

2. The phrase "your arms too short to box with God" is an example of which form of figurative language?

   A. metaphor

   B. simile

   C. personification

   D. irony

3. Which sentence from the passage refers to those who suffer rather than those who give aid?

   A. *It is to write relief checks, donate blood, volunteer material and time and to fear, even in the doing, that these gestures are small against the need, inconsequential against the ache of a people whose turn seems never to end.*

   B. *To crawl the planet's skin, scanning for tornadoes in Oklahoma, charting storm tracks in Florida, running from wildfires in California, is to understand this in a primal, personal way.*

   C. *We are hamstrung by our own limitations, so we can only do what we always do, only send prayers and help.*

   D. *And watch, staggered by the courage it takes, as Haitians do what human beings always do, the thing at which they have become so terribly practiced.*

Continue the performance task by reading a second and third source and answering questions.

Source #2

Read the poem "Mother to Son" by Langston Hughes, which you read in Chapter 7.

Well, son, I'll tell you:

Life for me ain't been no crystal stair.

It's had tacks in it,

And splinters,

And boards torn up,

And places with no carpet on the floor—

Bare.

But all the time

I'se been a-climbin' on,

And reachin' landin's,

And turnin' corners,

And sometimes goin' in the dark

Where there ain't been no light.

So, boy, don't you turn back.

Don't you set down on the steps.

'Cause you finds it's kinder hard.

Don't you fall now—

For I'se still goin', honey,

I'se still climbin',

And life for me ain't been no crystal stair.

4. Who is the speaker and what is she speaking about?

5. What is meant by the "crystal stair"?

continued on next page

6. Describe the tone of the poem.

Source #3

Read the following excerpt from *Narrative of the Life of Frederick Douglass, an American Slave* from Chapter 8.

I had at one time over forty scholars, and those of the right sort, ardently desiring to learn. They were of all ages, though mostly men and women. I look back to those Sundays with an amount of pleasure not to be expressed. They were great days to my soul. The work of instructing my dear fellow-slaves was the sweetest engagement with which I was ever blessed. We loved each other, and to leave them at the close of the Sabbath was a severe cross indeed. When I think that these precious souls are to-day shut up in the prison-house of slavery, my feelings overcome me, and I am almost ready to ask, "Does a righteous God govern the universe? and for what does he hold the thunders in his right hand, if not to smite the oppressor, and deliver the spoiled out of the hand of the spoiler?" These dear souls came not to Sabbath school because it was popular to do so, nor did I teach them because it was reputable to be thus engaged. Every moment they spent in that school, they were liable to be taken up, and given thirty-nine lashes. They came because they wished to learn. Their minds had been starved by their cruel masters. They had been shut up in mental darkness. I taught them, because it was the delight of my soul to be doing something that

©Perfection Learning® • No Reproduction Permitted

looked like bettering the condition of my race. I kept up my school nearly the whole year I lived with Mr. Freeland; and, beside my Sabbath school, I devoted three evenings in the week, during the winter, to teaching the slaves at home, And I have the happiness to know, that several of those who came to Sabbath school learned how to read; and that one, at least, is now free through my agency.

7. Based on the context, what does the word *agency* mean in the final sentence?

   A. a business

   B. an action or force

   C. someone who represents another person

   D. a spy organization

8. Which sentence best supports the idea that the slaves who attended Douglass's classes wanted to be there?

   A. *I look back to those Sundays with an amount of pleasure not to be expressed.*

   B. *They were great days to my soul.*

   C. *I had at one time over forty scholars, and those of the right sort, ardently desiring to learn.*

   D. *They had been shut up in mental darkness.*

9. Which word best characterizes the tone of the passage?

   A. sullen

   B. irritable

   C. disinterested

   D. inspirational

Your Assignment

In this unit, you read a scene from the play *The Diary of Anne Frank*. For this task, you will be reading two excerpts from the diary on which the play was based. Study the writing prompt below. Then review the text in Chapter 10, and carefully read the excerpt below.

WRITING PROMPT

Write two well-organized paragraphs that compare and contrast the biographical play *The Diary of Anne Frank* and *The Diary of a Young Girl* by Anne Frank.

On a separate sheet of paper, create your own Venn diagram like the one in Chapter 10 of this unit. Make notes about the similarities and differences between the play you previously read and the diary entries below. Consider how Anne's personality is conveyed in each version and whether both versions seem to present the same person by considering the following.

- the inclusion of her thoughts, beliefs, and attitudes
- the dialogue and interaction with other characters
- the events portrayed and the theme expressed

The Diary of a Young Girl: The Definitive Edition
by Anne Frank

Wednesday, February 23, 1944

. . . The weather's been wonderful since yesterday, and I've perked up quite a bit. My writing, the best thing I have, is coming along well. I go to the attic almost every morning to get the stale air out of my lungs. This morning when I went there, Peter was busy cleaning up. He finished quickly and came over to where I was sitting on my favorite spot on the floor. The two of us looked out at the blue sky, the bare chestnut tree glistening with dew, the seagulls and other birds glinting with silver as they swooped through the air, and we were so moved and entranced that we couldn't speak. . . .

"As long as this exists," I thought, "this sunshine and this cloudless sky, and as long as I can enjoy it, how can I be sad?" The best remedy for those who are frightened, lonely or unhappy is to go outside, somewhere they can be alone, alone with the sky, nature and God. For then and only then can you feel that everything is as it should be and that God wants people to be happy amid nature's beauty and simplicity.

As long as this exists, and that should be forever, I know that there will be solace for every sorrow, whatever the circumstances. I firmly believe that nature can bring comfort to all who suffer . . . .

Saturday, July 15, 1944

. . . It's utterly impossible for me to build my life on a foundation of chaos, suffering and death. I see the world being slowly transformed into a wilderness, I hear the approaching thunder that, one day, will destroy us too, I feel the suffering of millions. And yet, when I look up at the sky, I somehow feel that everything will change for the better, that this cruelty too shall end, that peace and tranquility will return once more. In the meantime, I must hold on to my ideals. Perhaps the day will come when I'll be able to realize them!

Use the following flowchart to organize your writing.

Paragraph 1: Similarities

Introduction: Begin with a statement about Anne Frank.

↓

Thesis: What is the main *similarity* between the ways in which the two texts convey Anne's character?

↓

Evidence 1: Explain with evidence from the play.

↓

Evidence 2: Explain with evidence from the diary.

↓

Concluding sentence: Comment on which aspect of her character stands out in both texts.

©Perfection Learning® • No Reproduction Permitted

Paragraph 2: Differences

Introduction/transition/thesis: What is the main *difference* between the ways in which the two texts convey her character?

↓

Evidence 1: Explain with evidence from the play.

↓

Evidence 2: Explain with evidence from the diary.

↓

Concluding sentence: Comment on the overall effect of a diary versus a play. Think about why a reader might prefer one or the other.

©Perfection Learning® • No Reproduction Permitted

Your Assignment (continued)

Read the prompt again carefully. Underline words that indicate how to write your compare and contrast paragraphs. Use the flowchart to help you explain your ideas in a way that draws the readers in and allows them to understand your points. Your goal is to explain your thoughts using evidence from the text. Study the rubric below to understand how your writing will be evaluated before you begin to write.

REFLECT

Would you rather write an autobiography (a book about your life) or a biography (a book about someone else)?

Your paragraphs will be scored using the following criteria.

Reading Comprehension:
- How well did you understand the texts?
- Were you able to infer aspects of Anne Frank's character?
- Were you able to compare and contrast the two genres and demonstrate understanding of each?

Writing Expression:
- Does your writing address the requirements in the prompt?
- Does your writing use specific language? (Avoid general words like *good*, *great*, *fantastic*, or *wonderful*.)
- Does your evidence have ideas from both sources?
- Do you use a transition to connect the two paragraphs?
- Is your tone formal and your voice your own?

Writing Conventions:
- Does your writing follow the rules of standard English with few errors in grammar, usage, and spelling?

Write a first draft, focusing on your ideas more than the conventions of writing. Then go back and edit your writing for clarity and structure. When you are finished, evaluate your essay using the list above. Revise your writing as needed.

Unit 3

Essential Question
What power do words have?

Do words have the power to change lives or just the way we perceive our lives? If a friend uses a word that offends you, would your view of that person change? Can you think of words that you could say right now that have the ability to heal or hurt someone? What about words someone could say to you that would transform you as a person? Think about how words can change the relationships in your life.

Take apart a word and you simply have individual letters. A, B, C . . . . Separately, letters are just packages of possibility. Shaped into words, letters take on a world of meaning. Group words into phrases and sentences and paragraphs and stories and fortunes are made or lost, friendships are built or destroyed, and revolutions are started or prevented.

Today, average people have more opportunities than ever to share their points of view through Facebook, Twitter, and other forms of social media. Our words travel faster and farther than ever before, and they endure in cyberspace for years to come. It makes one wonder; will our hastily written posts come back to haunt us?

In this chapter you will learn how language influences and affects our understanding of the world. You will reflect on a poem that celebrates language and then read about how words saved one girl's life. You will learn how leaders use words to manipulate an entire country. Finally, you will read a famous speech that inspired a nation. As you work through the unit, think about the power and influence of language. Consider your own relationship to words—do you use them to hurt or to heal? Do they gush rapidly from your mouth, or are you often gripped by speechlessness? How can you use words to empower yourself and others?

GOALS

- To analyze a poem for sensory language, mood, and structure
- To understand how episodes in a novel reveal conflict and character
- To analyze points of view in a memoir
- To compare and contrast authors' presentations of events
- To analyze how the meanings of words change over time and identify claims and supporting evidence in an informational text
- To write an analysis of a speech that impacted the world in a positive way

Chapter 11

Analyzing Sensory Language and Structure in Poetry

Preview Concepts

Colors are associated with different emotions. For example, sunny yellow communicates happiness and positivity. Black, however, is often associated with sadness. Perhaps this is because people wear black to funerals. Have you ever wondered why no professional football teams choose powder pink for their team color? It's because colors have emotional connotations that go beyond what we see with our eyes. What emotions are associated with each of the color words below? Write two or three next to each color.

Color	Emotional Connotations
Red	
Green	
Blue	
Gray	
White	
Gold	
Pink	

Share your answers with a partner. Note any different ideas you have in the connotations of the colors. Try to discover why a color impacts you differently than it does your partner.

CHAPTER GOALS

In this chapter you will

- determine the theme of a poem.
- analyze how sensory language and color communicate mood.
- analyze how structure communicates the meaning of a poem.
- use commas with direct address.

PREVIEW ACADEMIC VOCABULARY

connotation

direct address

free verse

mood

onomatopoeia

sensory language

Making Connections

Read the following quotation.

> If I read a book and it makes my whole body so cold no fire can warm me, I know that is poetry. If I feel physically as if the top of my head were taken off, I know that is poetry. These are the only ways I know it. Is there any other way?
>
> —Emily Dickinson

What type of reaction does Emily Dickinson have to poetry?

Have you ever read poetry or a book and had this type of reaction? If you have, write the title of the poem or the book below.

With a partner share your own experiences of reading poetry. Do you enjoy it or not? Explain.

MAKING CONNECTIONS

In this chapter you will analyze how a poem uses sensory language to create vivid word pictures and convey emotions.

First Read: Determining Theme

Pat Mora, a writer, teacher, and public speaker, believes that bilingual poetry reflects the constant changing nature of language. In the poem below, she celebrates the beauty of words.

Objective: Before you begin reading a new text, preview it by reading the title and quickly scanning the text. Use clues from the title to predict what you think the poem is about. For example, what is confetti? What do you do with confetti? What does it look like? As you read the poem, underline phrases that describe how words are like confetti.

Words Free as Confetti
by Pat Mora

	My Thoughts

1   Come, words, come in your every color.

       I'll toss you in storm or breeze.

       I'll say, say, say you,

       taste you sweet as plump plums,

5   bitter as old lemons.

       I'll sniff you, words, warm

       as almonds or tart as apple-red,

       feel you green

       and soft as new grass,

10   lightwhite as dandelion plumes,

       or thorngray as cactus,

       heavy as black cement,

       cold as blue icicles,

       warm as **abuelita's** yellowlap.

15   I'll hear you, words, loud as searoar's

       purple crash, hushed

       as **gatitos** curled in sleep,

---

abuelita: Spanish for *grandma*

gatito: Spanish for *little cat*

as the last goldlullaby.

I'll see you long and dark as tunnels,

20   bright as rainbows,

playful as chestnutwind.

I'll watch you, words, rise and dance and spin.

I'll say, say, say you

in English,

25   in Spanish,

I'll find you.

Hold you.

Toss you.

I'm free too.

30   I say **yo soy libre**,

I am free

free, free

free as **confetti**.

---

yo soy libre: Spanish for *I am free*

confetti: small pieces of colored paper thrown during a celebration such as a wedding or party

My Thoughts

FIRST RESPONSE: KEY IDEAS AND DETAILS

In a paragraph in your response journal, summarize the ways in which the author says words are like *confetti*.

TECH-CONNECT

Download a vocabulary app for your phone or computer to learn ten new words.

Focus on Determining Theme

As indicated by the title, the entire poem is comparing words to confetti. How are words like confetti? Complete the chart that begins on the next page to answer this question. The first column identifies qualities of confetti from the poem. In the second column, explain how words are similar to confetti. Use the questions in the chart to help you.

continued on next page

©Perfection Learning® • No Reproduction Permitted   Chapter 11 • Unit 3   **211**

Confetti	Words
every color (line 1)	Do words come in different colors? How?
I'll toss you in storm or breeze (line 2)	How do you "toss" words?
I am free, free, free free as confetti (lines 31–33)	How can saying words be free like confetti?

Speak and Listen Share your answers to the chart with a partner. Then write a statement together that expresses the theme of the poem. Use these sentence starters to help you:

- Pat Mora believes words are similar to confetti because they . . . .

- Like confetti, words are . . . .

Second Read: Analyzing Sensory Language

Listen as your teacher reads the poem aloud.

Objective: Draw a box around words associated with the five senses: sight, hearing, touch, smell, and taste. Circle words that describe colors.

Focus on Analyzing Sensory Language

Words that appeal to the five senses are called *sensory language.* Sensory language is very descriptive. It uses specific words that help the reader experience what the writer is describing.

©Perfection Learning® • No Reproduction Permitted

One example for each sense is provided for you. Add a second example from the poem that describes the sense in the first column. The chart is continued on the next page.

Sense	Lines from the poem (Add one more example for each sense.)	Color words used	What emotions are communicated? (mood)
Sight	1. *see you long and dark as tunnels* 2.		
Hearing	1. *I'll hear you, words, loud as searoar's purple crash* 2.		
Touch	1. *feel you green and soft as new grass* 2.		

continued on next page

Sense	Lines from the poem (Add one more example for each sense.)	Color words used	What emotions are communicated? (mood)
Smell	1. *warm as almonds* 2.		
Taste	1. *sweet as plump plums* 2.		

Pat Mora uses many color words in her descriptions. As you discovered in the Preview Concepts section of this chapter, colors convey emotions. When analyzing literature, the emotional feeling of a work of literature is called the *mood*. The mood of a work of literature may be sad, joyful, anxious, fearful, or any number of emotions. The words the author chooses create the mood of the poem.

Now complete the second and third columns in the chart. Identify the colors being described, and then write the mood(s) that the lines and the colors convey.

⟨Speak and Listen With a group of three or four students, discuss how sensory language contributes to the theme of the poem. Consider the following question.

Why does the poet use sensory and color words to describe how she experiences words?

REFLECT

Why does the author use made-up, compound words such as *lightwhite*, *thorngray*, and *yellowlap*?

©Perfection Learning® • No Reproduction Permitted

Use the chart below to monitor your participation in the group discussion. Place a mark in the appropriate column each time you participate.

Made a comment	Asked a question	Connected my idea with another person's idea

Summarize your discussion below.

Third Read: Analyzing Structure

As you read the poem a third time, notice its structure.

Objective: Note any lines that rhyme. Write notes about lines that are longer or shorter in length. Underline words or phrases that are repeated.

Focus on Analyzing Structure

Some poems have a specific pattern of rhyme or number of lines. For example, a haiku does not rhyme but has three lines that contain 5, 7, and 5 syllables. In a limerick, lines 1, 2, and 5 rhyme and have the same rhythm, or meter, and lines 3 and 4 rhyme and have the same meter.

Free verse poetry does not follow a set pattern of rhyme or rhythm. Instead, the poet varies the length of the lines to make the poem flow. Poets also consider how the appearance of the poem supports the theme.

continued on next page

Use the following questions to help you analyze the structure of "Words Free as Confetti."

1. Do any of the lines rhyme?

2. What repeated words or phrases are used?

3. Which lines are longer and sound smoother?

How does the length of the longer lines communicate their meaning?

©Perfection Learning® • No Reproduction Permitted

4. Which lines are shorter and sound clipped?

How does the length of the shorter lines communicate their meaning?

5. Onomatopoeia are words whose sounds imitate their meanings. Examples include *buzz* and *pow*. Are there any words that are onomatopoeia?

6. Why do you think the author uses free verse to write about words being free as confetti?

Write With each read of this chapter, you have been diving deeper into understanding the poem "Words As Free as Confetti."

- First, you identified the theme.
- Then you analyzed the author's use of sensory language to communicate the mood.
- Finally, you analyzed how the structure of a poem communicates the theme.

Use the information you gathered from all three reads to write a literary analysis of the poem. Use the following sentence frames to help you write two or three paragraphs explaining how the author uses sensory language and structure to communicate the theme.

- In the poem ____, the author Pat Mora describes . . . .
- The theme of the poem is . . . .
- The author communicates the theme by using . . . .
- An example of this is . . . .
- Another way the author emphasizes the theme is through . . . .
- For example, ...
- In conclusion, ...

REFLECT

Why does the author use Spanish words and phrases in the poem?

Language: Using Commas with Direct Address

Direct address is when a speaker is talking *to* someone or something. Use a comma to set off a person's name at the beginning of a sentence.

> Example: Jack, would you please bring me the book?

If the name is in the middle of the sentence, use a pair of commas to set off the direct address.

> Example: Send me a text, Dontaye, when you are ready to walk home.

Notice how Pat Mora uses direct address to speak to "words" as if they were a person.

> Come, words, come in your every color.
> I'll hear you, words, loud as searoar's purple crash,
> I'll watch you, words, rise and dance and spin.

REFLECT

Does moving the name in the direct address to the beginning of the sentence change the rhythm of the sentence? How might this affect the rhythm of the poem?

Rewrite the three lines from the poem so that the direct address falls at the beginning of the sentence. Use commas correctly.

TECH-CONNECT

Write a simile to capture your relationship to words. Fill in the following: Words as

_____ (Adjective)

as _____ (Noun). Share your simile by tweeting it or posting it on your class website.

Project-Based Assessments

Poetry Puzzle

With a group of three to four students, choose a poem by Pat Mora, Emily Dickinson, Langston Hughes, or another poet your class has studied. Get your teacher's approval for your chosen poem. Then type (or copy and paste) the poem into a new document. Enlarge the words to 20-point type or larger and print the poem. (You can also write the poem in big letters on paper. Cut up the poem so each word and punctuation mark is separated. Place the poem words in an envelope. Write the title of the poem on the envelope. Trade envelopes with another group.

Follow these steps to put your poem together.

1. Look at the title and think about what the poem could be about.
2. Spread the words on the floor or a table.
3. Begin arranging the words in a way that makes sense.
4. Pay attention to structure and punctuation. Think about what you already know about this poet and his or her style.
5. Rearrange the words until the poem makes sense and all the words are used.
6. Read your poem to the other group, and then have them read you the original. How close did you come to the original?
7. Listen to the other group's poem and read them the original. How close did they come to the original?
8. Discuss what you noticed about the structure and style of the poems.
9. Write a few paragraphs reflecting on what you learned about the poem from this experience.

CONNECT TO ESSENTIAL QUESTION

Is there a word for everything? Think about a situation or a feeling that does not have a word. If you speak another language, think about a word that doesn't quite translate into English.

continued on next page

	Use the following guidelines for your poetry puzzle.
To receive the highest score (4.0), your poem must meet all of these criteria.	**Your poem** • demonstrates knowledge of poetry. • uses punctuation correctly. • reflects an understanding of the poet and his/her style. • makes sense, even though it may not be similar to the original. **Your group** • works together to complete the poem, with everyone taking a part in the selection, reconstruction, and discussion of the poem. **Your written reflection** • discusses what you learned about the structure and style of the poem from putting it back together.

Free Verse Poem

Write a free verse poem addressed to an important person, idea, place, or object. Use the following steps:

1. Decide on a topic.
   - Think of an object, idea, or person who is important to you, and write the name of the person or object at the top of your paper.

      Examples: a pet, friendship, a brother, the ocean

2. Brainstorm for ideas.
   - Make a list of seven to ten words that describe or define your topic.

   - Next, write five phrases that highlight a quality about your topic that appeals to each of the five senses. Refer to sentences from "Words Free as Confetti" as a model.

      Examples: I feel ears, soft like flower petals.
      I see your nose, shaped like a pink heart.

   Use commas correctly when addressing the object.

3. Define your purpose.
   - Once you have completed your brainstorming, think about what you would like to communicate about your topic. Go beyond the literal meaning of your topic, and think of its power to influence people or cause change. This will be the purpose of your poem.

   - Write a clear purpose statement, using this sentence frame: The purpose of my poem is to . . . .

©Perfection Learning® • No Reproduction Permitted

Example: The purpose of my poem is for the reader to see beauty in something that is not always considered beautiful.

4. Develop the structure.
   - Arrange the words on the page to fit the meaning and emotions of the words. Think about how you would like the structure of your poem to look. This will take time, so write at least three drafts of the poem, rearranging words and ideas until the structure fits the meaning. Think about using long and short sentences, onomatopoeia/sound words, repetition, and punctuation effectively.

5. Type or write your poem so that it is neat in appearance. Include your purpose statement at the bottom of the page.

	Use the following guidelines for your free verse poem.
To receive the highest score (4.0), your poem must meet all of these criteria.	Your poem • demonstrates knowledge of free verse poetry. • uses punctuation intentionally. • experiments with repetition, line breaks, and sentence length. • is focused on one topic and its significance. • uses direct address. • uses sensory language to describe the qualities of the object. • uses correct spelling, punctuation, and usage.

On Your Own: Integrating Ideas

1. Select one form of poetry and write an original poem. Possibilities include acrostic, limerick, diamante, haiku, tanka, ode, terza rima, or sonnet. Research these types of poetry and read a few model poems before beginning your own. Share your poem with a friend or parent.

2. Find out how new words are accepted into the Merriam-Webster and Oxford English dictionaries every year. Does the word have to appear in speech or writing first, or do people make suggestions for new words? What words do you think should be added?

3. Visit the Poetry Foundation's learning lab at poetryfoundation.org to read and listen to poems online. Find three poems you like and share them with your class. Explain why you chose them.

> **REFLECT**
>
> If you were disagreeing with a friend, how would you prefer to communicate with them—text, email, cell phone, face to face, Facebook, or a handwritten note? Why?

Connect to Testing

In this chapter, you analyzed the meaning and structure of a poem. This Connect to Testing section will provide practice answering the types of questions that may appear on standardized reading tests.

1. Which of the following lines from "Words Free as Confetti" is the best example of sensory language?

    A. *Come, words, come in your every color.*

    B. *I'll toss you in storm or breeze.*

    C. *I'll say, say, say you,*

    D. *taste you sweet as plump plums,*

2. Which of the following lines appeals to the sense of hearing?

    A. *I'll toss you in storm or breeze.*

    B. *and soft as new grass,*
       lightwhite as dandelion plumes

    C. *I'll watch you, words, rise and dance and spin.*

    D. *I'll say, say, say you*
       in English,
       in Spanish,

3. Explain two ways in which the writer compares words to confetti. Support your answer by quoting lines from the poem.

4. **Part A:** The best word to describe the mood of the poem is

    A. anxious.

    B. disbelieving.

    C. celebratory.

    D. reflective.

    ©Perfection Learning® • No Reproduction Permitted

Part B: Which of the following lines provides the strongest evidence for the answer for Part A?

A. *I'll say, say, say you,*
   taste you sweet as plump plums,

B. *I'll sniff you, words, warm*
   as almonds or tart as apple-red,

C. *I'll see you long and dark as tunnels,*

D. *I'll find you.*
   Hold you.
   Toss you.
   I'm free too.

Read the following poem and answer the questions that follow.

A Word Is Dead
by Emily Dickinson

A WORD is dead

When it is said,

Some say.

I say it just

Begins to live

That day.

5. **Part A:** Which of the following lines from "Words Free as Confetti" best support the theme of the poem "A Word Is Dead."

A. *Come, words, come in your every color.*

B. *I'll sniff you, words, warm*
   as almonds or tart as apple-red,

C. *I'll watch you, words, rise and dance and spin.*
   I'll say, say, say you

D. *I'll hear you, words, loud as searoar's*
   purple crash, hushed
   as gatitos curled in sleep,

Part B: Support your answer to Part A by explaining the theme from "A Word Is Dead."

Chapter 12

Understanding How Episodes in a Novel Reveal Conflict and Character

Preview Concepts

Think about a time when you really wanted to speak but couldn't. What was it that you wanted to say and why couldn't you speak? Write your response below.

CHAPTER GOALS

In this chapter you will

- understand the role of the exposition of a text.
- analyze how episodes in a story reveal conflict and character.
- analyze how a character grows and changes throughout a story.
- use objective and subjective pronouns correctly.

PREVIEW ACADEMIC VOCABULARY

conflict

dynamic character

exposition

nominative pronouns

possessive pronouns

reflexive pronouns

static characters

subjective pronouns

©Perfection Learning® • No Reproduction Permitted

Making Connections

Christy Brown was born in 1954 with cerebral palsy, which left him unable to stand, walk, or speak. Doctors assumed that Brown was mentally disabled, but his mother refused to believe this diagnosis and spent hours reading to him. The following excerpt from Christy's autobiography, *My Left Foot*, describes the moment when his mother encourages ten-year-old Christy to write the letter A—with his foot.

"Try again, Chris," she whispered in my ear. "Again."

I did. I stiffened my body and put my left foot out again, for the third time. I drew one side of the letter. I drew half of the other side. Then the stick of chalk broke and I was left with a stump. I wanted to fling it away and give up. Then I felt my mother's hand on my shoulder. I tried once more. Out went my foot. I shook, I sweated and strained every muscle. My hands were so tightly clenched that my fingernails bit into the flesh. I set my teeth so hard that I nearly pierced my lower lip. Everything in the room swam till the faces around me were mere patches of white. But—I drew it—the letter "A". . . .

I had done it! It had started—the thing that was to give my mind its chance of expressing itself. True, I couldn't speak with my lips. But now I would, speak through something more lasting than spoken words—written words.

How does Brown feel about being able to communicate with his family?

What does he mean by the phrase "But now I would, speak through something more lasting than spoken words—written words"?

MAKING CONNECTIONS

In this chapter you will read about a character who has cerebral palsy and is unable to speak.

First Read: Analyzing Exposition

Read the following excerpt from the novel *Out of My Mind* by Sharon Draper, an educator and award-winning author. Her novel *Out of my Mind* tells the story of Melody Brooks, an eleven-year-old girl who has cerebral palsy, a disability resulting from damage to the brain.

Objective: As you read, underline words that describe Melody's character. Write questions you have in the My Thoughts column.

excerpt

Out of My Mind
by Sharon Draper

Chapter 1

	My Thoughts

1 **Words.**

I'm surrounded by thousands of words. Maybe millions.

Cathedral. Mayonnaise. Pomegranate.

Mississippi. Neapolitan. Hippopotamus.

5 *Silky. Terrifying.* **Iridescent**.

Tickle. Sneeze. Wish. Worry.

Words have always swirled around me like snowflakes—

each one delicate and different, each one melting untouched

in my hands.

10 Deep within me, words pile up in huge drifts. Mountains of

phrases and sentences and connected ideas. Clever expressions.

Jokes. Love songs.

From the time I was really little—maybe just a few months

old—words were like sweet, liquid gifts, and I drank them like

15 lemonade. I could almost taste them. They made my jumbled

thoughts and feelings have substance.

---

iridescent: showing bright or shining colors that seem to change from different angles

©Perfection Learning® • No Reproduction Permitted

My parents always blanketed me with conversation. They chattered and babbled. They verbalized and vocalized. My father sang to me. My mother whispered strength into my ear.

20   Every word my parents spoke to me or about me I absorbed and kept and remembered. All of them.

I have no idea how I untangled the complicated process of words and thought, but it happened quickly and naturally. By the time I was two, all my memories had words, and all my

25   words had meaning.

But only in my head.

I have never spoken one single word. I am almost eleven years old.

My Thoughts

_____
_____
_____
_____
_____
_____
_____
_____
_____

FIRST RESPONSE: KEY IDEAS AND DETAILS

Based on your first reading of Chapter 1, what can you infer about Melody and her family? Write your answer in your response journal. Be prepared to support your answers with evidence from the text.

Focus on Analyzing Exposition

Exposition is a literary device used to introduce readers to the setting, characters, or historical context of a story. The exposition comes at the beginning and provides the reader with the necessary details to understand the background of the story. A good exposition draws the reader in by introducing interesting characters who must overcome challenges.

Use the web on the next page to make inferences about the characters and the conflict in _Out of My Mind_. Add to the web by connecting your own circles to the three topic circles. Record inferences related to Melody, her parents, and the conflict or problem. Be prepared to support your inferences with evidence from the text.

> **REFLECT**
>
> Like Melody, do you have certain words that you love? What is it you love about them? Their meaning? Their sound? How they look?

continued on next page

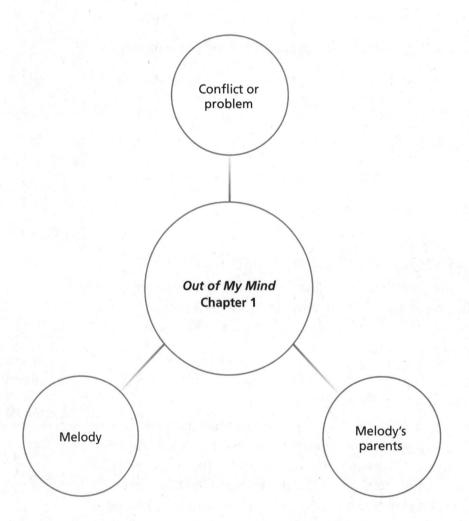

Conflict or problem

Out of My Mind
Chapter 1

Melody

Melody's parents

©Perfection Learning® • No Reproduction Permitted

Speak and Listen With a partner or the class, discuss the following questions:

- At which point did you learn that Melody could not speak?
- What inferences did you make about Melody?
- What inferences did you make about her parents?
- Are you interested in her story? Why or why not?

Second Read: Analyzing Character Development

Listen as your teacher or a classmate reads the excerpt from the First Read aloud. Then read the following excerpt from Chapter 3.

Objective: Underline examples of Melody's inability to communicate with her mother.

excerpt
Chapter 3

	My Thoughts

1   Once, when I was about four, Mom and I were in one of those superstores that sells everything from milk to sofas. I was still small enough to fit in the child seat in the front of the cart. Mom always came prepared and stuffed pillows on each

5 side of me so I wouldn't tilt. Everything was fine. She tossed toilet paper and mouthwash and detergent into the cart, and I looked around, enjoying the ride.

    Then, in the toy section, I saw them. Brightly colored packages of plastic blocks. Just that morning I had seen

10 a warning on television about that toy—they were being recalled because the blocks had been painted with lead paint. Several children had already been hospitalized with lead poisoning, the report had said. But there they were—still on the shelf.

15   I pointed to them.

    Mom said, "No, sweetie. You don't need those. You have enough toys."

I pointed again and screeched. I kicked my feet.

"No!" Mom said more forcefully. "You are not going to

20   have a tantrum on me!"

I didn't want the blocks. I wanted to tell her they were

dangerous. I wanted her to tell somebody to get rid of them

before a child got sick. But all I could do was scream and point

and kick. So I did. I got louder.

25   Mom rushed out of the toy section, pushing the cart real

fast. "Stop it!" she cried out at me.

I couldn't. It made me so angry that I couldn't tell her. The

tornado took over. My arms became fighting sticks, my legs

became weapons. I kicked at her with my feet. I screamed. I

30   kept pointing in the direction of those blocks.

People stared. Some pointed. Others looked away.

Mom got to the door of the store, yanked me out of the

cart, and left it with all her selections sitting there. She was

almost in tears when she got to the car. As she buckled me

35   in my seat, she almost screamed at me, "What is wrong with

you?" . . .

I don't think Mom ever figured out what I was trying to say

that day.

Focus on Analyzing Character Development

Most stories are told in episodes. Writing everything the
character does every single day would make for a boring
story. Instead the author chooses important episodes from the
character's life—episodes that move the plot forward and reveal the
character's personality and motivation.

In the first chapter, you were introduced to the central
conflict—Melody loves words but cannot speak her mind. This
episode in Chapter 3 reveals more about Melody's character and
how the central conflict affects her life and her relationships.

My Thoughts

Answer the questions below to analyze this episode from Chapter 3.

1. Describe what happens in this episode from Chapter 3.

2. What does this episode reveal about Melody's character that you didn't learn in Chapter 1?

3. How does this scene further develop the central conflict of the novel?

continued on next page

4. As a reader, what are your feelings toward Melody after reading this episode?

(Speak and Listen Imagine you are a part of a team of writers and directors who are planning to film the scene you just read. Brainstorm with a partner or small group how you would shoot this scene so that it portrays Melody's desire to communicate and her mother's misunderstanding. Consider the following.

- Who is narrating the scene?

- What images would the camera focus on during different parts of the scene?

- How would you portray Melody and her mother so that the movie is true to what you know about their characters from the book?

REFLECT

What assumptions do you make about people with disabilities that affect their ability to speak?

Third Read: Analyzing an Episode in a Novel

Listen as your teacher or a student rereads the excerpts from the first two reads. Then read the following excerpt from Chapter 16 of *Out of My Mind.* In this chapter Melody gets a Medi-Talker. This is a computer that enables her to talk to fellow students and the teachers for the first time.

Objective: As you read, place a star by how the teacher and students respond to Melody. Write a word or phrase that describes their response in the My Thoughts column.

    ©Perfection Learning® • No Reproduction Permitted

excerpt

Chapter 16

1   I shiver with excitement. When I roll into Miss Gordon's room, as usual, nobody looks up, except for Rose, who flashes me a smile.

But then I turn the volume up real loud and I push a

5   button: **"Hi, everybody. I have a new computer."**

Heads turn and voices whisper.

"They make computers for the special eddies?"

"It talks? Mine doesn't do that."

"You don't need yours to talk!"

10   "It sounds weird."

"So do you."

"What could she possibly have to say, anyway?"

But Connor jumps up, his shaggy blond hair flopping into his eyes, and says loudly, "That's awesome, Melody!"

15   And because he's one of the popular kids, and probably the biggest and tallest kid in the fifth grade, I think because he gives his okay, the rest of the students decide to leave it alone.

Well, most of them. Claire, who was the first in the class to get her own laptop and who makes sure everybody knows

20   it when she gets a new iPhone or a Wii game, sniffs and says, "That sure is a funny-looking computer! But I guess it's perfect for a kid like you." She and Molly exchange looks. I swear they think I am blind.

Miss Gordon, who looks like she wants to squeeze Claire

25   like an empty toothpaste tube, tells her, "Claire, I don't allow rudeness in my classroom. Now sit down and hush!"

But even Claire can't dim my good mood. I push another button for a sentence Mrs. V and I prepared ahead of time.

Somehow I knew I would need it! The machine says, **"I talk to**
30 **everybody now—Claire, too!"**

I see her scowl, but everyone else laughs. They all want
to touch the machine or push a button or try to operate
it, but Catherine keeps them away and lets me do all the
demonstrating.

35 I go to the green level—the jokes. **"Knock, knock!"**

"Who's there?" several people reply together.

"Isabel," the Medi-Talker says.

"Isabel who?" the kids surrounding me reply.

"Isabel out of order? I had to knock!"

40 Everybody laughs at the silly joke with me. Even though my
arms and legs flail out and I drool a little as I laugh, it is the first
time in my entire life that I feel like I'm part of the group. . . .

Claire raises her hand.

"Yes, Claire," Miss Gordon says, a look of warning in her
45 eyes.

"I'm not trying to be mean—honest—but it just never
occurred to me that Melody had thoughts in her head."

A couple of other kids nod slightly. Miss Gordon doesn't
raise her voice. Instead, she responds thoughtfully: "You've
50 always been able to say whatever came to your mind, Claire.
All of you. But Melody has been forced to be silent. She
probably has mountains of stuff to say."

"Yes. Yes. Yes," I make the machine say.

. . . Rose pulls her desk close to my chair. "This is so
55 awesome, Melody," she says softly, and I let her touch the
shimmery keys.

"Oh, yes," I reply. Then I look at her. **"Friends?"** I type.

"Friends!" she answers without hesitation.

©Perfection Learning® • No Reproduction Permitted

"Happy," I type, then I tense. I hope I won't do anything
60 stupid like knock something over with excitement. Rose is
looking intently at me. "I can't imagine what it must be like to
have all my words stuck inside," she finally says.

"It sucks!" I type in.

Rose chuckles. "I feel you!"

My Thoughts
_____
_____
_____
_____

Focus on Analyzing an Episode of a Novel

When reading a longer work of literature such as a novel, think
about how the plot unfolds in a series of episodes. With each
episode, ask yourself why the author included it. What does it
reveal about the character, the conflict, and ultimately, the theme
of the story?

When analyzing characters in a story, consider whether they
are dynamic and static. Dynamic characters grow and change in
response to conflict; static characters don't. For example, a fearful
character who finds the courage to stand up to bullies with the
help of a new friend is a dynamic character.

In this chapter, you have read three different episodes from
three chapters of *Out of My Mind*. Think about how each chapter
provides a little more information about the characters and
conflict in the story. Fill in the chart below to analyze how each
chapter adds to the story as a whole. Return to the excerpts as you
complete the chart.

> **REFLECT**
>
> As you read this scene, do you feel sorry for Melody or are you cheering for her? Explain your answer.

Summary of events—What happens in this chapter?	What does this episode reveal about Melody's character and the other characters in the story?	How does this chapter develop the conflict?
Chapter 1		

continued on next page

Summary of events—What happens in this chapter?	What does this episode reveal about Melody's character and the other characters in the story?	How does this chapter develop the conflict?
Chapter 3		
Chapter 16		

Is Melody a static or dynamic character? Explain your answer with details from the text.

©Perfection Learning® • No Reproduction Permitted

Based on the events in Chapter 16, what new conflicts might develop between Melody and her classmates now that Melody has the ability to communicate her thoughts and feelings?

What further conflicts might Melody struggle with as she makes friends with the students in her class?

Speak and Listen With a partner, discuss how each chapter excerpt from the three reads reveals Melody's character and the conflict of the story. Use these sentence starters to help you.

- Chapter 1 reveals that Melody . . . .
- Chapter 3 describes . . . .
- This is important because . . . .
- Chapter 16 is important to the story because it . . . .
- Because _____, the conflict . . . .
- Melody changes because . . . .

Language: Using Pronouns in the Correct Case

A pronoun is a word that takes the place of a noun, such as *I, me, he, him, she, her,* or *they.* Pronouns are organized into cases depending on how they are used in a sentence—as a subject or an object.

If a pronoun is the subject of a sentence, it must be in the subjective case. If a pronoun is the object of a sentence, it must be in the objective case. Refer to the chart on the next page and read the examples.

continued on next page

	First Person		Second Person		Third Person	
	Singular	Plural	Singular	Plural	Singular	Plural
Subjective (Subject)	I	We	You	You	He, She, It	They
Objective (Object)	Me	Us	You	You	Him, Her, It	Them
Possessive	My, Mine	Our, Ours	Your, Yours	Your, Yours	His, Her, Hers, Its	Their, Theirs
Reflexive	Myself	Ourselves	Yourself	Yourselves	Himself, Herself, Itself	Themselves

Incorrect: Her and me went to the school play. (The pronouns are the subject of the sentence, but *Her* and *me* are in the objective case.)

Correct: She and I went to the school play. (*She* and *I* are the subjects of the sentence. *She* and *I* are pronouns in the subjective case.)

Incorrect: Give the results of the game to he and myself. (The pronouns are the object of the preposition *to*, but *he* is subjective case and *myself* is reflexive.)

Correct: Give the results to him and me. (*Him* and *me* are both objective case.)

Notice how Sharon Draper used pronouns correctly.

- She and Molly exchange looks. (Subjective case)
- Rose is looking intently at me. (Objective case)

Answer the following questions using pronouns correctly. Follow the directions in parentheses.

1. Who wants to go outside for class?
   (Write an answer using two pronouns as subjects.)

©Perfection Learning® • No Reproduction Permitted

2. Whom can I walk home with?
   (Write an answer using an objective pronoun correctly.)

REFLECT

Spend some time walking around your school and just listening. Which people are being heard and which are not? Is there a way for us all to be better listeners?

3. Who will take this note to the office?
   (Write an answer using two pronouns as subjects.)

4. Whose book is this?
   (Write an answer using a possessive pronoun correctly.)

CONNECT TO ESSENTIAL QUESTION

Think of a time when you wanted to say something but couldn't. How did it feel? What did you do instead?

5. To whom should I give these cookies?
   (Write an answer using two objective pronouns correctly.)

Project-Based Assessments

Add a Chapter

Imagine another episode in the book *Out of My Mind.* The episode might be before or after Melody gets her Medi-talker. You might consider what a day in the classroom is like for Melody before she gets the talking computer or how her doctors might treat her at an appointment.

Take an everyday occurrence, such as going up stairs or eating, and see it from Melody's point of view. In what new ways can you understand her character? How does she react to the situation you created and why?

Brainstorm for ideas by answering the following questions.

- What is the situation or scene?

- How does Melody act?

- How do others around her act or react?

- How does the scene further develop the conflict?

- How does the scene further develop Melody's character?

Use your answers to the questions to write your new chapter. Remember to be true to Melody's voice as you write her thoughts in first person. Share your chapter on your class website, or read it aloud to the class.

Use the following guidelines for your chapter.	
To receive the highest score (4.0), the new chapter must meet all of these criteria.	Your chapter • adds an episode with a clear setting and situation. • is consistent with Melody's voice as created in the original text. • develops the conflict and character. • reveals a sensitivity to the main character and others with disabilities. • uses correct grammar, usage, punctuation, and spelling.

Podcast

Create a podcast to promote the book *Out of My Mind.* Include an analysis of Melody's character and the conflict in the story based on the excerpts in this chapter. Use Garageband, Audacity, AudioBoo, or an app on your phone or iPad to record and edit your podcast.

©Perfection Learning® • No Reproduction Permitted

Follow these steps to create your podcast.

- Introduce your podcast by giving your name, the title of the book, and the author.

- Include two or three paragraphs analyzing how Melody and the conflict she faces change in the three excerpts you read in this chapter.

- Choose a short section of the book that supports one of the points you are making about Melody. Read it aloud as a way to introduce the character or to support one of your conclusions about Melody and the story's conflict.

- Close the podcast by encouraging listeners to read the book themselves.

- Practice several times before recording yourself.

- Upload your podcast to the class website so others can listen and comment.

> **CONNECT TO ESSENTIAL QUESTION**
>
> What does Melody's story communicate about the power of communication?

Use the following guidelines for your podcast.	
To receive the highest score (4.0), the podcast must meet all of these criteria.	Your podcast • analyzes the characters and conflict in *Out of My Mind*. • includes a section from the book as an example. • features a fluent reading/speaking voice. • engages the reader with appropriate vocal volume, tone, and variety. • uses correct grammar and pronunciation.

On Your Own: Integrating Ideas

1. Research cerebral palsy or another disability. What can you learn about people with different abilities? How has technology helped people overcome physical and mental challenges?

2. Read the entire novel *Out of My Mind* by Sharon Draper. Go to sharondraper.com and read about why the author wrote the book.

3. Spend time with a person with disabilities who goes to your school or lives in your community. Take time to learn the way he or she communicates. What can you learn from him or her? What activity can you do together?

Connect to Testing

Questions on reading tests will test your ability to understand how episodes in a story develop characters and conflict. Many questions will require you to provide evidence to support your conclusions about the text.

1. **Part A:** Based on all three episodes from the book *Out of My Mind*, Melody can be described as

   A. smart and observant.

   B. frustrated and out of control.

   C. anxious and shy.

   D. gentle and withdrawn.

   Part B: Which of the following best supports the answer to Part A?

   A. *Even though my arms and legs flail out and I drool a little as I laugh, it is the first time in my entire life that I feel like I'm part of the group. . . .*

   B. *The tornado took over. My arms became fighting sticks, my legs became weapons.*

   C. *She and Molly exchange looks. I swear they think I am blind.*

   D. *"It sucks!" I type in.*

2. **Part A:** What does Rose do that shows she is genuinely supportive of Melody?

   A. She tells the other students to be quiet.

   B. She stands up and tells Melody that the computer is awesome.

   C. She doesn't touch the computer.

   D. She moves her desk closer to Melody and speaks softly.

   Part B: Which of the following sentences provides further evidence for your answer to Part A?

   A. *I shiver with excitement.*

   B. *When I roll into Miss Gordon's room, as usual, nobody looks up, except for Rose, who flashes me a smile.*

   C. *Everybody laughs at the silly joke with me.*

   D. *"That sure is a funny-looking computer! But I guess it's perfect for a kid like you."*

©Perfection Learning® • No Reproduction Permitted

3. **Part A:** The central conflict of the story is Melody's struggle to

  A. communicate her thoughts and feelings.

  B. make friends with the kids at school.

  C. get along with her parents.

  D. control her temper.

Part B: Which of the following provides the best evidence for the answer for Part A? (Choose all that apply.)

  A. *all my words had meaning.*
     But only in my head.
     I have never spoken one single word.

  B. *I didn't want the blocks. I wanted to tell her they were dangerous. I wanted her to tell somebody to get rid of them before a child got sick.*

  C. *It made me so angry that I couldn't tell her. The tornado took over.*

  D. *I shiver with excitement. When I roll into Miss Gordon's room, as usual, nobody looks up, except for Rose, who flashes me a smile.*

  E. *"It sounds weird."*
     "So do you."
     "What could she possibly have to say, anyway?"

4. In a few sentences, explain why the episode from Chapter 16 is important in the development of the conflict. Support your answer with evidence from the text.

Chapter 13

Analyzing Points of View in a Memoir

Preview Concepts

Words have connotations and denotations. The *denotation* of a word is its dictionary definition, or what it means. A word's *connotation* is its implied meaning, or the feelings associated with it. Although words may be synonyms, or mean nearly the same thing, their connotations can be very different. Would you rather be thought of as cautious or afraid? Consider these word pairs. Write a + above words with a positive connotation and a – above those with a negative connotation.

1. The watch was (cheap / inexpensive).

2. The little boy was (sensitive / a crybaby).

3. The (antique / old) chair needed to be recovered.

4. The politician (lied / used alternative facts).

5. The principal called the (rebellious / high-spirited) girl into her office.

With a partner, discuss why some words above seem more positive than others. Writers choose their words carefully to communicate their point of view to the reader. They want the reader to feel a certain way about ideas and events described.

CHAPTER GOALS

In this chapter you will

- determine the central idea of a text.
- provide a summary.
- identify the various points of view of characters in a narrative.
- integrate information presented in different mediums.

PREVIEW ACADEMIC VOCABULARY

central idea

memoir

propaganda

summary

Making Connections

Think about a political ad you've seen on television, or watch a political ad with your class. Describe the advertisement below.

What persuasive words does the advertisement use? Write them below.

Next to the words above, write the emotions the words create in the viewer.

Read this definition of propaganda.

propaganda: *the spreading of ideas, information, or rumor for the purpose of helping or injuring an institution, a cause, or a person*

Is the ad you viewed an example of propaganda? Why or why not?

MAKING
CONNECTIONS

In this chapter you will identify how words can be used as propaganda to influence the actions of people.

First Read: Using Details to Determine the Central Idea

Red Scarf Girl, a historical memoir, tells Ji-li Jiang's story of her childhood during the Cultural Revolution in China. In 1966, Mao Zedong, China's Communist leader, began the Cultural Revolution as a way to change Chinese society and assert his power. China's youth became a key part of Chairman Mao's plan. In this excerpt, Ji-li, her brother Ji-yong, and her friend An Yi are part of a protest in which crowds tear down a store sign considered "superstitious."

Objective: As you read, notice how words are used to influence the actions of the people in China. Underline the words that have positive connotations. Place a plus sign next to them (+). Also, underline negative words and mark them with a minus sign (-).

excerpt
Red Scarf Girl
Chapter 2: "Destroy the Four Olds!"
by Ji-li Jiang

My Thoughts

1   Our beloved Chairman Mao had started the Cultural Revolution in May. Every day since then on the radio we heard about the need to end the evil and pernicious influences of the "Four Olds": old ideas, old culture, old customs, and old habits.

5   Chairman Mao told us we would never succeed at building a strong **socialist** country until we destroyed the "Four Olds" and established the "Four News." The names of many shops still stank of old culture, so the signs had to be smashed to make way for the coming of new ideas.

10   The Great Prosperity Market was on Nanjing Road, Shanghai's busiest shopping street, only two blocks from our alley. Nanjing Road was lined with big stores and always bustled with activity. The street was full of bicycles and

---

socialist: a follower of socialism; a system of government in which the state controls the means of production; private property is allowed and the government redistributes wealth to narrow the gap between rich and poor

©Perfection Learning® • No Reproduction Permitted

pedicabs and trolleys, and the sidewalks were so crowded

15 with shoppers, they spilled on the sidewalk into the street. We were still quite a distance away when we heard the hubbub and ran faster.

A big crowd had gathered outside the Great Prosperity Market, one of the most successful food stores in the city. It

20 was full of good things to eat, with rare delicacies from other provinces and delicious items like dried duck gizzards strung up in its window. But today the window was bare. The store was deserted. All eyes were riveted on a dense ring of people in the street. Some young men were cheering excitedly for

25 the people inside the circle, but half the crowd were merely craning their necks and watching.

We wriggled our way between the bodies.

Lying on the dirty ground inside the circle was a huge wooden sign, at least twelve feet long. It was still impressive,

30 although the large golden characters GREAT PROSPERITY MARKET had lost their usual shine and looked dull and lifeless on the red background.

Two muscular young men in undershirts, probably salesmen from the store, were gasping next to it.

35 "Come on. Try again!" shouted the taller of the two.

He spat into his palms and rubbed them together. Then, with the help of the other, he lifted the board to shoulder height. "One, two, three!" They threw the board to the ground.

40 The board bounced twice but did not break. The two men threw the board again. Nothing happened.

---

pedicabs: a bicycle with a small seat on the back for hauling passengers

"Put one end on the curb. Stamp on it. That's bound to work," someone suggested.

"Good idea!"

45 "Come on! Try it!"

Amid a clamor of support, the two men moved the board half onto the sidewalk. Then they jumped onto it. "One... two... three..." We heard their shoes strike the hard wood. But the board did not yield.

50 ". . . This fourolds is really hard. Hey! Come on. Let's do it together!" the tall fellow shouted at the crowd.

I looked at An Yi to see if she would like to join me, but while I was hesitating, the board became fully occupied. Ji-yong had moved faster and was one of the dozen people on

55 it. They stamped, bounced, and jumped with excitement. One stepped on another's shoes. Hips and shoulders bumped. We all laughed.

The board refused to break. Even under a thousand pounds it did not give way. The crowd became irritated and started

60 shouting suggestions.

"Take it to a carpenter and let him use it for something!"

"Let's get a truck and drive over it!"

Someone started pushing through the circle.

"Hey, I've got an ax. Let me through! I've got an ax."

65 We stood back to give the man room. He lifted the ax to his shoulder and paused. The blade flashed in the sunlight as it began to move faster and faster in a shining arc until it crashed into the sign. The wood groaned with the impact, and we all cheered. The man gave the sign another blow, and another.

70 At last the sign gave way. With another groan and a crack it broke in two.

©Perfection Learning® • No Reproduction Permitted

Everyone cheered. People rushed forward to stamp on what remained of the sign. An Yi and I had found a few classmates in the crowd, and we all embraced, jumped, and shouted. Although what we had smashed was no more than a

75 piece of wood, we felt we had won a victory in a real battle.

Bathed in the evening's glow, we jumped and giggled all the way home. Inspired by what we'd seen, we noticed that other stores we passed also needed to change their names.

"Look. This is called the Good Fortune Photo Studio.

80 Doesn't that mean to make a lot of money, just like Great Prosperity? Chairman Mao told us that was exploitation. Don't you think this is fourolds?" Ji-yong asked enthusiastically.

"Right. We should change it to the **Proletarian** Photo Studio."

85 "Here's another one. The Innocent Child Toy Shop," An Yi exclaimed. "Innocent is a neutral word. It shows a lack of **class** awareness. What should we change it to?"

"How about the **Red** Child Toy Shop?"

"That's great," I said. "And we should change the

90 Peace Theater to the Revolution Theater. After all, without revolution, how can we have peace?"

We felt proud of ourselves. We were certain that we were bringing a new life to China.

So Grandma's reaction was a surprise to me. At dinner I

95 told her and my parents all about what had happened.

"My goodness!" she blurted out. "That sign cost the owner a fortune. They always said that since an especially auspicious

---

Proletarian: related to the working class

class: a division of a society based on social and economic status; Mao believed that the poor working classes must rise up and overthrow the rich, landowning classes.

Red: the color red was a symbol of the Communist government in China, used in its propaganda posters and worn by supporters of Chairman Mao.

date was chosen to hang the sign, the store has been

prosperous for more than thirty years. What a shame! What a

100 shame!"

"But Grandma, we have to get rid of those old ideas,

old culture, old customs, and old habits. Chairman Mao said

they're holding us back," I informed her.

"Besides, Grandma, there's no such thing as an auspicious

105 date. That's superstition, and superstition is fourolds. And the

name Great Prosperity is very bad. Great prosperity means to

make a fortune, and making a fortune is what bad people do.

Right?" Ji-yong tilted his head toward Mom and Dad.

Mom and Dad looked at each other and then turned to

110 Grandma.

"Yes, Ji-yong is right," Mom said, and shook her head.

My Thoughts

FIRST RESPONSE: KEY IDEAS AND DETAILS

Based on the positive and negative words you underlined,
explain the message Chairman Mao is promoting to Ji-li Jiang,
her family, and the people of China. Refer to specific words in
your answer. Write your answer in your response journal.

TECH-CONNECT

Post your examples
of words with
positive and negative
connotations to
Poll Everywhere
according to your
teacher's instructions.

Focus on Using Details to Determine the Central Idea

You've just read a true story, a narrative, of events experienced
by Ji-li Jiang while growing up in China under Chairman Mao. The
excerpt opens with an explanation of the ideas Mao's government
was promoting. The rest of the excerpt describes events that
resulted from Mao's philosophy.

When reading narratives—both real and imagined think about
events and ideas that caused other events. Understanding causes
and effects in a story is crucial to understanding the central idea
and to writing a good summary of the events.

Use the following chart to help you analyze the causes and resulting events in the excerpt.

Chairman Mao's message (Use direct quotes and line numbers)	Effects of Mao's message (Paraphrase, use direct quotes, and line numbers)

▼ **Write** Write a summary of the excerpt from *Red Scarf Girl*. Include the causes and effects in your paragraph. Use appropriate transitional words, such as *because*, *as a result*, and *so*.

Here is a checklist of ideas to include in a good summary.

✓ Who is the passage about?

✓ When and where does the event take place?

✓ What event happens in the passage?

✓ Why does the event in the passage happen?

✓ How do the characters react to each other and/or to the event?

Remember to keep your summary brief (four to six sentences) and to use your own words. Also, do not include your own personal opinions, since a summary covers only the ideas found in the text. Trade summaries with a partner and use the checklist to check your partner's work.

Second Read: Analyzing Varying Points of View in a Narrative

Read the text again with a partner. Take turns reading paragraphs aloud.

Objective: As you read the passage, think about how characters in the passage respond differently to ideas promoted by the revolution. Write the POV (point of view) next to lines from the text that help you infer the point of view of the following characters:

- Ji-li and her friends
- the men breaking the sign and the crowd
- Ji-li's grandmother
- Ji-li's parents

Focus on Analyzing Varying Points of View in a Narrative

Differing points of view among characters cause conflict. So it's important that you understand characters' points of view. This understanding also helps you determine the writer's purpose.

To determine point of view, look at what characters say and do and their reactions to events in the story.

Using your annotations from the second read of the passage, infer how the author and other characters viewed the ideas of the Revolution. Fill in the following chart.

Characters	What is their point of view of Chairman Mao and the Cultural Revolution?	Supporting Evidence
Ji-li and her friends		
the sign breakers and the crowd		
Ji-li's grandmother		
Ji-li's parents		

©Perfection Learning® • No Reproduction Permitted

Ji-li's story is written in first-person limited point of view. The reader only hears Ji-li's thoughts about the events. However, there is another point of view to take into account. You, as a reader, stand apart from the characters and events in the story. As you read, you have thoughts and feelings about the events described. You also bring your own background and experiences to the story. You may agree or disagree with the point of view of the narrator.

What is your point of view about the revolution and the breaking of the sign?

REFLECT

Which characters were supportive of the ideas of the revolution? Who was least supportive of the revolution? Explain your answer.

Do you agree with the ideas that Mao is promoting? Why or why not? What details from the text support your point of view? What knowledge from outside the text supports your point of view?

Do you think Ji-li will continue to support the revolution? Why or why not?

Speak and Listen In a group of two to three people, write three to five questions you would like to ask Ji-li about the events described in the excerpt. Write the questions as if you had the chance to interview her in person. All group members should agree on all the questions. Record them on a separate sheet of paper.

continued on next page

As a group, pass your questions to another group. Then work with your group to write an answer to one of the questions. Answers should reflect Ji-li's point of view from the excerpt. Continue passing your papers until all questions are answered. Share the answers to your questions with your group and the entire class.

Third Read: Integrating Visuals and a Text

Reread the text. Then study the poster below. Many propaganda posters like this were commissioned by the Chinese government and were circulated to spread the ideals of the Cultural Revolution to the Chinese people.

Objective: As you examine the poster, think about what words and objects remind you of details found in the excerpt.

The caption to this poster from 1968 said, "Destroy (or Scatter) the Old World. Forge the New World."

Focus on Integrating Visuals and a Text

Much like the thinking process you use when analyzing a text, you can analyze an image and determine its central idea. Answer these questions to analyze the image.

Who is in the image?

What is happening in the image?

Where does the image take place?

What meaning or main ideas does it convey?

continued on next page

How do the details contribute to the meaning of the image?
Consider these things:

- size (what elements are large or small)

- words in the caption

Why does the image matter and for whom was it made?

Speak and Listen With a partner, return to the excerpt from *Red Scarf Girl*. Scan the text together, stopping to identify details that relate to something on the poster—either words or visuals. Next to the detail on the poster, identify an event or detail from the text that relates to the image.

Write How does Chairman Mao use propaganda to influence the people of China? Write several paragraphs explaining how words are used to manipulate people to do what Mao wants and how Ji-li and her friends also become involved in creating propaganda.

REFLECT

Are commercials propaganda? Why or why not?

©Perfection Learning® • No Reproduction Permitted

Language: Capitalization of Proper Nouns

Proper nouns are names of a specific person, place, or thing. The first letter of a proper noun should be capitalized.

Notice Ji-li's use of proper nouns:

✓ Our beloved <u>Chairman Mao</u> had started the <u>Cultural Revolution</u> in <u>May</u>.

✓ This is called the <u>Good Fortune Photo Studio</u>.

✓ The <u>Great Prosperity Market</u> was on <u>Nanjing Road</u>, <u>Shanghai</u>'s busiest shopping street, only two blocks from our alley.

Note that the title and the name of the leader of China is capitalized as are the names of the movement in history, the month, the store, the market, the road, and the city.

Write four sentences about your school or city. Include at least one proper noun in each sentence. Be sure to correctly capitalize each proper noun.

1.

2.

3.

4.

> **CONNECT TO ESSENTIAL QUESTION**
>
> Are there any posters hanging in your school? If so, notice the words used and the purpose of the poster. How well do the posters achieve their purpose?

Project-Based Assessments

Poster of Protest

Follow the steps below to create a digital poster of protest.

Think of some ideas or policies you have a strong objection to. Choose a topic that is appropriate, current, and important. Brainstorm two to three ideas below.

Follow these steps for your poster:

1. Select the idea you feel most strongly about and get your teacher's approval. In your response journal, write your objection to the issue. Then think about your audience. Who would you like to send a message to, and what would you like them to know about this issue? Brainstorm a purpose for your poster, and write it in one clear statement.

   Purpose statement:

©Perfection Learning® • No Reproduction Permitted

2. Search online for propaganda posters. Study famous examples of posters used to influence people to fight for a cause, think a certain way, or join a movement. Consider how artists use words and visuals to influence people. Which designs seem overly dramatic? Which ones are subtly effective?

3. Consider the words on your poster. Think of a slogan you can use to communicate your purpose. Use words with positive and negative connotations to influence your audience. Write a few possible slogans below.

Think about the poster design. Which image(s) will best convey your idea? Consider using the following:

- photos, cartoons, symbols, or other images
- colors with emotional appeal
- size to emphasize important words or concepts

4. In your response journal make a sketch of your design and get approval from your teacher.

5. Use a computer program to produce and publish your poster. Share your final draft with your class by publishing the poster on the class website.

Use the following guidelines for your poster.	
To receive the highest score (4.0), the poster must meet all of these criteria.	Your poster • clearly communicates your point of view about a current issue. • has a slogan. • has a central image. • uses writing, color, sizing, and details to communicate a clear message. • is appropriate and professional. • is uploaded to a class website where others can view it. • uses correct grammar, usage, punctuation, and spelling.

Roundtable Discussion

Participate in a roundtable discussion on the following question.

> What can we as students in America learn about propaganda from reading the *Red Scarf Girl*?

In a roundtable discussion, all students are equal and everyone participates. Arrange your seats in a circle so that all participants can see one another. Your teacher or a discussion leader may sit in the middle. Come to the discussion with an open mind, and be prepared for a challenge! You will be evaluated on the following:

Expectations for Discussion	
Listening	**Speaking**
Listen respectfully.	Speak at least two times.
Look at speaker.	Offer reasons to support your point of view.
Follow text references.	Ask questions.
Take notes on what the speaker is saying.	Refer to text to support your conclusions.
Write follow-up questions.	Be open to other students' comments and questions.

Instructions for a Roundtable Discussion

1. The discussion leader (teacher or student) begins by asking the question.

> What can we as students in America learn about propaganda from reading *Red Scarf Girl*?

2. Allow each member the chance to reply to the question.

3. Take notes on comments you disagree with or you have questions about. Write what was said and who said it.

4. Go around the circle again and allow everyone to ask a follow-up question. Questions should be directed to the person who made the original comment. Try phrasing your questions in this way:
   • Can you explain what you mean by . . . ?

5. Then continue the discussion by having everyone respond to the following question, using steps 2–4 above.

> Where do you see and hear propaganda today? How do you know it's propaganda?

©Perfection Learning® • No Reproduction Permitted

On Your Own: Integrating Ideas

1. Read the entire memoir *Red Scarf Girl*. Use a recording device to make an audio advertisement for the book and share it with your friends. What does the book say about discrimination, injustice, conformity, and obedience? What parts were the most interesting or gripping? Does Ji-li change her point of view about the revolution?

2. Consider reading the following titles to learn more about the Chinese Cultural Revolution:

   Mao's Last Dancer: Young Reader's Edition by Li Cunxin. This is the story of a young Chinese boy born in 1961, who was chosen to leave his small town in China to become a dancer.

   Revolution is Not a Dinner Party by Ying Chang Compestine. The author grew up during the revolution and was happy in her childhood until Comrade Li, one of Mao's political officers, moves into her home when she is nine-years-old, and her life changes.

   Little Green: Growing Up During the Chinese Cultural Revoltuion by Chun Yu. The author uses poetry to explain her lack of understanding of what is happening around her.

   Snow Falling in Spring by Moying Li is another memoir of adolescence in the People's Republic of China.

Portrait of Mao Zedong from Chinese currency

Connect to Testing

In this chapter, you identified the central idea of a text, analyzed different points of view, and integrated details from a memoir and a poster. Questions on reading tests will test your ability on these skills. Answer the following questions. Return to the excerpt in the chapter as needed.

1. **Part A:** The Great Prosperity Market most likely got its name because it

   A. was the only market in Shanghai.

   B. brought crowds to an unpopulated street.

   C. sold items of luxury and comfort.

   D. was Chairman Mao's way of bringing wealth and success to China.

   Part B: Which of the following lines provides the strongest evidence for the answer for Part A?

   A. *Our beloved Chairman Mao had started the Cultural Revolution in May.*

   B. *The names of many shops still stank of old culture, so the signs had to be smashed to make way for the coming of new ideas.*

   C. *the sidewalks were so crowded with shoppers, they spilled on the sidewalk into the street.*

   D. *It was full of good things to eat, with rare delicacies from other provinces and delicious items like dried duck gizzards.*

2. Why was the crowd destroying the sign to the Great Prosperity Market? Use evidence from the text to support your answer.

©Perfection Learning® • No Reproduction Permitted

3. Which of the following quotations from the excerpt are the best examples of Mao's propaganda? Choose all that apply.

A. *to end the evil and pernicious influences of the "Four Olds"*

B. *The names of many shops still stank of old culture, so the signs had to be smashed to make way for the coming of new ideas.*

C. *But today the window was bare. The store was deserted.*

D. *Lying on the dirty ground inside the circle was a huge wooden sign, at least twelve feet long.*

E. *It was still impressive, although the large golden characters GREAT PROSPERITY MARKET had lost their usual shine and looked dull and lifeless on the red background.*

Read the excerpt below from *Red Scarf Girl*, and then answer the questions that follow. Use details from the text to support your answer.

So Grandma's reaction was a surprise to me. At dinner I told her and my parents all about what had happened.

"My goodness!" she blurted out. "That sign cost the owner a fortune. They always said that since an especially auspicious date was chosen to hang the sign, the store has been prosperous for more than thirty years. What a shame! What a shame!"

"But Grandma, we have to get rid of those old ideas, old culture, old customs, and old habits. Chairman Mao said they're holding us back," I informed her.

"Besides, Grandma, there's no such thing as an auspicious date. That's superstition, and superstition is fourolds. And the name Great Prosperity is very bad. Great prosperity means to make a fortune, and making a fortune is what bad people do. Right?" Ji-yong tilted his head toward Mom and Dad.

Mom and Dad looked at each other and then turned to Grandma.

"Yes, Ji-yong is right," Mom said, and shook her head.

continued on next page

4. Explain the points of view of the following characters regarding the destruction of the sign: Ji-li, Ji-yong, Grandma, Mom, and Dad. Use evidence from the text to support your answer.

5. Both the excerpt and the poster promote

   A. using violence to destroy objects that represent old customs.

   B. children's respect for ancestors.

   C. changing the names of stores to reflect the new ways.

   D. the lower class overthrowing the rich upper classes.

Chapter 14

Comparing and Contrasting Authors' Presentations of Events

Preview Concepts

Think about the term *revolution*. What does the word mean or suggest? What are some of the positive and negative aspects of a revolution? Write your thoughts below.

CHAPTER GOALS

In this chapter you will

- identify the central idea in an informational text.
- identify the author's purpose for writing a nonfiction text.
- compare and contrast how a memoir and a nonfiction article treat the same events.

Discuss your response with a partner. Then summarize your conclusions below.

PREVIEW ACADEMIC VOCABULARY

author's purpose

central idea

summary

Making Connections

In the last chapter you read Ji-li Jiang's memoir about the revolution in China. In this chapter you will read an informational text on the same topic. These sources are different because one was written by a girl who lived through the events and other was written by a person who researched the events many years after they happened. Ji-li Jiang's memoir and the poster on p. 254 are primary sources. Primary sources include letters, artwork, books, advertisements, and other sources written by people who lived through the events being described. Secondary sources are written by people who researched events but did not live during the historical events. What might be the advantages and disadvantages of reading primary and secondary sources?

Under each genre below, write a description of what you expect when you read each. Consider the kinds of details included, point of view, purpose, and writing style.

Memoir/Autobiography:

Informational article:

MAKING CONNECTIONS

In this chapter you will compare how a memoir and an informational text each present details about the Chinese Cultural Revolution.

Discuss your answers with a partner. Then discuss the following questions:

- Which type of text do you think would be more accurate or reliable? Why?

- Which type of text do you prefer to read? Why?

First Read: Identifying the Central Idea

In *Red Scarf Girl*, you read about one girl's experiences during the Chinese Cultural Revolution, and you analyzed a propaganda poster from the revolution. Read the article below to find out more about propaganda during the revolution.

Objective: As you read, underline a sentence in each paragraph that conveys the main idea of the paragraph.

On to Victory in China
by Gloria W. Lannom
Calliope
October 2013

	My Thoughts

1   "Come rally in Beijing!" The year was 1966, and Mao Zedong, chairman of the Chinese Communist Party, was summoning a million students from around the country to come to China's capital city. Throngs came, and the Red Guards

5   movement was born. Revolutionary music played an important role in its propaganda activities. Red Guard choirs sang in the streets and recorded their performances for nationwide distribution.

Love and Hate

10   Songs such as the "Red Guards Battle Song" and "Sailing the Seas Depends on the Helmsman" praised Mao lavishly. **Buzzwords** such as "struggle," "battle," "capitalists," "criticize," and "steel" were repeated over and over to inspire absolute devotion to Mao in both singers and audiences.

15   Historians note that two emotions appear in Red Guard songs: love for Chairman Mao and hatred for his enemies. The well-known Red Guard song "The East is Red" borrows the melody of a familiar folk song about farming. Traditionally, the sun rising in the East is a symbol of the Chinese emperor. The new

---

Buzzwords: terms or phrases that are associated with a specialized field or group. They usually sound important or technical and are used primarily to impress people who are not part of the field or group.

20   version, however, linked the sun with Mao as the godlike ruler
      on earth.

Red It Is

      For the Chinese, red is the color of joy, good luck, and
      prosperity. The Chinese Communists used red for badges
25   and banners. They also used it for "The Little Red Book,"
      which included selected statements from Mao's speeches
      and writings. In propaganda paintings, a bright red sun was
      depicted shining behind Mao, who was praised in print and
      song: "You are the reddest red sun in our hearts." As the Red
30   Guards movement evolved, opposing factions emerged that
      Mao believed would hinder his Cultural Revolution, so he
      ordered them suppressed. His revolution continued a while
      longer but, for the Red Guards, the music stopped in 1968.

My Thoughts

FIRST RESPONSE: KEY IDEAS AND DETAILS

In your response journal, finish the following sentence:
    This article is mainly about . . . .

Focus on Identifying the Central Idea

    The central idea of an informational text is like the theme in
a fictional text. The following can help you determine the central
idea.
    1. Read the title and any subheadings.
    2. Pay attention to the first and last sentences of the first
       paragraph.
    3. Look for words or information that is repeated.
    4. Think about the most important point of the passage.
    5. Think about the idea that the details or examples work
       together to support.

TECH-CONNECT

Search for the
definition of the
word *propaganda*,
and record it in your
reader response
journal. Tweet, text,
or post the definition
on your class website.

©Perfection Learning® • No Reproduction Permitted

Answer the following questions to help you determine the
central idea of the text.

1. What is a rally? What is the purpose of a rally?

2. What population does Chairman Mao focus on when he
organizes his rallies?

3. What method do the students use to share their message of
revolution and the importance of change?

continued on next page

4. How is Chairman Mao portrayed in songs and other forms of propaganda?

▼**Write** Write a summary of the passage in your response journal. Remember that a summary should

✓ clearly state the central idea.

✓ include details that support the central idea.

✓ not include personal opinions or judgments.

(**Speak and Listen** Trade paragraphs with a partner and compare central ideas. Discuss any differences in your answers.

CONNECT TO ESSENTIAL QUESTION

What words and phrases were used to define and promote Mao Zedong's Cultural Revolution?

Second Read: Understanding Author's Purpose

As your teacher reads the passage aloud, focus on the writer's purpose.

Objective: Why do you think Gloria W. Lannom wrote this article? Place a star by sentences that reveals the author's purpose.

REFLECT

Are revolutions usually violent or peaceful? Why do you think this is?

Focus on Understanding Author's Purpose

We are surrounded by more information today than ever before. When you read an informational text, it is important to question the source and the author's purpose. Remember that most writing reflects an author's bias, which means an interest or prejudice in favor of or against something. Remember the acronym PIE to help you decide an author's purpose:

✓ to **p**ersuade or convince

✓ to **i**nform or explain

✓ to **e**ntertain or amuse

Use the chart on the next page to determine the author's purpose in writing the article in this chapter. Choose examples (sentences or phrases) from the passage, and write each one in the appropriate box. Then analyze the graphic organizer as a whole to determine the author's overall purpose for writing.

To inform me
Examples:

To persuade me
Example:

To entertain me
Examples

The writer's overall purpose for writing this passage is to _____ .

Speak and Listen In small groups, discuss this question:

> What is the purpose of the text "On to Victory in China" by Gloria W. Lannom? Explain by using evidence from the text.

Discussion Steps

1. Each person answers the question.
2. Then each person asks a follow-up question or comments on another group member's answer.
3. Use the guidelines below to evaluate your own participation.

Put a check in the appropriate box each time you complete an action. Remember that the goal is for your group to come to an answer as a whole. It is not a competition to see who can talk the most or who knows the most.

It may help you to think about *Red Scarf Girl* and what you did *not* learn about the Cultural Revolution in that passage that you did learn in this passage.

Speaking and Listening Goals	Check Yourself
Respond to question	
Cite text for support	
Ask a question	
Respond to a question	
Listen to peers	
Involve others by inviting comment and encouraging participation	

Third Read: Comparing and Contrasting Presentations of Events

Review the excerpt from *Red Scarf Girl* in Chapter 13. As you read, pay attention to the author's presentation of the Cultural Revolution in contrast to Lannom's description in this chapter.

Focus on Comparing and Contrasting Presentations of Events

An author's presentation of information affects the way a reader understands it. A writer can influence the reader to think about an event or a person in a way that may be one-sided, naïve, or biased. After all, writing is a form of communicating one's opinions.

     ©Perfection Learning® • No Reproduction Permitted

Fill in the chart below to compare and contrast the presentation of the Cultural Revolution in the two texts. Pay careful attention to each writer's choice of words and details. Decide what the information presented shows about each author's point of view. If there is no comment given for an event or detail, write *not shown.*

Event, person, or detail	How is it presented in *Red Scarf Girl?*	How is it presented in "On to Victory in China"
Start of the revolution	exciting, full of energy and enthusiasm	
Chairman Mao		
How the message was being shared		
The significance of the color red		

continued on next page

Event, person, or detail	How is it presented in *Red Scarf Girl?*	How is it presented in "On to Victory in China"
How the youth and the parents/elders felt		
Why the revolution ended		

Speak and Listen Share your answers to the chart above with a partner. Then discuss these questions:

1. How is Ji-li Jiang's purpose for writing different from Gloria Lannom's purpose?

2. Do the texts disagree on any points of detail?

3. How is the experience of reading the memoir different from reading the informational article?

4. How did the texts work together to enhance your understanding of the Chinese Cultural Revolution? Refer to specific details from both texts in your answer.

Write Write several paragraphs contrasting *Red Scarf Girl* and the informational excerpt from this chapter. Consider the purposes of each excerpt, the way information is presented, and the experience of reading each.

©Perfection Learning® • No Reproduction Permitted

Language: Commas with Lists

Use commas to separate words and word groups in a simple series of three or more items. The final comma is known as the *serial comma* or *series comma*, and it comes before the coordinating conjunction, usually *and* or *or*.

Note how the excerpt uses commas between items in a list.

> Buzzwords such as "struggle," "battle," "capitalists," "criticize," and "steel" were repeated over and over to inspire absolute devotion to Mao in both singers and audiences.

> For the Chinese, red is the color of joy, good luck, and prosperity.

Finish the following sentences with a list of three items or more. Use commas correctly.

1. My three favorite foods are

2. The names of my closest friends are

3. The three purposes for writing are

REFLECT

Imagine what it would be like to have a country's youth running a revolution. In what ways could this be negative? In what ways could it be positive?

CONNECT TO ESSENTIAL QUESTION

Have you ever been involved in a protest? If so, what was it like?

Project-Based Assessments

Write a Protest Song

Work with a partner to write lyrics for your own protest song. Determine something you'd like to see changed at school. The change doesn't need to be meaningful or even possible. Make sure that your proposed change doesn't involve a person or offend or upset anyone. Get approval from your teacher.

Changes to consider include the following:

- The school day should be shorter.

- Sixth graders should stay with the same teacher all day.

- Sixth graders should have recess every day.

continued on next page

- Sixth graders should never have to work in groups.

- Report cards should only be sent out at the end of the year.

- Students should be allowed to retake tests.

Once you and your partner have decided on the topic of your protest song, decide on a tune to use. In the excerpt from this article, Gloria W. Lannom indicated that a song from the Chinese Cultural Revolution borrowed the melody of a familiar folk song. Consider the melody of a well-known childhood song or folk song.

"Row, Row, Row Your Boat"

"The Wheels on the Bus"

"If I Had a Hammer"

"Farmer in the Dell"

"Old MacDonald Had a Farm"

"Home on the Range"

"This Land Is Your Land"

"You Are My Sunshine"

Or you may prefer to become "Weird Al" Yankovich and choose a contemporary tune for your protest song.

Once you have chosen a tune, work with the melody to create your lyrics. You may want to use a recording of the song to guide your lyrics writing.

Once your lyrics are written, record your protest song. You may choose to sing the song with your partner or convince someone else to sing your lyrics.

Use the following guidelines for your protest song.	
To receive the highest score (4.0), the song must meet all of these criteria.	Your protest song • clearly states the change you want to see. • offers reasons for the proposed change. • has lyrics in written form. • has lyrics that match the melody of your chosen song. • is recorded for presentation.

    ©Perfection Learning® • No Reproduction Permitted

On Your Own: Integrating Ideas

1. Watch the film *To Live* by Zhang Yimou, which covers the end of the Qing dynasty to the end of the Cultural Revolution. Focus on the last 50 minutes if you don't have time to watch the entire film. What new information can you learn about the causes and effects of the Cultural Revolution in China?

2. View more examples of propaganda posters from the Cultural Revolution. Identify words and images that promote the revolution in a positive light.

3. Look at a timeline of the Cultural Revolution and modern China to gain further understanding of this significant period in world history. What are some of the lasting effects of the revolution? In what ways has China changed? In what ways has China remain unchanged?

4. Watch Part 2 of the film *China: A Century of Revolution* directed by Sue Williams to learn more about Mao Zedong and the years in which China was under his rule.

Connect to Testing

In this chapter, you practiced the skills of finding the central idea of a text, understanding the author's purpose, and comparing two authors' presentations of events. Questions on reading tests will test you on these skills.

Read the following and answer the questions that follow.

> "Come rally in Beijing!" The year was 1966, and Mao Zedong, chairman of the Chinese Communist Party, was summoning a million students from around the country to come to China's capital city. Throngs came, and the Red Guards movement was born. Revolutionary music played an important role in its propaganda activities. Red Guard choirs sang in the streets and recorded their performances for nationwide distribution.

1. **Part A:** Based on the context, the word *throngs* as used in the third sentence most likely refers to

   A. people who edited propaganda for the Cultural Revolution.

   B. students from around the country who came to the rally.

   C. the Red Guards.

   D. people who played revolutionary music.

   Part B: Which of the following provides the strongest evidence to support the answer to Part A?

   A. *summoning a million students*

   B. *Red Guards movement was born*

   C. *Red Guard choirs sang in the streets*

   D. *recorded their performances*

2. The quotations in this excerpt serve what purpose?

   A. to indicate the language spoken during the Chinese Revolution

   B. to indicate the words of the call that went out

   C. to show actual words from party officials and intellectuals

   D. to highlight the most important words for the reader

©Perfection Learning® • No Reproduction Permitted

3. Which of the following best communicates the main idea of this section of the text?

    A. The Red Guard were cruel to the youth who didn't support Chairman Mao Zedong.

    B. Chairman Mao Zedong did not have the support of the Chinese people.

    C. Young people showed their support by rallying behind Chairman Mao Zedong.

    D. Chairman Mao Zedong was a cruel dictator.

4. According to this article, the Cultural Revolution in China can best be described as

    A. drawn out and tedious.

    B. violent and destructive.

    C. short and not well attended.

    D. organized and popular.

5. Underline two details from the passage that are also supported by events from *Red Scarf Girl*. Number them 1. and 2. For each underlined detail, explain how the idea is shown in *Red Scarf Girl*. Write your explanations below.

Chapter 15

Analyzing Word Meaning

Preview Concepts

Did you know that words are continually being added to the English language? In September of 2016, 477 new words were added to Oxford English Dictionary. Some of the new words are related to changing technology. Some have been around but were never included in the dictionary. And others are just new. Who knew that so many words are continuing to come into the English language! Here are a couple of examples. Write a definition for what you think each means.

bocconcini (noun)

clickbait (noun)

freemium (noun)

scrumdiddlyumptious (adjective)

spanakopita (noun)

uptalk (noun)

Now work with a partner and compare your definitions. Then together find the definitions for each word. Use a different-colored ink to write the definition.

CHAPTER GOALS

In this chapter you will

• define key terms in a historical document and argumentative essay based on a historical document.
• identify claims in an argument.
• identify supporting evidence.

PREVIEW ACADEMIC VOCABULARY

argument

claim

evidence

Making Connections

Read the following inspirational quotes.

"Believe you can and you're halfway there."

—Theodore Roosevelt

"When I was 5 years old, my mother always told me that happiness was the key to life. When I went to school, they asked me what I wanted to be when I grew up, I wrote down *happy*. They told me I didn't understand the assignment, and I told them that they did not understand life."

—attributed to John Lennon

"The most effective way to do it is to do it."

—Amelia Earhart

"A person who never made a mistake never tried anything new."

—attributed to Albert Einstein

"You miss 100% of the shots you don't take."

—Wayne Gretzky

"Remember, no one can make you feel inferior without your consent."

—Eleanor Roosevelt

"I've learned that people will forget what you said, people will forget what you did, but people will never forget how you made them feel."

—Maya Angelou

The inspirational quotes illustrate the power of words. Which of the above quotes held the most power for you? Explain below.

First Read: Defining Key Terms

The Preamble to the Constitution is the introduction to the document that contains the most important words in American government. When the Constitutional Convention met in May 1787, representatives of twelve of the thirteen colonies were present. Among those in attendance were George Washington, Benjamin Franklin, James Madison, and Alexander Hamilton. The words that these men wrote over the next few months have become known as the "supreme law of the land." And the document they created is still the basis of American democracy today, more than two centuries later. However, many of those words carried a different meaning in 1787 than they do today.

Objective: The first three words that begin the Preamble to the Constitution are "We the People." As you read the Preamble and the excerpt from the essay about these three important words, underline unfamiliar terms.

Preamble to the Constitution

We the People of the United States, in Order to form a more perfect Union, establish Justice, insure domestic Tranquility, provide for the common defence, promote the general Welfare, and secure the Blessings of Liberty to ourselves and our Posterity, do ordain and establish this Constitution for the United States of America.

excerpt
The Words We Live By
by Linda R. Monk
"The Preamble: We the People"

	My Thoughts

1   The first three words of the Constitution are the most important. They clearly state that the people—not the king, not the legislature, not the courts—are the true rulers in American government. This principle is known as popular
5   sovereignty.

But who are "We the People"? This question troubled the nation for centuries. As Lucy Stone, one of America's first advocates for women's rights, asked in 1853, " 'We the People'? Which 'We the People'? The women were

10 not included." Neither were white males who did not own property, American Indians, or African Americans—slave or free. Justice Thurgood Marshall, the first African American on the Supreme Court, described the limitation:

> for a sense of the evolving nature of the constitution,
15 we need look no further than the first three words of the document's **preamble:** "we the people." When the founding fathers used this phrase in 1787, they did not have in mind the majority of America's citizens . . . the men who gathered in Philadelphia in 1787 could
20 not . . . have imagined, nor would they have accepted, that the document they were drafting would one day be construed by a Supreme Court to which had been appointed a woman and the descendant of an African slave.

25 Through the Amendment process, more and more Americans were eventually included in the Constitution's definition of "We the People." After the Civil War, the Thirteenth Amendment ended slavery, the Fourteenth Amendment gave African Americans citizenship, and the
30 Fifteenth Amendment gave black men the vote. In 1920, the Nineteenth Amendment gave women the right to vote nationwide, and in 1971, the Twenty-sixth Amendment extended **suffrage** to eighteen-year-olds.

---

preamble: introduction
suffrage: right to vote in political elections

My Thoughts

FIRST RESPONSE: KEY IDEAS AND DETAILS

Which adults in your life wouldn't have been part of "We the People" when the Constitution was drafted ? Write your answer in your response journal.

Focus on Defining Key Terms

The Preamble to the Constitution, as with any formal or legal writing that is more than two hundred years old, contains difficult and sometimes outdated academic vocabulary. Additionally, the excerpt, which is based on the Preamble, also contains academic vocabulary. Understanding this vocabulary is important to comprehending the text.

Complete the following chart. Use context clues to determine what you think each word means. Then check the definition in a dictionary. Add terms that you underlined in the empty cells. Some terms may not be found in the dictionary and will take a bit of online research to find the definitions.

TECH-CONNECT

Text, tweet, or post on the class website your response to the First Response question.

Academic Vocabulary	What I Think It Means (from context and from what I already know)	Dictionary Definition
domestic Tranquility		
general Welfare		
Blessings of Liberty		
Posterity		
ordain		
popular sovereignty		

©Perfection Learning® • No Reproduction Permitted

Academic Vocabulary	What I Think It Means (from context and from what I already know)	Dictionary Definition
founding fathers		
Amendment process		
suffrage		

Speak and Listen Share your definitions with a partner. Discuss the following questions.

1. How is domestic tranquility achieved today?
2. Why is the amendment process important?

Second Read: Identifying Claims

Objective: Listen as your teacher reads the text aloud, or read it on your own a second time. Think about what the author wants you to understand or remember. What is her purpose for writing the essay?

Focus on Identifying Claims

The central idea of an informational text is the main point the author wants you to understand or remember. Since this is an argumentative essay, the author's central idea is also known as a claim. A claim is the main argument.

A claim is

- a statement that an author is trying to prove is true.

- based upon an opinion.

- sometimes clearly stated and sometimes must be inferred.

In analyzing (or writing) an argument, use the PEELS approach. The PEELS approach stands for the following:

1. Make a **p**oint
2. Support it with **e**vidence. (and examples).
3. **E**xplain the evidence.
4. **L**ink the points.
5. Maintain a formal **s**tyle.

The first step in the PEELS approach—make a **p**oint—is the central claim in an argument. As noted above, sometimes the central claim is inferred and not stated. That is the case in this excerpt. Answer the following questions to uncover the author's claim.

1. Why does the author focus on the first three words of the Preamble to the Constitution?

2. Why does Monk say that Lucy Stone's question has troubled the nation for decades?

©Perfection Learning® • No Reproduction Permitted

3. How does Justice Marshall add evidence to the troubling nature of the words "We the People"?

The author's claim is

(Speak and Listen Share your central idea or claim with a partner.

Third Read: Identifying and Explaining Supporting Evidence

Read the Preamble and the excerpt a third time.

Objective: Pay particular attention to the quote by former Supreme Court Justice Thurgood Marshall. How does his quote support the author's claim?

Focus on Identifying and Explaining Supporting Evidence

Now that you have identified the author's central claim, return to the PEELS chart and steps 2, 3, and 4 to identify and explain supporting evidence and how the points are linked.

Support it with **e**vidence (and examples).

Explain the evidence.

Link the points.

Use the chart below to identify and explain the author's supporting evidence.

continued on next page

Analysis Questions	Answers
What claim is the author making in her essay?	The meaning of the first three words in the Preamble to the Constitution has changed over time.
What is the purpose of Lucy Stone's question from 1853?	
What is the purpose of the quote from Supreme Court Justice Thurgood Marshall?	
How does the final paragraph support the author's central claim?	

©Perfection Learning® • No Reproduction Permitted

⟨Speak and Listen With two or three classmates, discuss whether you find the claims made in this article convincing. Discuss the following questions.

1. How does the quote from Lucy Stone support the central claim?
2. How does the quote from Supreme Court Justice Thurgood Marshall support the central claim?
3. How does the information in the last paragraph about the amendment process link the points?
4. Do you think the author's central claim extends beyond the first three words of the Preamble to the Constitution? Why or why not?

▼Write Write a paragraph explaining whether you think the author's central claim extends beyond the first three words of the Preamble to the Constitution.

Here are some sentence frames to help you get started.

- The author's central claim is . . . .

- I think the author's central claim extends/doesn't extend beyond the first three words because . . . .

CONNECT TO ESSENTIAL QUESTION

Do you think our founding fathers could have imagined that the words they were writing more than two hundred years ago would be some of the most powerful words today?

Language: Dashes

Dashes are used to set off extra, yet important, words or a group of words in a sentence. If the words are removed, the sentence is still complete. These extra words are called *parenthetical elements* or *interrupters* because they interrupt the flow of the sentence. Notice the following example of the author's use of dashes from the excerpt in this chapter.

> They clearly state that the people—not the king, not the legislature, not the courts—are the true rulers in American government.

When the interrupter is in the middle of the sentence, a dash is used before the words and another after the words. Read the sentence without the interrupter. It is still a complete sentence. Notice the effect of the dashes and the interrupter. The information between the dashes adds emphasis to the fact that the people are the true rulers in American government.

continued on next page

Below is another example of the author's use of dashes. This time, only one dash is needed because the interrupter is at the end of the sentence. The author is adding clarifying information with the words after the dash. You, as a reader, are more likely to notice this extra information because you naturally pause when you come to the dash.

Neither were white males who did not own property, American Indians, or African Americans—slave or free.

Practice adding dashes where they belong in the sentences below to set off the interrupters. Use a carot (^) with a dash above where the dashes belong. Then write your own sentence with a dash or pair of dashes.

1. Harry Potter novels all seven of them are my favorite books of all time.

2. There are 4,100 pages in all of the seven novels, with *Harry Potter and the Order of the Phoenix* at 766 pages the longest.

3. I saw all of the movies even *Fantastic Beasts and Where to Find Them* as soon as they came out in the theaters.

Now write your own sentence with dashes.

Project-Based Assessments

Timeline

Conduct research and create a timeline that traces the beginning of the Constitutional Convention to the end when the Constitution was signed. Search online for information related to this important event in American history.

    ©Perfection Learning® • No Reproduction Permitted

Remember to use only reliable sources for your information. Websites that end in *.gov*, *.edu*, or *.org* usually have more reliable information than sites with muny contributors such as Wikipedia.

Gather the following information for your timeline.

- When and where did the convention take place?

- How many delegates were in attendance? Who were they? How were they chosen? Who was in charge?

- How long did the convention last?

- When was the Constitution completed? How many delegates signed it?

Create your timeline digitally or draw it yourself. Include screenshots or images of the original documents. If you choose to create a digital timeline, search for software that specializes in timelines. Add descriptions and art to mark each point on your timeline.

Use the following guidelines for your timeline.	
To receive the highest score (4.0), the timeline must meet all of these criteria.	**Your timeline** • traces the Constitutional Convention from beginning to end. • includes the important dates of the convention. • has a description and graphic for each point on the timeline. • is organized and presented in a professional manner. • is free from typos and grammatical errors.

On Your Own: Integrating Ideas

1. Research changes to the Constitution since it was drafted in 1787. What was the first amendment and when was it added? How many amendments have been added to date?

2. What is the Bill of Rights? When was this document drafted and why? Explain the rights included.

3. Learn more about the "founding fathers" or the framers of the Constitution. Who was Gouverneur Morris and what role did he play?

Connect to Testing

In this chapter, you read an argumentative essay on the Preamble to the Constitution. Answer the following questions based on your close reading of the excerpt in this chapter.

1. One of the purposes of the first paragraph of the essay is to

   A. teach the first three words of the Constitution.

   B. explain how the Constitution was written.

   C. emphasize the importance of the first three words of the Constitution.

   D. introduce the true rulers of American government.

Read the following excerpt and answer the question that follows.

> But who are "We the People"? This question troubled the nation for centuries. As Lucy Stone, one of America's first advocates for women's rights, asked in 1853, " 'We the People'? Which 'We the People'? The women were not included."

2. What is the part of speech and meaning of the word *advocates* as it is used in the quote from the excerpt above?

   A. noun, supporter

   B. verb, supports

   C. noun, justice

   D. verb, opposes

3. **Part A:** What is the author's purpose in including the quote from former Supreme Court Justice Thurgood Marshall in her essay? Choose all that apply.

   A. He attended the Constitutional Convention in 1787.

   B. As a decendant from an African American slave, Marshall is a personal example supporting the author's claim.

   C. As a Supreme Court justice, he knows more about the Constitution than the author.

   D. His quote offers supporting evidence to the author's central claim.

   E. He was an early supporter of popular sovereignty.

©Perfection Learning® • No Reproduction Permitted

Part B: Which of the following lines provides the strongest evidence for the answers in Part A? Choose all that apply.

A. *Justice Thurgood Marshall, the first African American on the Supreme Court*

B. *for a sense of the evolving nature of the constitution, we need look no further than the first three words of the document's preamble*

C. *When the founding fathers used this phrase in 1787*

D. *the men who gathered in Philadelphia in 1787*

E. *document they were drafting would one day be construed by a Supreme Court*

4. Rewrite the Preamble to the Constitution in your own words below. Replace the outdated language with current terms, but don't lose the meaning or the structure of the writing.

Writing a Literary Analysis

In this unit, you reflected on the power of words in a variety of texts—a poem, excerpts from a novel, a memoir, an informational article, and an essay based on a historical document. The selections showed how words can be appreciated as an art form or used as protest, as propaganda, or as the supreme law of the land. In this chapter, you will apply what you've learned about the power of words.

WRITING PROMPT

We can learn about our country by analyzing historical documents. Historical speeches are another piece of history. The power of the words and the art of their delivery give historical speeches the power to inspire, to incite change, and to chase ideals. They offer moments of motivation and years of historical impact.

Choose a well-known speech and analyze its impact on the world. Research the background of the speech as well as the orator, and learn how the speech fits into history. Think about the immediate and lasting effects. What made the speech powerful, and how did it affect the audience and perhaps even change the world?

Your analysis should be two to three pages long. It should be typed, double-spaced, and using a standard-size font.

Prepare to Write:

Carefully read the prompt. Underline key words that explain the requirements of the task. Break it down based on purpose, audience, content, and additional requirements by filling in the chart below.

Purpose	
Audience	
Content Requirement	
Additional Requirements	

▼ The Writing Process

Brainstorm

Choose a famous historical speech from the list below, or find another that you are familiar with. You can also consult the book *Speeches That Changed the World* (2005) for additional options, or search online for one on a subject of interest. For longer speeches, choose the first three to five paragraphs (about a page) to review and analyze.

- the Gettysburg Address by Abraham Lincoln

- "I Have a Dream" by Martin Luther King Jr.

- "We Choose to Go to the Moon" speech by John F. Kennedy

- speech on women's suffrage by Emmeline Pankhurst

- "There Is No Salvation for India" speech by Mohandas Gandhi

- "Women's Rights Are Human Rights" by Hillary Clinton

- farewell address by General Douglas MacArthur

- "Their Finest Hour" speech by Winston Churchill

- victory speech (2008) by Barack Obama

Read several speeches before deciding on one. Choose a speech that captures your interest or ignites a passion. If the speech is longer and you aren't sure which part to analyze, ask your teacher for help choosing a smaller section to write about.

Generate Ideas

When writing an analysis, it is important to identify and understand all of the ideas of the text before evaluating them. Use the close reading practices you've been taught in this book to read and reread the text. During your first read, annotate as suggested below.

✓ Underline main ideas.

✓ Note places where main ideas are supported with examples, reasons, a story or anecdote, data, or other supporting details.

✓ Draw arrows to show the development of the ideas.

✓ Star any words you do not know the meaning of and look these up.

✓ Mark the text with question marks where you are unsure about the meaning of something.

✓ Jot down any comments in the margins about how the speech makes you feel or what makes it remarkable.

> **REFLECT**
>
> Which part of the research process do you struggle with the most? Which part do you enjoy the most? What would help you be more effective in the research process?

continued on next page

Then fill in the chart below to analyze the text. If any of the elements are not addressed, write *none* in the third column.

Element of Speech	Explanation	Example from Speech
Historical context	Understand the time period and setting of the speech. Why was the speech necessary? Was there any opposition to the speech?	
Subject	What is the topic of the speech?	
Audience	For whom was the speech written?	
Purpose	What is the speaker's purpose?	

©Perfection Learning® • No Reproduction Permitted

Read the speech again and focus on logical and rhetorical appeals. Good logical appeals are based on accurate reasoning and avoid fallacies such as bandwagon and prejudice. Annotate the following in the speech.

✓ Highlight convincing words or phrases.

✓ Underline persuasive logical reasons.

✓ Circle any repeated words or phrases with similar structure.

Then fill in the charts below and on the next page to analyze both the logical and emotional appeals.

Logical Appeals	Explanation	Example from Speech
Central idea/ Claim	What is the main idea? What claim is the speaker making?	
Supporting evidence	What evidence does the speaker give to support the main idea?	
Counterclaim	What is the opposing viewpoint?	
Response to counterclaim	What reasons does the speaker give to disprove the counterclaim?	

Rhetorical Appeal	Explanation	Example from Speech
Rhetorical questions	Questions used to make the audience think but that don't require a response.	
Imagery metaphors	Descriptive language that creates a picture in the audience's mind Comparisons	
Emotional language	Words with strong negative or positive connotations	
Parallel structure	Repetition of phrases for emphasis	

Don't confuse rhetorical appeals and some types of logical fallacies. One logical fallacy is loaded language, which means using words with strong emotional appeal instead of reasons and evidence. Emotional words can be used effectively but using them as the sole method of persuasion is a serious logical fallacy.

Organize Ideas

When writing an analysis, you should explain the text and evaluate how well the text communicates. Use the outline on the next page to help you organize your ideas.

I. Introductory paragraph: Give the context and purpose of the speech. Identify the speaker and make a claim about the importance of the speech.

> For example: Martin Luther King Jr.'s "I Have a Dream" speech inspired not only the American civil rights movement but also civil rights movements in South Africa and around the world.

REFLECT

In you were to give a speech about something important, what would you like it to be about?

II. Body paragraphs:

   A. Explain what the speech says by writing one to two paragraphs. This is a summary of the main ideas. Explain the central claim and the supporting reasons.

   B. Explain how the speech says what it says by writing one to two paragraphs. This is an analysis of the speaker's methods. Explain how he or she appeals to logic and also emotions.

III. Conclusion: Restate the central idea of the speech and its purpose. Then comment on the immediate and lasting effects of the speech. Show how the words spoken changed the world in some way.

First Draft

Use your outline to write a draft of your analysis. The purpose of the first draft is to get your ideas down on paper in an organized way. Here are some helpful hints:

- Refer to your outline as well as the notes you wrote in the brainstorming activities.

- Write quickly so you don't lose your train of thought. You will revise and proofread later. Try to write as much as you can in one sitting. You can set a timer if that helps you.

- Write on every other line or double-space if working on a computer. This will make it easier to add changes.

- If you take a break and then return to writing, reread what you have written before continuing. This will help you resume the flow of thought.

- Mark this Draft #1.

CONNECT TO ESSENTIAL QUESTION

Have you used powerful words in your essay? Use a dictionary or a thesaurus, and choose strong words that mean exactly what you wish to say.

Revision

There is great benefit to having other people read your writing. Shown on the next page are three ways to revise your paper. Choose at least one way and then mark the revision as Draft #2.

continued on next page

First Peer Review

This review will evaluate whether your ideas are clear and whether they flow together in a logical order. With a group of two to three people, complete the following steps.

Steps for Peer Review

1. Select a timekeeper. Each writer gets fifteen minutes. Stick to the time.
2. One person begins by reading aloud his or her first paragraph while other members listen.
3. Pause for questions.
4. Writer asks, "Is the central idea of my essay clear?" Each member responds as the writer takes notes on his or her draft.
5. Writer reads the rest of the essay, pauses, and then reads it again.
6. As the writer reads a second time, the other members take notes.
7. Writer asks, "Do I explain why this is a good speech? Do I show how the speech impacted the world? Do I support my points with details from the speech?"
8. Peers offer constructive comments and the writer makes note of their suggestions.
9. Repeat steps 1–7 with the next writer.

As soon as possible after the peer review, revise your draft based on your peers' questions and comments.

Second Peer Review

With a partner, trade essays and use the following checklist to evaluate:

Think big. Look at the draft as a whole.

- ❏ Have I covered everything required by the prompt?
- ❏ Is the flow between paragraphs smooth or choppy?
- ❏ Is my point of view consistent throughout?

Think medium. Look at the draft paragraph by paragraph.

- ❏ Does my introduction introduce the speech, the speaker, the occasion, and the purpose?
- ❏ Does each paragraph support my claim?
- ❏ Are my ideas supported by evidence from the speech?

Think small. Look at your draft sentence by sentence.

- ❏ Are any sentences long and confusing? short and choppy?
- ❏ Are any sentences unclear?
- ❏ Are there errors in spelling, grammar, or usage?

> **REFLECT**
>
> Have you chosen a formal tone and word choice to fit your audience? Avoid slang words, addressing your reader, and contractions.

Final Peer Review

Ask another student to read your essay and rate it using the rubric.

Use the following guidelines for your analysis.	
To receive the highest score (4.0), the analysis must meet all of these criteria.	Your analysis should • explain and summarize the ideas found in an important historical speech. • evaluate specific elements of the speech to show why it is considered a great speech. • be organized logically. • have varied sentence types and lengths. • include an introduction, body, and conclusion. • use correct grammar, usage, punctuation, and spelling.

Proofread

As you prepare a final draft, make sure you have included standard grammar and punctuation. Proofread carefully for omitted words and punctuation marks, especially when using a direct quotation. If you used a computer, run a spell-check but be aware of its limitations. Proofread your essay again, reading it from the last sentence to the first in order to catch errors in fluency. By taking the sentences out of context, you are more likely to find mistakes. Mark this Draft #3.

Final Essay

Make all the necessary changes from Draft #3 to complete your final essay. If your teacher requires you to turn in your paper digitally, allow enough time to upload your essay before the due date in case you have any technical problems.

If you are comfortable, share your completed essay with audiences beyond your classroom. Read it to your family and friends, or share your ideas in a conversation. Upload your finished digital copy to your class website or personal blog.

FLUENCY CHECK

Before submitting your paper, check for the following:

1. Count the number of words in four consecutive sentences. Do they vary in length?

2. List the main verbs in four consecutive sentences. Do they vary?

3. Underline the first five words of four consecutive sentences. Do they vary?

Practice Performance Task

A performance task evaluates your ability to comprehend selections of literature and informational texts and then demonstrate your knowledge in writing. The task often begins with several multiple-choice or short-answer questions on key vocabulary and the main ideas of the passage(s). The task culminates with a writing assignment.

Complete the following performance task based upon selections from Unit 3.

Source #1

Read the following poem, "Words Free as Confetti" by Pat Mora, which you read in Chapter 11.

Come, words, come in your every color.

I'll toss you in storm or breeze.

I'll say, say, say you,

taste you sweet as plump plums,

bitter as old lemons.

I'll sniff you, words, warm

as almonds or tart as apple-red,

feel you green

and soft as new grass,

lightwhite as dandelion plumes,

or thorngray as cactus,

heavy as black cement,

cold as blue icicles,

warm as *abuelita's* yellowlap.

I'll hear you, words, loud as searoar's

purple crash, hushed

as *gatitos* curled in sleep,

as the last goldlullaby.

I'll see you long and dark as tunnels,

bright as rainbows,

playful as chestnutwind.

I'll watch you, words, rise and dance and spin.

I'll say, say, say you

in English,

in Spanish,

I'll find you.

Hold you.

Toss you.

I'm free too.

I say *yo soy libre*,

I am free

free, free

free as confetti.

1. Read the following lines and then answer the question.

   I'll see you long and dark as tunnels,

   bright as rainbows,

   The lines show that according to the speaker, words

   A. are colorful and long.

   B. are scary and dark.

   C. can have negative and positive meanings.

   D. can be found anywhere.

2. Read the following lines and then answer the question.

   I'll hear you, words, loud as searoar's

   purple crash, hushed

   as gatitos curled in sleep,

   as the last goldlullaby.

   The lines show that words can be

   A. harsh or gentle.

   B. heard from far away.

   C. big or small.

   D. happy or sad.

continued on next page

3. What is the theme of the poem?

    A. There are so many words in the world that we could never know all of them.

    B. Words offer so many possibilities and meanings, including the feeling of freedom.

    C. Spanish and English words are similar, which is freeing.

    D. Words stimulate the senses just like items in the natural world.

Continue the performance task by reading a second source and answering the questions.

Source #2

Read the following passage from "On to Victory in China" by Gloria W. Lannom, which you read in Chapter 14. Then answer the questions that follow.

Red It Is

For the Chinese, red is the color of joy, good luck, and prosperity. The Chinese Communists used red for badges and banners. They also used it for "The Little Red Book," which included selected statements from Mao's speeches and writings. In propaganda paintings, a bright red sun was depicted shining behind Mao, who was praised in print and song: "You are the reddest red sun in our hearts." As the Red Guards movement evolved, opposing factions emerged that Mao believed would hinder his Cultural Revolution, so he ordered them suppressed. His revolution continued a while longer but, for the Red Guards, the music stopped in 1968.

4. Read the following sentence and then answer the question.

    As the Red Guards movement evolved, opposing factions emerged that Mao believed would hinder his Cultural Revolution, so he ordered them suppressed.

This sentence suggests which of the following?

    A. The Red Guard did not support the Chinese Cultural Revolution.

    B. Not everyone in China supported Mao Zedong.

    C. Mao Zedong was opposed to the Red Guard.

    D. Everyone in China supported the Chinese Cultural Revolution.

5. **Part A:** What is the meaning of *suppressed* as used in the passage on the previous page?

   A. supported

   B. forcibly put an end to

   C. spread the word

   D. returned

   Part B: Which of the following provides the strongest evidence to support the answer to Part A? Choose two.

   A. *As the Red Guards movement evolved*

   B. *opposing factions emerged*

   C. *Mao believed would hinder his Cultural Revolution*

   D. *His revolution continued a while longer*

Your Assignment

WRITING PROMPT

"What power do words have?" Write a well-organized essay in which you answer the chapter's Essential Question. Explain how words can influence people's behavior for good or bad and ultimately have the power to change lives. Your essay should refer to at least three texts from the unit. Organize your ideas clearly into a well-developed essay with a clear thesis statement included in your introduction. Your essay should also contain a body and a conclusion. Write your essay using a formal tone and style.

Read the prompt carefully. Underline words that indicate what to include and how to write your essay. Study the guidelines at the end of this performance task before you begin to write. This will help ensure you are meeting all the requirements of the essay.

Plan your essay by brainstorming for examples from the texts. It may be helpful to create a graphic organizer like the following.

Text from Unit 3	Quotation from Text	What does this say about the power of words?

What power do words have?

My answer:

continued on next page

Your Assignment (continued)

Write a first draft, focusing on your ideas more than the conventions of writing. Then go back and edit your writing for clarity and structure. When you are finished, evaluate your essay using the list below. Revise your writing as needed.

Your essay will be scored using the following guidelines:

Reading Comprehension:

- How well did you understand the texts?
- Does your writing reflect your understanding of the sources?

Writing Expression:

- Does your writing address the requirements of the prompt?
- Does your essay contain a thesis statement that answers the unit Essential Question?
- Does your essay refer to at least three texts from the chapter?
- Is your essay well organized with ideas that fit together logically?
- Does your essay contain an introduction, body, and conclusion?
- Does the writing style contain precise, accurate language and content appropriate to the prompt?

Writing Conventions:

- Does your writing follow the rules of standard English with few errors in grammar, usage, and spelling?

©Perfection Learning® • No Reproduction Permitted

Unit 4

Essential Question
Why should you protect Earth and its creatures?

BRRIINNNNNGGGG! Your alarm goes off and you crawl out of bed. (Or if you're a morning person, you *jump* out of bed.) You head to the bathroom to brush away your nasty dragon breath. A few minutes later you pop into the shower. The warm water washes over you, chasing away the fogginess in your brain. Your favorite sweatshirt is missing from its usual spot on your bedroom floor. Foraging through the clean laundry, you discover it among the clean clothes. Quickly, you run downstairs and grab some breakfast, remembering to fill up a water bottle to help you stay hydrated during school. Your day has begun.

This morning routine is completed day in and day out by middle schoolers all over the world. For each task that makes up your morning routine, think of all the times you rely on water. What would happen if you didn't have clean water to wash your clothes, to brush your teeth, or to drink? What if all the sources of water became polluted or dried up due to environmental changes? Think of how that would affect you and your family, your pets and other animals, and the plants you eat for food.

Water is just one vital part of our natural environment, which is made up of a complex mix of elements that supports life on our planet. Often we take water, soil, sun, and other elements for granted—until something happens to shift the fragile balance of our world.

In recent years, scientists have warned that humans are impacting the environment in negative ways. People have different ideas about how to protect the earth and its creatures. In this unit, you will explore how humans help and hurt this planet, and you will engage in activities to write, speak, and debate about protecting the earth and its creatures.

GOALS

- To analyze character development and interaction
- To make inferences based on textual evidence
- To evaluate claims and support for claims
- To determine main ideas and compare themes
- To write an argumentative essay

Chapter 16

Analyzing Characters and Point of View

Preview Concepts

Think about an interesting main character from a story you enjoyed reading. Write the name of the character and the book title below. Write three of four sentences that describe the character.

What do you like about the character? What don't you like about the character?

With a partner, share what you each wrote about your chosen characters. Then imagine that your characters were stuck in an elevator that suddenly stopped working. What would each character do to solve the problem? What would they say to each other? Write your response below.

One of the ways that authors reveal characters is by having them interact with other characters. When reading a story, pay attention to dialogue between characters. Make inferences about the personality traits of the characters based upon their reactions to other characters.

CHAPTER GOALS

In this chapter you will

• write a summary of chronological events.

• analyze characters by making inferences about their personalities.

• analyze how an author develops the point of view of a narrator.

• write a biopoem or write from a new point of view.

PREVIEW ACADEMIC VOCABULARY

character

chronological

first-person point of view

inference

point of view

textual evidence

summary

©Perfection Learning® • No Reproduction Permitted

Making Connections

Read the following passage about an interaction between Tom Sawyer and his aunt.

There was a slight noise behind her and she turned just in time to seize a small boy by the slack of his **roundabout** and arrest his flight.

"There! I might 'a' thought of that closet. What you been doing in there?"

"Nothing."

"Nothing! Look at your hands. And look at your mouth. What IS that **truck**?"

"I don't know, aunt."

"Well, I know. It's jam—that's what it is. Forty times I've said if you didn't let that jam alone I'd skin you. Hand me that switch."

The switch hovered in the air—the peril was desperate—

"My! Look behind you, aunt!"

The old lady whirled round, and snatched her skirts out of danger. The lad fled on the instant, scrambled up the high board-fence, and disappeared over it.

— *The Adventures of Tom Sawyer* by Mark Twain

---

roundabout: a coat or jacket
truck: trash or rubbish

Underline lines from the text that show character qualities of Tom's aunt. Based upon the sentences you underlined, describe her character in a few sentences.

MAKING CONNECTIONS

In this chapter you will be making inferences about characters based on evidence from a text.

First Read: Summarizing Events

Noah Underwood lives in Key West, Florida, with his father, mother, and sister Abbey. Noah's father has been arrested for sinking a riverboat casino called the *Coral Queen*. In the following excerpt from the novel *Flush*, Noah and his sister survey the damage to the riverboat.

Objective: As you read the story, focus on the events that have led up to Noah's current situation. Underline events that are important to understanding the story. Think about which events came before others in the story.

from

Flush

by Carl Hiaasen

		My Thoughts

1   The *Coral Queen* had gone down stern first in twelve feet

of water. Her hull had settled on the marly bottom at a slight

angle with the bow aiming upward.

She was a big one, too. Even at high tide, the top two

5   decks were above the water line. It was like a big ugly

apartment building had fallen out of the sky and landed in

the basin.

Abbey hopped off my handlebars and walked to the

water's edge. She planted her hands on her hips and stared at

10   the crime scene.

"Whoa," she said. "He really did it this time."

"It's bad," I agreed.

The *Coral Queen* was one of those gambling boats where

passengers line up to play blackjack and electronic poker,

15   and to stuff their faces at the all-you-can-eat buffet. It didn't

sound like a ton of fun to me, but the *Coral Queen* was packed

to the rafters every night. . . . My dad had waited until three

in the morning, when the last of the crew was gone, to sneak

aboard. He'd untied the ropes and started one of the engines

20 and idled out to the mouth of the basin, where he'd opened

the seacocks and cut the hoses and disconnected the bilge

pumps and then dived overboard.

The *Coral Queen* had gone down crosswise in the channel,

which meant that no other vessels could get in or out of the

25 basin. In other words, Dusty Muleman wasn't the only captain

in town who wanted to strangle my dad on Father's Day.

I locked my bike to a buttonwood tree and walked down

to the charter docks, Abbey trailing behind. Two small skiffs

and a Coast Guard inflatable were nosing around the *Coral*

30 *Queen*. We could hear the men in the skiffs talking about what

had to be done to float the boat. It was a major project.

"He's lost his marbles," Abbey muttered.

"Who—Dad? No way," I said.

"Then why did he do it?"

35 "Because Dusty Muleman has been dumping his holding

tank into the water," I said.

Abbey grimaced. "Yuck. From the toilets?"

"Yep. In the middle of the night, when there's nobody

around."

40   "That is so gross."

"And totally illegal," I said. "He only does it to save money."

According to my father, Dusty Muleman was such a pathetic cheapskate that he wouldn't pay to have

45   the *Coral Queen's* sewage hauled away. Instead his crew had standing orders to flush the waste into the basin, which was already murky. The tide later carried most of the filth out to open water.

"But why didn't Dad just call the Coast Guard?" my

50   sister asked. "Wouldn't that have been the grown-up thing to do?"

"He told me he tried. He said he called everybody he could think of, but they could never catch Dusty in the act," I said. "Dad thinks somebody's tipping him

55   off."

"Oh, please," Abbey groaned.

Now she was starting to annoy me.

"When wind and the current are right, the poop from the gambling boat floats out of the basin and

60   down the shoreline," I said, "straight to Thunder Beach."

Abbey made a pukey face. "Ugh. So that's why they close the park sometimes."

"You know how many kids go swimming there? What

65 Dusty's doing can make you real sick at both ends. Hospital-

sick, Dad says. So it's not only disgusting, it's dangerous."

"Yeah, but—"

"I didn't say it was right, Abbey, what Dad did. I'm only

telling you why."

70 My father hadn't even tried to get away. After swimming

back to the dock, he'd sat down in a folding chair, opened a

can of root beer, and watched the *Coral Queen* go down. He

was still there at dawn, sleeping, when the police arrived.

"So, what now?" Abbey asked.

75 A dark bluish slick surrounded the boat, and the men in

the Coast Guard inflatable were laying out yellow floating

bumpers, to keep the oil and grease from spreading. By sinking

the *Coral Queen*, my father himself had managed to make

quite a mess.

80 I said, "Dad asked me to help him."

Abbey made a face. "Help him what—break out of jail?"

"Get serious."

"Then what, Noah? Tell me."

I knew she wasn't going to like it. "He wants me to help

85 him nail Dusty Muleman," I said.

A long silence followed, so I figured Abbey was thinking up

something snarky to say. But it turned out that she wasn't.

"I didn't give Dad an answer yet," I said.

"I already know your answer," said my sister.

90   "His heart's in the right place, Abbey. It really is."

"It's not his heart I'm worried about, it's his brain," she

said. "You'd better be careful, Noah."

"Are you going to tell Mom?"

"I haven't decided." She gave me a sideways look that told

95   me she probably wouldn't.

Like I said, my sister's all right.

My Thoughts

_____

_____

_____

_____

_____

_____

_____

_____

FIRST RESPONSE: KEY IDEAS AND DETAILS

Based on your first reading of this text, what key event is being explained? Describe an image that would illustrate your answer to this question. Write your answer in your response journal.

TECH-CONNECT

As instructed by your teacher, post your response and a GIF that illustrates the event on your class website, or tweet your response and GIF to your teacher. Read two other students' responses and comment positively on them.

Focus on Summarizing Events

Stories are made up of a series of events. Often these events are described in chronological, or time, order, but sometimes the author chooses to describe events that happened before the current action in the story. The author will drop the reader into an exciting part of a story and then flash back to explain earlier events.

In order to summarize a story, it's important to be able to understand the order of events and which events caused others to happen. Fill in the graphic organizer on the next page with the events from the excerpt. Use the phrases in each box to guide your answers. The first and last events are already completed for you.

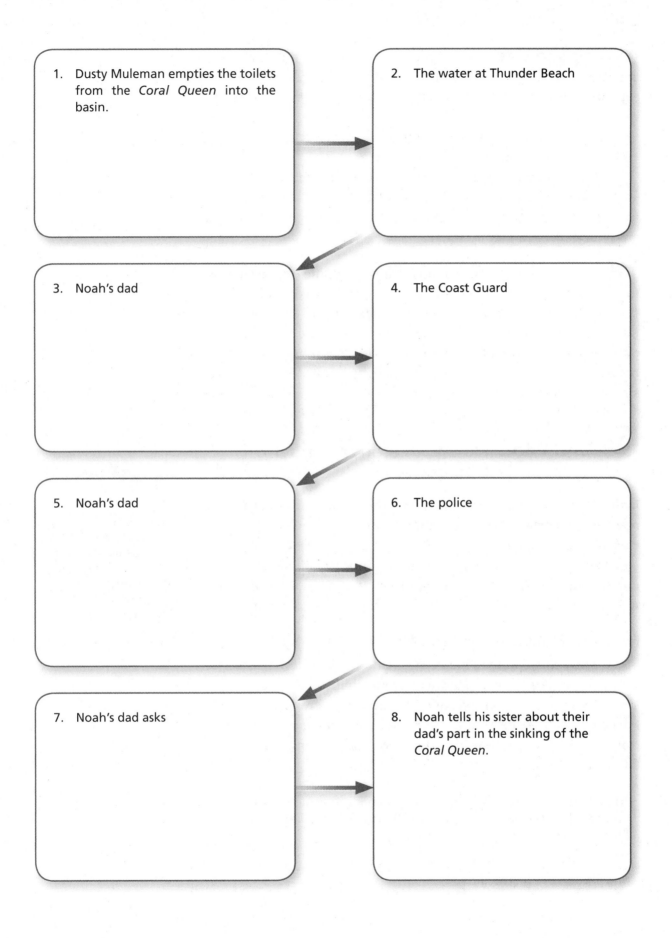

1. Dusty Muleman empties the toilets from the *Coral Queen* into the basin.

2. The water at Thunder Beach

3. Noah's dad

4. The Coast Guard

5. Noah's dad

6. The police

7. Noah's dad asks

8. Noah tells his sister about their dad's part in the sinking of the *Coral Queen*.

⸮Speak and Listen Share your answers to the graphic organizer with a partner. If you disagree with a classmate's answer, explain your opinion politely. Note any differences in answers in the organizer.

Then discuss this question: Why are the events in the story not explained in linear or chronological order?

A good summary focuses on the most important events in a story and does not include minor details. Which of the events from your graphic organizer are important enough to include in a summary? Place a star by them.

⸮Write Use your starred events from the graphic organizer to write a summary of the excerpt. Do not merely copy the sentences from the organizer. Rewrite them in your own words. Use transitional words and phrases to indicate how the events progressed. Here are a few possibilities: *first, next, then, as a result, after, finally.* Underline all of the transition words in your summary.

Second Read: Making Inferences About Characters

REFLECT

Many of Carl Hiaasen's novels are set in his home state of Florida. Why is the setting important to this story?

Listen as two of your classmates read the excerpt, taking turns reading the parts of Noah and Abbey. This time focus on these two characters.

Objective: Consider how Noah and Abbey feel about their father's actions. Underline phrases that help you infer Noah's and Abbey's opinions, and label them N for Noah and A for Abbey.

Focus on Making Inferences About Characters

As you read, you make inferences about characters in stories. An inference is a conclusion drawn from what the story directly states and your own background knowledge. Inferences should be based on what is stated in the text, called *textual evidence.* Textual evidence is based on details in the story. For example, read the following passage.

"He told me he tried. He said he called everybody he could think of, but they could never catch Dusty in the act," I said. "Dad thinks somebody's tipping him off."

"Oh, please," Abbey groaned.

Now she was starting to annoy me.

Notice what the text says—Noah is feeling annoyed at Abbey's reaction to his explanation. What can we infer about his character? Think about your own experience when you interact with siblings.

1. Noah is probably Abbey's older brother since he is doing most of the explaining and she is doing the questioning.

2. Abbey's groaning reaction is because she thinks her dad's idea that someone is tipping off the owner of the *Coral Queen* is far-fetched. Noah doesn't agree.

3. Noah is probably sympathetic to his father.

What other examples of Noah's and Abbey's words and actions help you draw inferences about their opinions of their father's behavior? Return to the excerpt to find examples, and fill in the chart below. A few have been completed for you.

What Abbey Says/Does (include line numbers)	What I Infer About Her Opinion of Her Father's Actions
Abbey hopped off my handlebars and walked to the water's edge. She planted her hands on her hips and stared at the crime scene. *"Whoa," she said. "He really did it this time."* (lines 8–11)	She is amazed at her father's extreme actions, but this isn't the first time he's been in trouble for going too far.
"He's lost his marbles," Abbey muttered. (line 32)	

continued on next page

What Abbey Says/Does (include line numbers)	What I Infer About Her Opinion of Her Father's Actions
"It's bad," I agreed. (line12)	Noah knows the situation is serious.

Write Write a short paragraph that answers the question: What are Noah's and Abbey's opinions about their father's sinking of the *Coral Queen?*

One strategy for writing paragraphs using textual evidence is called ACES, which stands for

Answer the question.
Cite examples.
Explain/elaborate on your example.
Summarize your ideas.

REFLECT

How does your background knowledge of siblings and family relationships help you understand the character of Noah?

©Perfection Learning® • No Reproduction Permitted

Here is how ACES can be used to write a paragraph on Noah's and Abbey's opinions of their father's actions. Use the suggestions to write your own paragraph.

Sentence 1: Explain how Noah's and Abbey's opinions are similar or different.

Sentence 2: Cite an example of Noah's opinion with a quotation from the chart.

Sentence 3: Explain or elaborate on the example in sentence 2.

Sentence 4: Cite an example of Abbey's opinion with a quotation from the chart.

Sentence 5: Explain or elaborate on the example in sentence 4.

Sentence 6: Restate the idea from sentence 1 using different words.

Third Read: Understanding Point of View

Objective: Read through the story again. Focus on the conflicts in the story. Circle examples of characters with conflicting opinions about the environment and how to protect the environment.

Focus on Understanding Point of View

When studying literature, the term *point of view* indicates who is telling the story. In this excerpt, Noah, who is one of the characters, is telling the story. This is *first-person limited point of view*.

As a reader, you learn information from Noah's thoughts and experiences. You learn about Dusty Muleman, the *Coral Queen*, and Noah's father through Noah. If Noah's dad or Noah's sister were telling the story, his or her descriptions of the events might be different.

Authors choose a story's point of view to accomplish their purpose and communicate the theme. Readers tend to sympathize with the character who is telling the story. The author could have written the story from *third-person omniscient point of view*, which means a narrator tells the story and reveals the thoughts and feelings of multiple characters.

Be aware that the term *point of view* has multiple meanings in the context of reading. Sometimes we use *point of view* in a more general way to mean a person's opinion, or perspective on a topic. A parent and a child have different points of view, or opinions, about what the family should eat for dinner. A parent wants healthy meat and vegetables; a child wants tasty fast food.

Think about how the story develops the point of view of Noah.
Answer the following questions.

1. What is Noah's point of view about protecting water supplies
   from pollution?

What evidence from the text supports your inference about
Noah's point of view?

REFLECT

How would this
excerpt be
different if Noah's
sister were telling
the story?

2. What is Noah's point of view about doing something illegal to
   protect humans and animals from harm?

©Perfection Learning® • No Reproduction Permitted

What evidence from the text supports your inference about Noah's point of view?

3. What is Noah's point of view of parents asking children to take risks that might put them in harm's way?

What evidence from the text supports your inference about Noah's point of view?

4. How would the reader experience the story differently if the book were written from omniscient point of view?

©Perfection Learning® • No Reproduction Permitted

Speak and Listen With a group of three, role-play a discussion between Noah, Abbey, and their father. Imagine Noah's father has been released from jail and the three are having a conversation about the sinking of the *Coral Queen* and whether Noah is going to help bring Dusty Muleman to justice. Prepare for the role play by writing down what you infer about your character's point of view of the events in the excerpt.

Language: Idioms

An idiom is a group of words that has a meaning other than what its individual words mean. You can't discover the meaning of an idiom from looking up the individual words in a dictionary. Sometimes you can figure out the meaning from the context. Consider this line from the excerpt:

> "He's lost his marbles," Abbey muttered.

Lost his marbles does not mean that their father had some marbles and now doesn't know where they are. It means he's *not acting normally* or *not in his right mind.*

See the chart below for some examples of common idioms.

REFLECT

Is committing a crime to stop or reveal another crime justified? Why or why not?

Idiom	Meaning
a piece of cake	very easy
a rip off	too expensive
bite off more than you can chew	taken on a task that is too big to complete
feel like a million bucks	feel great
hit the hay	go to sleep
kill two birds with one stone	accomplish two things at once
sit tight	wait patiently until further notice

Idioms are used in everyday, casual speech. How does the use of idioms in *Flush* make the dialogue more realistic?

©Perfection Learning® • No Reproduction Permitted

Fill in the chart with two more idioms from the excerpt. Then add two idioms from your own research.

Idiom	Meaning

©Perfection Learning® • No Reproduction Permitted

Project-Based Assessments

Biopoem

A biopoem is poem that describes a character or a person. It uses carefully chosen words and short phrases to describe important characteristics about a person. Here is an example of a biopoem about Superman's alter ego, Clark Kent.

> Clark
>
> Nerdy, intelligent, awkward
>
> Son of Smallville farmers Jonathan and Martha Kent
>
> Who believes that good will triumph over evil
>
> Who feels lonely because he has to keep his real identity hidden
>
> Who fears that he will never be able to tell Lois Lane that he loves her
>
> Who wants to declare his true identity to the world
>
> Kent

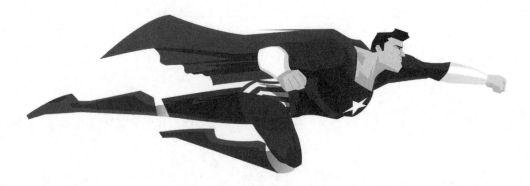

Write a biopoem about the character of Noah. Use the following guidelines.

How to Write a Biopoem
Line 1: First name
Line 2: Three or four adjectives that describe the person
Line 3: Important relationship (son of . . . , daughter of . . .)
Line 4: Who believes in (Describe something the person believes in.)
Line 5: Who feels (Describe feelings the person experiences.)
Line 6: Who fears (Describe fears the person experiences.)
Line 7: Who wants (Describe something the person wants to see happen or wants to experience.)
Line 8: Last name

REFLECT

How would the biopoem be different if it were written about Superman?

Use a word processing or design program to publish your biopoem. Consider drawing a picture of Noah based on your imagination, or include a picture that represents the ideas in your poem.

Use the following guidelines for your biopoem.	
To receive the highest score (4.0), the poem must meet all of these criteria.	Your biopoem • contains the content explained in the directions. • demonstrates an understanding of the character of Noah. • uses specific phrases and interesting language to describe the character. • is free from spelling errors.

Change the Point of View

The story is told from Noah's point of view through his conversation with Abbey. He explains his father's actions in his own words. Think about how their father might explain what he has done and why he did it. Write a few paragraphs with his father as the speaker instead of Noah. Have him explain his thoughts and actions. Use the following rubric to guide your writing.

Use the following guidelines for your new point of view.	
To receive the highest score (4.0), the story must meet all of these criteria.	Your paragraphs • are true to the plot, characters, and theme of the passage of the story. • are clearly organized and easy to follow. • use a variety of sentence types and lengths and have engaging and interesting writing. • contain specific words, creating details that draw the reader into the story. • is free from grammar, spelling, and punctuation errors.

On Your Own: Integrating Ideas

1. Read the rest of *Flush* to learn about what happens to Noah and his family. First, make a prediction of how the novel will end. See if your prediction is correct.

2. Read Carl Hiaasen's novel *Hoot*, and then watch the movie based on it. Compare how the book and movie portray characters and how different details are emphasized.

3. Read other works by Carl Hiaasen, such as *Scat*, or other novels with environmental themes. Possibilities include *Flight or Fight* by Diane Haynes, *The Missing 'Gator of Gumbo Limbo* by Jean Craighead George, or *The True Blue Scouts of Sugar Man Swamp* by Kathi Appelt.

4. How dangerous to the environment is illegal dumping? Read or listen to online discussions about illegal dumping and toxic waste. Search the Internet for information, beginning with the United States Environmental Protection Agency at www.epa.gov.

5. Find a local recycling facility and take a tour. How do the recycling products become separated correctly, and what are they then used for? What happens to garbage that is not recycled?

©Perfection Learning® • No Reproduction Permitted

Connect to Testing

In this chapter you practiced analyzing characters and making inferences. When you take assessments, you will be tested on these skills. Often you will be asked to identify details in paragraphs or passages that support your answers to previous questions. Below is an example. Answer the following questions on your own before reading the explanation.

1. **Part A:** Which inference is best supported by the text?

   A. Noah knows that he and his father cannot catch Dusty.

   B. Noah is angry that Abbey questions their father's actions.

   C. Noah wants to change his father's mind about catching Dusty.

   D. Noah has a close relationship with his father.

   Part B: Cite at least two details from the text to support your inference.

2. **Part A:** How would you describe Noah and Abbey's relationship?

   A. strained

   B. distant

   C. trusting

   D. sensitive

   Part B: Cite at least two details from the text to support your answer.

3. Read the following passage from the selection. Describe Abbey's reaction. Then explain why she reacts as she does.

> I knew she wasn't going to like it. "He wants me to help him nail Dusty Muleman," I said.
>
> A long silence followed, so I figured Abbey was thinking up something snarky to say. But it turned out that she wasn't.
>
> "I didn't give Dad an answer yet," I said.
>
> "I already know your answer," said my sister.
>
> "His heart's in the right place, Abbey. It really is."
>
> "It's not his heart I'm worried about, it's his brain," she said. "You'd better be careful, Noah."

4. **Part A:** The author does not directly state that Noah's father cares about protecting the environment and the people in it, but the reader can infer it. Quote two sentences from the passage that together support this inference.

©Perfection Learning® • No Reproduction Permitted

Part B: Explain your reasoning for your answer in Part A. Why did you choose that textual evidence to support your inference?

5. Which choice below best describes Abbey's reaction to learning that their father asked Noah to help catch Dusty?

A. worry

B. terror

C. anger

D. indifference

6. **Part A:** Which of the following best describes what Noah feels about why his father sank the *Coral Queen*?

A. dismay

B. suspicion

C. understanding

D. comfort

Part B: Read the quotes from the text below. Check all that support your answer to number 6.

"It's bad," I agreed. ☐

"You know how many kids go swimming there? What Dusty's doing can make you real sick at both ends. Hospital-sick, Dad says. So it's not only disgusting, it's dangerous." ☐

"I didn't say it was right, Abbey, what Dad did. I'm only telling you why." ☐

"I didn't give Dad an answer yet," I said. ☐

"His heart's in the right place, Abbey. It really is." ☐

Chapter 17

Analyzing How Central Ideas Are Developed

Preview Concepts

Think about disasters that have been in the news. Fill in the chart with at least three disasters.

Disaster	Who was affected by it?	Caused by nature, humans, or both?

Share your answers with a partner. In the space below, summarize your conclusions from your discussion.

CHAPTER GOALS

In this chapter you will

- use context clues and word parts to determine the meaning of unfamiliar words.
- determine central ideas of a passage.
- analyze how sections of a text introduce and develop central ideas.
- analyze text structures used in a passage.

PREVIEW ACADEMIC VOCABULARY

advantage/disadvantage

cause/effect

central idea

chronology

classification

comparison

context clues

contrast

definition

prefix

problem/solution

root

suffix

text structure (organizational patterns)

©Perfection Learning® • No Reproduction Permitted

Making Connections

Texts can be organized in different ways including chronologically (time order), cause/effect, definition, and comparison/contrast. As you read this short excerpt, think about how the information is organized.

The course of history would forever change for Centralia, [Pennsylvania,] on May 27, 1962. According to David DeKok in his book *Fire Underground*, on this day the local firefighters set the town landfill on fire in order to clean it up. This was in preparation for the upcoming Memorial Day holiday.

The landfill sat atop an old strip mining pit. When it was not fully extinguished, the fire was able to continue burning and entered the abandoned mines around the pit. As time went on, the fire grew and spread. Efforts to control it failed. Slowly, the fire moved under the town and directly affected the residents.

By the early 1980s after two decades of uncontrolled burning, the fire presented real health and safety hazards to the people of Centralia. Carbon monoxide gas seeped into homes and sinkholes opened up as the land subsided.

In 1984, a voluntary program was begun to move residents from their homes. Many accepted buyout offers for their properties and moved elsewhere. After leaving, their homes were leveled. In 1992, the Commonwealth of Pennsylvania used eminent domain to take control of all the property within the town. The remaining buildings were condemned and the residents asked to leave. Many did, but a few remained and sued for their right to stay.

> —from "About Centralia PA and the Mine Fire,"
> www.centraliapa.org

MAKING CONNECTIONS

In this chapter you will analyze how sections of a text develop central ideas.

How is the information in this text organized? Underline words and phrases that helped you determine how the text is organized.

First Read: Determining Word Meanings

The following article describes the aftermath of the 2010 *Deepwater Horizon* oil spill.

Objective: As you read, circle unfamiliar or confusing words and phrases. Write questions you have about the oil spill and its effects in the My Thoughts column as you read.

from

Saving Our Sea Turtles

After the oil spill in the Gulf of Mexico,
their fate is in our hands.

by Elizabeth Preston

	My Thoughts

1   "Already, this oil spill is the worst environmental disaster America has ever faced," President Obama said on June 15, 2010. It would still be another month before oil stopped gushing from a ruptured seafloor well into the Gulf of

5   Mexico.

As oil spread across the ocean's surface, residents of nearby states braced for it to reach their shores. Hotel owners and fishermen feared they would lose all their business for the season. Then there were the Gulf's other

10   inhabitants: the birds, fish, dolphins, and other animals living in the water or on the shores. Oil could coat the creatures and their habitats, poison them, choke them, and drown them. And the Gulf's sea turtles, whose populations were already fragile and in danger, desperately needed our help.

    ©Perfection Learning® • No Reproduction Permitted

15 **The Damage**

Deepwater Horizon was an oil rig floating platform as long

as a football field that drilled oil wells in the ocean floor. It was

stationed off the coast of Louisiana on April 20, 2010, when

an explosion onboard started a massive blaze that firefighters

20 could not put out. Thirty-six hours later, the rig sank. Eleven

people had been killed in the explosion, but the disaster was

far from over.

When *Deepwater Horizon* sank, oil began gushing out

of the pipe that had connected the platform to the oil well

25 below. Government scientists would later estimate that more

than 60,000 barrels of oil (that's more than 2.5 million gallons,

or 9.5 million liters) were pouring out of the well every day.

The leak urgently needed to be plugged.

It's not easy, though, to stop a leak or to do much of

30 anything at 5,000 feet (1,500 meters) underwater. . . . Finally,

on July 15, BP announced that it had put a cap on the well and

stopped the leak for good.

But the well had leaked for 86 days, and the damage had

been done. With about 4.9 million barrels of oil pumped into

35 the ocean, this was the biggest accidental spill in history. The

oil formed a slick across thousands of square miles in the Gulf

of Mexico. Cleanup crews went to work: they used dispersant

chemicals to break up the oil, controlled fires to burn up

patches of it, floating barriers called booms to contain it, and

40   skimming devices to scoop it off the surface of the water.

Nevertheless, oil began to wash up on the beaches of

Louisiana, Mississippi, Florida, and Alabama. Fishing was

banned in a large portion of the Gulf. Contaminated fish

would be unsafe to eat and not just for humans. Small fish that

45   ingested oil and were then eaten by other animals could send

toxic chemicals all the way up the food chain. Birds could be

covered in oil and drown, or ingest or inhale oil as they tried

to clean their feathers. Sure enough, people began to discover

birds, dolphins, and turtles that were oiled or dead.

50   The U.S. Fish and Wildlife Service was most worried about

species that were already threatened or endangered. It listed

38 of them, from cranes to manatees to sturgeons. Some of the

most worrying animals on the list were the sea turtles.

All five species of sea turtle that live in the Gulf of

55   Mexico are threatened or endangered. Humans hunting

them for meat, gathering their eggs, killing them for their

shells, or accidentally catching them in fishing nets have

made sea turtles rare. After the spill, a new threat faced these

turtles, not just the ones swimming in oiled waters, but a

60   whole generation that hadn't even hatched yet.

In the Red Zone

Headquarters for sea turtle rescue was the Audubon
Aquatic Center in New Orleans, Louisiana. There, a dedicated
team cleaned off oiled turtles and nursed them back to health.

65   Mayela Alsina, a veterinary technician at Shedd Aquarium
in Chicago, traveled to New Orleans for two weeks to help
take care of the turtles. There were about 120 turtles at the
Audubon Aquatic Center when she arrived in July. Many of
them had been rescued by workers patrolling the ocean in
70   boats. When they spotted a turtle that was oiled or otherwise
in trouble, they scooped it up with a net, wiped it off as well as
they could, and sent it along to New Orleans.

The center was divided into areas called the red, yellow,
and green zones. Newly arriving turtles went to the red zone.
75   Here, veterinarians gave each turtle a quick checkup. A blood
sample told doctors right away whether a turtle needed any
fluids or supplements.

In their first night at the Audubon center, each turtle got
two baths. Turtle washers used Dawn soap and toothbrushes

My Thoughts

80 to scrub oil out of the folds of the turtle's skin, and cotton

swabs to remove oil from their throats. A wipe-down using

mayonnaise (believe it or not) helped to strip off the sticky oil.

Finally, the turtles were moved to the yellow zone.

The next day, after a checkup, veterinarians decided

85 whether each turtle was oil-free and ready to move

to the green zone. The zones weren't just for keeping

the turtles organized; they also told workers how much

protective equipment they needed to wear to keep themselves

safe from the toxic oil.

90 No matter which species they belonged to, most

of the oiled turtles were young. Barbara Schroeder,

national sea turtle coordinator for the National Oceanic

and Atmospheric Administration, says that's because

older turtles stay closer to shore, while young turtles live and

95 feed farther out in the ocean exactly where the oil leak took

place.

Thanks to the hard work of their caretakers, 99 percent of

the oiled turtles in rehabilitation facilities survived, Schroeder

says. On August 18, the first 23 turtles with a clean bill of

100 health were released back into the Gulf of Mexico. To keep

them safe, "They are being released in areas that are free

of oil, were never oiled, and are at some distance from

the oil spill site," Schroeder says. As of early September,

My Thoughts

109 rehabilitated turtles had been sent back into the ocean.

105 Eventually, as they recover, all the turtles will be released.

Alsina says that working with the turtles brought mixed feelings. "On a daily basis, I would think to myself, this is so cool, these animals are going to be around for years and years and years, and outlive me, and I've never been so close to so

110 many turtles at a time!" she says. "But then it would hit you . . . I would not be here if it wasn't for the situation we're in."

My Thoughts

_____

_____

_____

_____

_____

_____

_____

FIRST RESPONSE: KEY IDEAS AND DETAILS

What is the purpose of the passage? Who might be the intended audience? How might they use this information? Write your answers to these questions in your response journal.

TECH-CONNECT

As instructed by your teacher, post your First Response answers on your class web page. Compare your answer to those posted by other students.

Focus on Determining Word Meanings

This passage has words used by scientists who work with wildlife or by people who respond to environmental disasters. These words may be unfamiliar to you. You probably will not have enough time to look up all of the unfamiliar words, so focus on understanding terms that are repeated and are essential to understanding the central idea of the passage. Do your best to figure out the terms that will help you understand the key ideas.

Use the words around the unfamiliar word to determine its meaning. These context clues, or hints about a word's meaning, can be found in the same sentence as the unfamiliar word or a nearby sentence. There are four main types of context clues.

Definition: The unfamiliar word is defined in the sentence (or in a nearby sentence).

> The house wren, *a small, plain brown songbird,* was named for its habit of nesting around homes or in birdhouses.

Synonym: Another word or phrase has a similar meaning to the unfamiliar word.

> The knight's <u>oath</u> to his king was a *vow* he would not forsake.

Antonym: Another word or phrase has an opposite or contrasting meaning to the unfamiliar word.

> The storeowner's <u>outrage</u> was a marked contrast to the police officer's air of *calm*.

Inference: The word's meaning is not directly stated but can be figured out by the context.

> The *pirate* dumped his <u>plunder</u> of *gold and jewels* onto the table.

Add the unfamiliar words you circled during the First Read to empty spaces in the graphic organizer below. Then complete the rows by adding context clues, your inference of the definition, and finally a definition from a dictionary.

Word	Context Clues	What I Think It Means	Dictionary Definition
ruptured (line 4)	*gushing from*		broken
rig (line 16)	*onboard, stationed off the coast*		piece of equipment designed for a specific purpose
booms (line 39)	*floating barriers*		
contaminated (line 43)	*unsafe to eat*		

©Perfection Learning® • No Reproduction Permitted

Word	Context Clues	What I Think It Means	Dictionary Definition
toxic (line 46)			

©Perfection Learning® • No Reproduction Permitted

Another strategy for determining word meanings is to use common affixes and roots that come from Greek and Latin. Many English words are formed by taking a base word and adding a prefix (word part at the beginning) or a suffix (word part at the end). For example, a common prefix is *mis-*, which means *wrongly* or *badly*. Examples include *misspell*, *mistake*, *mismatch*, and *misinformed*.

Study this chart with common prefixes, roots, and suffixes.

Prefix	Definition	Examples
dis-	not; opposite of	disagree, discomfort, disagreeable
sub-	under	submarine, substandard
pre-	before	preexisting, preview
in-, im-	in	income, impulse

Root	Definition	Examples
micro	small	microbe, microscopic
bio	life	biography, biosphere
hab	live or reside	rehabilitate, habit
techno	skill	technology
mis/mit	send	submit
bene	good	beneficial
man	hand	manual
scrib/script	write	scribble
jur/jus	law	jury, justice

Suffix	Definition	Examples
-ion, -tion, -ation	act; process	determination, isolation, education
-ful	full of	helpful, meaningful
-able, -ible	is; can be	affordable, sensible
-ian	person	

▼**Write** In your response journal, explain the definitions of the following words from "Saving Our Sea Turtles": *inhabitants* (line 10), *habitats* (line 12), *ingest* (line 47), *inhale* (line 47), *technician* (line 65), and *rehabilitation* (line 98)—without looking them up in a dictionary. Explain how you used context and word parts to determine their definitions.

   ©Perfection Learning® • No Reproduction Permitted

(Speak and Listen Share your explanations of the words with a partner. Use an online or print dictionary to confirm your definitions. Discuss how the strategies you learned in this chapter could help you determine the meanings of words found in texts related to specific academic subjects such as science or math. Share any other helpful strategies you use to figure out unfamiliar words.

Second Read: Analyzing the Development of the Central Idea

Listen as your teacher or another student reads the text aloud.

    Objective: As you follow along, think about the purpose of the article. After you have heard the article again, write a purpose statement below. Finish the sentence frame as shown.

This text is mainly about

TECH-CONNECT

Search online for a few of the words you defined for this lesson. Click on three links for websites, and notice how the word is used in context. Add this new information to your knowledge of how to use the term.

Focus on Analyzing the Development of the Central Idea

    When you were younger, the goal of reading was to understand what a text said by understanding the key ideas. As you mature as a reader, you will move on from understanding *what* a text says to analyzing *how* a text communicates ideas and ultimately evaluating *how well* it communicates.

    Analyzing a text requires you to take it apart—paragraph by paragraph or even sentence by sentence—to determine how all parts work together to communicate the central idea of the text. The diagram on the next page will help you break down the first paragraphs of the text into individual key ideas. For each area in the triangle, write a short description of the key idea of the sentences. Sentence 1 has been completed for you.

REFLECT

How does understanding difficult words in the excerpt help you determine the main idea?

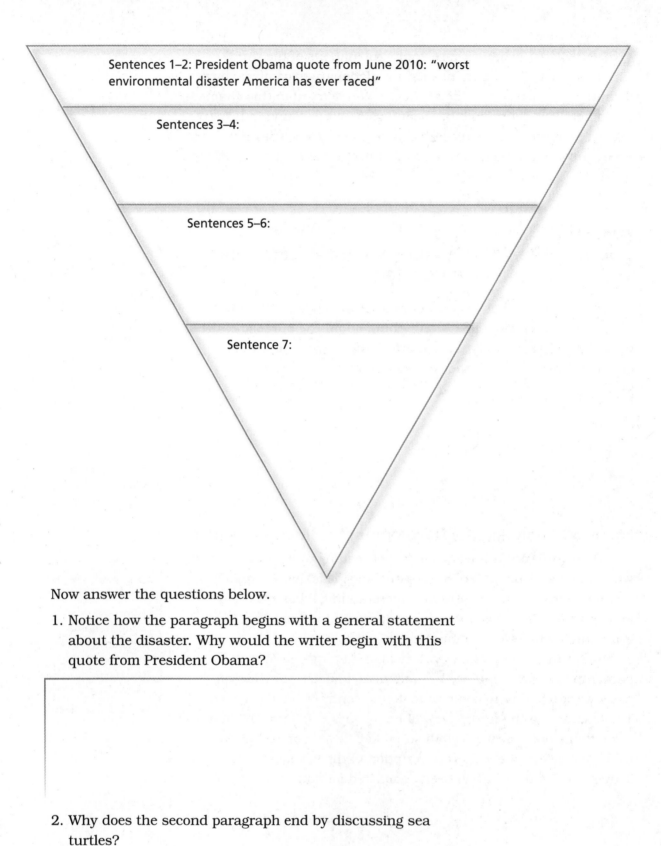

Sentences 1–2: President Obama quote from June 2010: "worst environmental disaster America has ever faced"

Sentences 3–4:

Sentences 5–6:

Sentence 7:

Now answer the questions below.

1. Notice how the paragraph begins with a general statement about the disaster. Why would the writer begin with this quote from President Obama?

2. Why does the second paragraph end by discussing sea turtles?

©Perfection Learning® • No Reproduction Permitted

3. How do the first paragraphs establish the central idea of the entire article?

Third Read: Analyzing the Structure of a Text

Read the text a final time.

Objective: Think about how the title and headers help you follow the key ideas in the text. For each of the two sections in the body of the text, write a sentence that explains what the section is mainly about.

Focus on Analyzing the Structure of a Text

Continue your analysis of the text by looking at the two main sections that follow the first paragraph.

Writers use different organizational patterns to structure ideas in a text. Here are a few examples:

- chronology—explaining events in the order that they happened

- comparison—showing how things or ideas are alike

- contrast—showing how things or ideas are different

- problem/solution—describing a problem and then the solution to the problem

- cause/effect—explaining the causes for an event and the effects that followed

- definition—explaining concepts and ideas

- classification—putting ideas into categories

- advantage/disadvantage—explaining the positives and negatives of a plan or idea

continued on next page

Use this chart to help you analyze the ideas and structures used in the passage. Finish the following sentence starters in the graphic organizer below.

The Damage
This section is mainly about
This section relates back to the sentence on lines _____ in the first paragraph that
Two sentences that provide strong evidence for my analysis of this section are
Organizational patterns used in this section are

In the Red Zone
This section is mainly about
This section relates back to the sentence on lines _____ in the first paragraph that explains
Two sentences that provide strong evidence for my analysis of this section are
Organizational patterns used in this section are

©Perfection Learning® • No Reproduction Permitted

(**Speak and Listen** Share your answers to the graphic organizer on the previous page with a partner. Discuss any differences in your answers, returning to the text to support your ideas. Work together to write the strongest answers and evidence.

Write Use your answers to the First and Second Reads to write an analysis of the text. Carefully read the prompt below and underline key words and phrases that tell you what to do and ideas to include.

WRITING PROMPT

Write an analysis of the key ideas from the excerpt. Explain how the body of the article develops the central idea that the *Deepwater Horizon* was one of the worst disasters to affect the sea turtle population in the Gulf of Mexico.

Use the sentence starters below to help you write a well-organized analysis.

- In the article "Saving Our Sea Turtles," author Elizabeth Preston explains . . . .

- The section called "The Damage" describes . . . .

- The author states that . . . . (provide a direct quotation as textual evidence)

- The text structures used include . . . .

- In "In the Red Zone," the author details . . . .

- For example, ...(provide a direct quotation as textual evidence)

- This article is . . . (provide a summary statement)

- The text structures used include . . . .

Language: Colons

The writer uses punctuation to show how ideas fit together. How do the commas and colons in the sentence below indicate how the sentence parts are related?

Then there were the Gulf's other inhabitants: the birds, fish, dolphins, and other animals living in the water or on the shores.

---

continued on next page

Study the following punctuation rules for colons and commas.

Commas in a Series
Use a comma (,) to separate words and groups of words in a series of three or more items.
Examples:
Earth is made up of three layers: the crust, mantle, and core.
Earth's crust is made up of igneous, metamorphic, and sedimentary rocks.

Colons
Use a colon (:) to introduce a list where the introduction can stand alone as a complete sentence. Colons often come after the phrase "the following."
Examples:
The dinosaurs lived during the Mesozoic Era, which is divided into three periods: the Triassic, Jurassic, and Cretaceous.
A canvas is a painting surface made of fabric and has three types: oil canvas for oil painting, absorbent canvas for tempera, and universal canvas for both oil and tempera.

Write Finish the following sentences with lists of three or more words and phrases. Use commas and colons correctly.

1. In the summer, I enjoy

2. On the camping trip, please remember to bring the following items

3. Three of my favorite weekend activities are

4. There are several foods I can't stand

5. Adjectives that could be used to describe my brother include all of the following

Project-Based Assessments

Pictorial Presentation

Create a pictorial presentation of the events in "Saving Our Sea Turtles."

- Possible formats include PowerPoint, a video, or a hand-drawn storyboard of each scene.

©Perfection Learning® • No Reproduction Permitted

- Use a minimum of six images presented in order. Write captions under each image to briefly explain the scene.

Ideas to help you in your research for this presentation:

- Read the rubric below carefully so that you know what is expected of you.

- Plan your images before you begin so you can research more effectively.

- Use keywords such as *sea turtles, Deepwater Horizon oil spill,* and *oil spill effects on wildlife.* (These words are only suggestions.) Even if you are creating your own illustrations, looking at images from the web can be helpful in making your drawings realistic.

CONNECT TO ESSENTIAL QUESTION

Should humans stop drilling for oil in places where potential spills could kill wildlife?

- Refine your search by clicking on *Videos* or *Images.*

- Once you find an image you like, save the image or capture a screenshot of it. Paste that image into your presentation and crop it. If you pause a video, you can capture an image as if it were a still shot.

- Consider adding music to support your visuals. Think about songs (with or without words) that communicate the feelings (emotional tone) of your presentation.

Use the following guidelines for your pictorial presentation.	
To receive the highest score (4.0), the project must meet all of these criteria.	Your pictorial presentation • uses appealing images or drawings. • contains interesting images that tell the events in the order they happened. • includes images appropriate for the intended audience. • includes short, interesting captions that are free from errors.

Brochure

Create a trifold brochure about an endangered species using a word processing or design program. Use three or more sources for the project. Include the following information in your brochure.

- name and description of the endangered species

- causes for endangerment and current and future effects

- plan or actions taken to protect the species

- historical population versus current population of the species

continued on next page

- the article's name and author, website, and date for your sources

- a chart, graph, or map that provides visual information

REFLECT

Which type of disasters impact the most animals: those caused by nature or humans?

Design your brochure so that readers will be able to learn about the endangered species and what actions are being taken for its protection. Use pictures to illustrate your writing. Include your list of sources on the back of the brochure. Make sure your information makes sense in the order that readers will look at the brochure. Include headers to call attention to key ideas.

Use the following guidelines for your brochure.	
To receive the highest score (4.0), the project must meet all of these criteria.	Your brochure • looks professional and appealing. • demonstrates an understanding of the endangered species, the cause of its endangerment, plans for its protection, and its population numbers. • includes photos and/or illustrations that support the text. • includes a chart, graph, or map. • is organized logically and includes headers. • uses correct grammar, usage, punctuation, and spelling.

On Your Own: Integrating Ideas

1. Learn more about endangered species in your area and the Endangered Species Act. What is the difference between *threatened* and *endangered*? Check out these websites: www.fws.gov and www.nmfs.noaa.gov.

2. Recently, the U.S. Fish and Wildlife Service identified the rusty patched bumblebee as an endangered species. This designation is the first for a bee species in the continental United States. Find out how a species becomes endangered and what actions are taken to protect it.

3. Watch an environmentally themed movie or documentary, such as *Over the Hedge*, *Free Willy*, Disneynature's *Oceans*, or *FernGully: The Last Rainforest*. Write a review of the movie or documentary and post it online.

4. Research other environmental disasters and their impact on humans and nature.

Connect to Testing

In this chapter, you learned to infer the meanings of unfamiliar words using context clues and word parts, to determine central ideas, and to analyze the content and structure of larger sections of a text. When you take reading assessments, you will be tested on these skills. Answer these questions to help you practice the types of questions that will appear on standardized tests.

1. **Part A:** Read this sentence from "Saving Our Sea Turtles." Then answer the questions that follow.

    > And the Gulf's sea turtles, whose populations were already <u>fragile</u> and in danger, desperately needed our help.

    What does the word *fragile* mean as it is used in the sentence?

    A. insecure

    B. undamaged

    C. indifferent

    D. unsteady

    Some tests will include a follow-up question in which you are asked to identify evidence to support the definition of the word.

    Part B: Which words or phrases from the passage best support the answer to Part A? Choose two answers.

    A. *the Gulf's sea turtles*

    B. *whose populations*

    C. *in danger*

    D. *desperately needed our help*

2. **Part A:** Which statement best describes how the section "The Damage" contributes to the development of the central idea of the article?

    A. It explains the methods taken to treat sea turtles affected by the oil spill.

    B. It compares the *Deepwater Horizon* spill to similar environmental disasters.

    C. It lists the five species of sea turtles that were affected by the *Deepwater Horizon* spill.

    D. It gives the chronology of the spill and its effects on wildlife.

continued on next page

Part B: Which **three** sentences from the article best support the answer to Part A?

A. *It would still be another month before oil stopped gushing from a ruptured seafloor well into the Gulf of Mexico.*

B. *It's not easy, though, to stop a leak or to do much of anything at 5,000 feet (1,500 meters) underwater.*

C. *Cleanup crews went to work: they used dispersant chemicals to break up the oil, controlled fires to burn up patches of it, floating barriers called booms to contain it, and skimming devices to scoop it off the surface of the water.*

D. *Sure enough, people began to discover birds, dolphins, and turtles that were oiled or dead.*

E. *Humans hunting them for meat, gathering their eggs, killing them for their shells, or accidentally catching them in fishing nets have made sea turtles rare.*

F. *After the spill, a new threat faced these turtles, not just the ones swimming in oiled waters, but a whole generation that hadn't even hatched yet.*

3. Read the following and then answer the questions that follow.

> All five species of sea turtle that live in the Gulf of Mexico are threatened or endangered. Humans hunting them for meat, gathering their eggs, killing them for their shells, or accidentally catching them in fishing nets have made sea turtles rare. After the spill, a new threat faced these turtles, not just the ones swimming in oiled waters, but a whole generation that hadn't even hatched yet.

Part A: Which of the following best explains the key ideas of the passage above?

A. Fishing has caused many animal species to be endangered.

B. The spill put already endangered turtles at even greater risk.

C. The gulf has more than one species of sea turtle.

D. Too many sea turtles were exposed to the oil.

Part B: Which phrase from the passage best supports the answer to Part A?

A. *five species of sea turtle that live in the Gulf of Mexico*

B. *Humans hunting them for meat*

C. *accidentally catching them in fishing nets*

D. *After the spill, a new threat faced these turtles*

©Perfection Learning® • No Reproduction Permitted

4. **Part A:** Which statement best describes how the section "In the Red Zone" contributes to the development of the central idea of the article?

   A. It explains the area where the most damage occured.

   B. It explains the process taken to save the sea turtles.

   C. It explains how to avoid oil spills in the future.

   D. It explains how the oil spill was prevented from spreading.

   Part B: Which **three** sentences from the article best support the answer to Part A?

   A. *Mayela Alsina, a veterinary technician at Shedd Aquarium in Chicago, traveled to New Orleans for two weeks to help take care of the turtles.*

   B. *When they spotted a turtle that was oiled or otherwise in trouble, they scooped it up with a net, wiped it off as well as they could, and sent it along to New Orleans.*

   C. *In their first night at the Audubon center, each turtle got two baths.*

   D. *A wipe-down using mayonnaise (believe it or not) helped to strip off the sticky oil.*

   E. *The zones weren't just for keeping the turtles organized; they also told workers how much protective equipment they needed to wear to keep themselves safe from the toxic oil.*

   F. *Alsina says that working with the turtles brought mixed feelings. "On a daily basis, I would think to myself, this is so cool, these animals are going to be around for years and years and years, and outlive me, and I've never been so close to so many turtles at a time!" she says.*

©Perfection Learning® • No Reproduction Permitted

Chapter 18

Comparing and Contrasting Texts

Preview Concepts

Have you ever had an experience with an animal that was not a pet? Perhaps you found an injured rabbit in your yard and nursed it back to health, or maybe there is a tame deer that wanders into your yard to eat your flowers. How do you feel about this animal? Describe your encounter and your response below.

CHAPTER GOALS

In this chapter you will

• summarize central ideas.

• analyze word choice.

• compare and contrast texts.

Share your answer with a partner. In the space below, summarize your conclusions from your discussion.

PREVIEW ACADEMIC VOCABULARY

connotation

denotation

genre

imagery

purpose

summary

Making Connections

Read the excerpt on the next page from a poem about Ross Sea, a deep bay of the Southern Ocean in Antarctica, which is covered with ice for most of the year. Underline places where animals or other nonhuman elements of nature act like humans.

But what if I told you I know of a place

where there is no noise, no clutter,

no pollution, no lies, no greed.

A space so precious—a pristine utopia

Imagine the edge of existence

like nowhere else on earth

Then would you lend me your ears?

Let me tell you about this place

A force of nature, the eye of purity

where whales and fish swim free

and penguins and seals clap for joy

This is The Last Ocean

This is The Ross Sea

She breathes

She gives life

But it's not enough

They want more

and more and more.

—"The Last Ocean" by Jamie Joseph

With a partner, share your underlined examples of nonhuman things doing humanlike things. How does this make you feel about these nonhuman things?

MAKING CONNECTIONS

In this chapter you will be analyzing the central ideas and word choice of a poem.

Who is the "They" in the next to last line? What evidence from the poem supports your inference?

First Read: Summarizing Central Ideas

In this poem, the narrator describes her interaction with a turtle affected by the *Deepwater Horizon* oil spill.

Objective: As you read, try to visualize the events the author is describing. Notice any repeated details. Underline details that describe the speaker's feelings toward the turtle, and mark them with an S for speaker. Write two or three questions you have in the My Thoughts column.

Song for the Turtles in the Gulf
by Linda Hogan

	My Thoughts
1 We had been together so very long,	
you willing to swim with me	
just last month, myself merely small	
in the ocean of splendor and light,	
5 the reflections and distortions of us,	
and now when I see the man from **British Petroleum**	
lift you up dead from the plastic	
bin of death,	
he with a smile, you burned	
10 and covered with red-black oil, torched	
and pained, all I can think is that I loved your life,	
the very air you exhaled when you rose,	
old great mother, the beautiful swimmer,	
the mosaic growth of shell	

British Petroleum: worldwide oil and gas company responsible for the *Deepwater Horizon* oil spill in the Gulf of Mexico in 2010

©Perfection Learning® • No Reproduction Permitted

15 so detailed, no part of you

simple, meaningless,

or able to be created

by any human,

only destroyed.

20 How can they learn

the secret importance

of your beaten heart,

the eyes of another intelligence

than ours, maybe greater,

25 with claws, flippers, **plastron**.

Forgive us for being thrown off true,

for our trespasses,

in the eddies of the water

where we first walked.

---

plastron: the under part of a tortoise shell

Which phrase from the poem created a lasting visual image in your mind? Record the phrase and describe or draw the image in your response journal.

Focus on Summarizing Central Ideas

Poetry communicates in very different ways from other types of literature and informational text. Instead of communicating specific details and facts, poetry uses a few carefully chosen words to paint images that create strong emotions.

Understanding who is speaking is often key to understanding the central ideas of the poem. Sometimes the speaker is giving a voice to the poet's thoughts and feelings. Other times the speaker in a poem is an imaginary character.

> **TECH-CONNECT**
>
> As instructed by your teacher, send a question you had about the poem to Poll Everywhere or post it on your class website.

1. To whom is the speaker in the poem speaking?

What words or phrases support your inferences?

2. What has happened in the poem?

©Perfection Learning® • No Reproduction Permitted

What words or phrases support your inferences?

3. How does the poet feel about the events in the poem? (What is her point of view about the events?)

What words or phrases support your inferences?

4. The author, Linda Hogan, is a Native American from the Chickasaw tribe and an environmentalist. Could the speaker be the poet herself?

What words or phrases support your inferences?

Speak and Listen Share your responses to the questions on the previous pages with a partner. Discuss the following questions, recording your answers in your response journals.

1. Who is the "they" in line 20?
2. Who is the "us," "our," and "we" in lines 26–29?
3. What does the author mean by phrase "Forgive us for being thrown off true"?
4. Look up the word *trespasses*. What is the denotation of the word? What is the connotation?
5. What do you think the "eddies of the water where we first walked" might refer to?

Write Based on your answers to the questions on the previous pages and your discussion with a partner, write a summary of the poem. Here are some sentence frames to help you get started. Use specific evidence from the poem in your answers.

- In "Song for the Turtles in the Gulf," the speaker describes . . . .

- The turtle . . . .

- The poem describes . . . .

- Next, the speaker wonders . . . .

- Finally, the speaker . . . .

TECH-CONNECT

Search online for images of sea turtles or other creatures caught in an oil spill. Post an image on your class website or on Pinterest. Then comment on a classmate's posting.

Second Read: Analyzing Word Choice

With a partner, take turns reading the poem aloud to each other. Try to read the poem so that you are communicating the emotions the lines communicate. Think about the following:

- pausing before and/or after important lines in order to emphasize them

- reading faster to communicate excitement or action

- reading slower to communicate sadness or to emphasize important words

- matching the sound of your voice to the meaning of the words. For example, you might say the word *dead* with a short, flat tone to emphasize the word's meaning.

Objective: Underline key words and phrases that describe interesting images. Draw a line where the speaker's voice changes focus from describing the turtle to offering an opinion about the events described.

REFLECT

How does viewing an image of a suffering creature differ from reading about it?

Focus on Analyzing Word Choice

Poets use language that is meant to create vivid images in the minds of the reader. Study the following chart that contains terms related to types of language and the use of words in poetry.

Term	Definition	Example
imagery	using language to create visual pictures of actions, objects, and ideas in such a way that they appeal to the senses	The sunlight sparkled on the water, creating shimmering prisms of light.
denotation	the dictionary definition of a word	The denotation of the word *home* is "the place (house or apartment) where someone lives."
connotation	an implied or associated meaning of a word	The word *home* has connotations of safety and comfort for some people.

Fill in the following chart with details from the poem in the first column and the emotions communicated by those images in the second column.

Imagery	Connotations/Emotions Communicated by Words
The turtle and swimming with the turtle: *in the ocean of splendor and light*	The experience of swimming with the turtle was beautiful.
Man from British Petroleum:	
Dead turtle:	

Third Read: Comparing and Contrasting Texts

Objective: As you read the poem again, think about the theme. Below the poem, write a sentence that explains the theme.

Focus on Comparing and Contrasting Texts

In Chapter 16 you read an informational article about rescuing sea turtles affected by the *Deepwater Horizon* disaster. In this chapter you read a poem about sea turtles affected by an oil spill. These two passages are different *genres*, or types of writing. Fill in the organizer below to analyze how these two works are similar and different. Use textual evidence to support your answers.

CONNECT TO ESSENTIAL QUESTION

Does a poem about an animal's struggle and suffering make you feel more sympathetic?

	"Saving Our Sea Turtles"	"Song for the Turtles in the Gulf"
Genre (type of writing)		
Purpose (What is the goal of the writing? Why did the writer write this?)		
Language (types of words used)		
Central Idea or Theme		

©Perfection Learning® • No Reproduction Permitted

Speak and Listen With a partner, compare and contrast the two texts by finishing the following sentences for each text. Use your answers to the table on the previous page to help you.

- (Title of text) was a _____, written for the purpose(s) of . . . .

- The words and language used by the writer are _____. An example of this is . . . .

- The central idea/theme of the work is . . . .

Then take turns finishing the following sentences.

- The two texts are similar in that they both . . . .

- One way the texts are different is . . . .

- The text I enjoyed more was _____ because . . . .

REFLECT

Why do people found and join animal protection agencies, such as the American Society for the Prevention of Cruelty to Animals (ASPCA), the Humane Society of the United States, or the American Humane Association?

Language: Pronouns

Pronouns are words that can be substituted for nouns. In other words, pronouns take the place of nouns.

Example: <u>Sean</u> saw <u>Nancy</u> yesterday, and **he** told **her** goodbye.

Pronouns can be subject or object pronouns. Subject pronouns are in the subjective case: *I, he, she, it, they.* Use subject pronouns when the pronoun is in the subject position in the sentence.

Examples: **She** and **I** went to the movie yesterday. (Not Her and me went)
We are going to play baseball at the park. (Not Us are going)

Object pronouns are in the objective case: *him, her, it, them, me.* Object pronouns should be used when the pronoun is in the object position (direct object, object of the preposition, indirect object).

Examples: Give the bike to **him**. (Not Give the bike to he.)
I want to eat lunch with **you** and **her**. (Not I want to eat lunch with you and she.)

Pronouns can also be possessive, or show ownership: *his, her, its, my, their, theirs, our.*

Examples: José got a new bike for **his** birthday.
Amadea and Sabina rode **their** bikes to school.

continued on next page

Pronouns need to match the noun, or *antecedent*, they refer to in a sentence or paragraph. What is the antecedent for the pronoun *they* in the following sentence?

> Eventually, as **they** recover, all the turtles will be released.

The antecedent is *turtles*.

Notice the use of pronouns in the first lines from the poem, and think about what nouns they are referring to:

> **We** had been together so very long,
> **you** willing to swim with me

The poem begins with the pronoun *we*, and based upon the title, the reader can infer that *we* refers to the sea turtles and the speaker. As the poem continues, the speaker clarifies this fact. The short-lived confusion comes from a lack of antecedent.

When writing in standard English, make sure pronouns have clear antecedents.

> Examples: When Alexander drove the car through the garage door, he damaged it. (Does it refer to the car or the garage door?)
>
> Luna told her mother that her sweater had a hole in it. (Is the sweater Luna's or her mother's?)

Rewrite the sentences above, correcting unclear antecedents.

CONNECT TO
ESSENTIAL QUESTION

Why do people devote their time and energy to helping sea creatures?

©Perfection Learning® • No Reproduction Permitted

Sometimes poets are intentionally vague when they use pronouns. Reread the following lines:

> How can **they** learn
> the secret importance
> of your beaten heart,
> the eyes of another intelligence
> than ours, maybe greater,
> with claws, flippers, plastron

Earlier in the chapter you discussed who *they* probably refers to. Why would the poet choose not to use a clear antecedent?

REFLECT

What animal group would be the easiest to live without? What animal group is the most important to human survival?

Project-Based Assessments

Compare/Contrast Essay

Write an essay comparing and contrasting "Saving Our Sea Turtles" and "Song for the Turtles in the Gulf." You have already analyzed the purpose, word choice, and theme during the Third Read. Include this information in a well-written comparison/contrast essay. Here is a basic outline.

- Introduction—Give background on the topic and then end with a clearly stated main idea statement (also called a thesis statement).

- Body Paragraph 1—Write about how they are similar.

  Writing frames: Both ____ and ____ . . . .

  > For example, both texts . . . .

  > Another way they are similar is . . . .

- Body Paragraph 2—Write about how they are different.

  Writing frames: However, the texts are different because they. . . .

  > An example of the difference _____ is . . . .

- Conclusion—Summarize your main ideas and restate your main idea.

  Writing frames: In conclusion, the texts are . . . .

Work through the writing process to write a first draft, to edit, and to proofread your paper.

continued on next page

Use the following guidelines for your essay.	
To receive the highest score (4.0), the essay must meet all of these criteria.	Your compare/contrast essay • includes a clear central idea (thesis) statement. • uses correct information about the purposes, language, and themes of the two texts. • includes textual evidence to support key points. • is clearly organized with a well-developed introduction, body, and conclusion. • uses correct grammar, usage, punctuation, and spelling.

Digital Presentation

The *Deepwater Horizon* spill affected not only sea turtles but also many other wildlife. Find out information about another animal group affected by the oil spill, and create a presentation to share with the class. In your presentation include

- a description of the bird, fish, or other animal.

- how this species was affected by the oil spill.

- what rescue efforts were undertaken to help them.

- visual images, including photos, maps, timelines, and/or graphs.

- background music that is appropriate for the subject. Create a well-organized presentation using Prezi, PowerPoint, or another presentation program. Read the guidelines below to know what to include:

Use the following guidelines for your digital presentation.	
To receive the highest score (4.0), the project must meet all of these criteria.	Your digital presentation • focuses on an animal affected by the oil spill. • is well organized so that the audience can easily follow the main ideas. • uses multimedia in a professional way and is visually appealing. • demonstrates that you clearly understand the topic. • uses correct grammar, usage, punctuation, and spelling.

©Perfection Learning® • No Reproduction Permitted

On Your Own: Integrating Ideas

1. Sea turtles have been around since the time of the dinosaurs. Discover how they survived for so long and why they are endangered now. Choose websites from reliable sources.

2. Watch *Turtle: The Incredible Journey* (G), a documentary released in 2009. What challenges does the loggerhead sea turtle face that are naturally occurring versus caused by human actions?

3. What is the difference between *turtles*, *tortoises*, and *terrapins*? Find out at livescience.com.

4. Listen to a version of "Big Yellow Taxi." It was written by Joni Mitchell and has been also recorded by Amy Grant, Bob Dylan, and Counting Crows. What point does the song make about preserving the environment? What other songs cover the topic of environmentalism?

5. In an interview, Linda Hogan explains, "I see so many disappointing environmental writers who are not writing about the environment at all. They're writing about themselves in the environment, and they often don't understand the world they're writing about. There are clearly writers who are more concerned with traveling around and checking everything out than they are with long-term survival of the habitats that they're working in." Discuss whether you agree or disagree with Hogan's quote, and read the rest of the interview at www.terrain.org.

Connect to Testing

In this chapter you analyzed a poem for central ideas and word choice. You also compared a poem and a nonfiction article. The following questions will help you understand how these skills might be tested on standardized tests.

1. **Part A:** Which statement best expresses a central idea of the poem?

   A. Humans can form relationships with wildlife.

   B. The oil spill could have been prevented with safety precautions.

   C. Sea turtles are one of the oldest creatures in the ocean.

   D. Oil companies pose a danger to sea creatures.

   Part B: Which of the following lines best supports the answer to Part A?

   A. *We had been together so very long,*
      you willing to swim with me
      just last month,

   B. *and now when I see the man from British Petroleum*
      lift you up dead from the plastic
      bin of death,

   C. *all I can think is that I loved your life,*
      the very air you exhaled when you rose,
      old great mother

   D. *How can they learn*
      the secret importance
      of your beaten heart,
      the eyes of another intelligence
      than ours,

©Perfection Learning® • No Reproduction Permitted

2. Which of the following paragraphs from the article "Saving Our Sea Turtles" expresses a similar idea to the central idea of the poem "Song for the Turtles in the Gulf" identified in question 1, Part A?

   A. *When Deepwater Horizon sank, oil began gushing out of the pipe that had connected the platform to the oil well below. Government scientists would later estimate that more than 60,000 barrels of oil (that's more than 2.5 million gallons, or 9.5 million liters) were pouring out of the well every day. The leak urgently needed to be plugged.*

   B. *The U.S. Fish and Wildlife Service was most worried about species that were already threatened or endangered. It listed 38 of them, from cranes to manatees to sturgeons. Some of the most worrying animals on the list were the sea turtles.*

   C. *There were about 120 turtles at the Audubon Aquatic Center when Alsina arrived in July. Many of them had been rescued by workers patrolling the ocean in boats. When they spotted a turtle that was oiled or otherwise in trouble, they scooped it up with a net, wiped it off as well as they could, and sent it along to New Orleans.*

   D. *On August 18, the first 23 turtles with a clean bill of health were released back into the Gulf of Mexico. To keep them safe, "They are being released in areas that are free of oil, were never oiled, and are at some distance from the oil spill site," Schroeder says.*

3. **Part A:** The speaker's words in "Song for the Turtles in the Gulf" create an overall feeling of

   A. remorse.

   B. anger.

   C. peacefulness.

   D. uncertainty.

   Part B: Which of the following best supports the answer to Part A?

   A. *in the ocean of splendor and light,*

   B. *he with a smile, you burned*
   and covered with red-black oil,

   C. *the secret importance*
   of your beaten heart,

   D. *Forgive us for being thrown off true,*

4. Read the following excerpt from "Saving Our Sea Turtles."

> Alsina says that working with the turtles brought mixed feelings. "On a daily basis, I would think to myself, this is so cool, these animals are going to be around for years and years and years, and outlive me, and I've never been so close to so many turtles at a time!" she says.

Which of the following lines from the poem express a similar point of view of sea turtles as the quotation above?

A. *and now when I see the man from British Petroleum*
   lift you up dead from the plastic
   bin of death,

B. *he with a smile, you burned*
   and covered with red-black oil, torched
   and pained,

C. *all I can think is that I loved your life,*
   the very air you exhaled when you rose,
   old great mother, the beautiful swimmer,
   the mosaic growth of shell
   so detailed, no part of you
   simple, meaningless,

D. *Forgive us for being thrown off true,*
   for our trespasses,
   in the eddies of the water
   where we first walked.

5. The speaker's question in lines 20 through 25 of the poem reveals the speaker's

A. lack of self-confidence.

B. determination to take action.

C. connection with the turtle.

D. desire to study turtles.

©Perfection Learning® • No Reproduction Permitted

Chapter 19

Analyzing Claims and Support

Preview Concepts

Watch an advertisement with your class, or think about an advertisement you have seen recently. Answer the following questions.

What product was being advertised?

What claims about the product did the advertisement make?

How did the commercial try to convince you to buy the product? Did it appeal to your emotions or your brain?

Were the claims persuasive? Why or why not?

Share your answers with a partner. Would you be more likely to buy a product based on seeing a commercial or based on a friend's positive recommendation? Why?

CHAPTER GOALS

In this chapter you will

- define academic terms related to science.

- analyze a central claim and supporting evidence.

- integrate information from a text and a graph.

PREVIEW ACADEMIC VOCABULARY

bias

claim

evidence

line graph

©Perfection Learning® • No Reproduction Permitted

Making Connections

Informational texts dealing with scientific or historical topics often include graphs, charts, or photos to illustrate and explain information in a visual way. Read the following passage and study the illustrations.

The effects of climate change are not the same in all parts of the world. While Earth's average temperature has risen 0.6°C (1.0°F) during the 20th century, some areas of our planet are warming faster than others. The Arctic is warming twice as fast as other parts of the world. In Alaska (USA) average temperatures have increased 3.0°C (5.4°F) between 1970 and 2000. The warmer temperatures

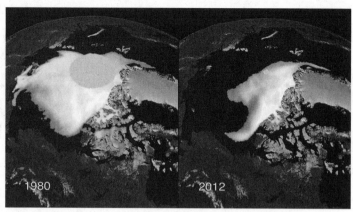

These images from NASA's ICESat satellite show the difference in ice cover in the Arctic between 1980 (left) and 2012 (right). NASA

have caused other changes in the Arctic region such as melting ice and shrinking polar bear habitat. In the opposite hemisphere, the Antarctic Peninsula has also warmed rapidly, five times faster than the global average. Meanwhile, temperatures of the interior of the Antarctic continent have remained stable or have cooled, which may be related to ozone depletion. Since 1945, the Antarctic Peninsula has warmed about 4.5°F (2.5°C). The Southern Ocean is also warming faster than expected.

—"Warming of the Polar Regions" by the National Earth
Science Teachers Association

> **MAKING CONNECTIONS**
>
> In this chapter you will identify a claim in an argument and analyze the support included.

How do the images show what is explained in the passage? Underline lines from the text that relate to the images.

Do the images support or contradict the text?

First Read: Defining Key Terms

The following is a nonfiction article from an online scientific journal. Some of the scientific vocabulary may be unfamiliar. Read at a slower pace to understand paragraphs with technical language or complex ideas. If your comprehension breaks down, go back and reread. Try to connect what you don't understand with ideas that you do understand.

Objective: As you read the text, circle any words you don't know. Write questions you have about the article in the My Thoughts column.

Climate Change: The Long Reach
Earth may face far warmer temperatures than previous estimates had indicated.
by Stephen Ornes
Science News for Students

August 22, 2013

	My Thoughts

1   Earth is warming. Sea levels are rising. There's more carbon in the air, and Arctic ice is melting faster than at any time in recorded history. Scientists who study the environment to better gauge Earth's future climate now argue that these changes may
5   not reverse for a very long time. Think millennia.

People burn fossil fuels like coal and oil for energy. That burning releases carbon dioxide, a colorless gas. In the air, this gas traps heat at Earth's surface. And the more carbon dioxide released, the more the planet warms. If current consumption
10   of fossil fuels doesn't slow, the long-term climate impacts could last *thousands* of years—and be more severe than scientists had been expecting. Climatologist Richard Zeebe of the University of Hawaii at Manoa offers this conclusion in a new paper. . . . in the *Proceedings of the National Academy of Sciences*.

15   Most climate-change studies look at what's going to happen in the next century or so. During that time, changes in the planet's environment could nudge global warming even higher. For example: Snow and ice reflect sunlight back into space. But

as these melt, sunlight can now reach—and warm—the exposed
20 ground. This extra heat raises the air temperature even more,
causing even more snow to melt. This type of rapid exaggeration
of impacts is called a "fast feedback."

Zeebe says it's important to look at fast feedbacks. However,
he adds, they're limited. From a climate change perspective, "This
25 century is the most important time for the next few generations,"
he told Science News. "But the world is not ending in 2100."

For his new study, Zeebe now focuses on "slow feedbacks."
While fast feedback events unfold over decades or centuries, slow
feedbacks can take thousands of years. Melting of continental ice
30 sheets and the migration of plant life—as they relocate to more
comfortable areas—are two examples of slow feedbacks.

Zeebe gathered information from previously published studies
investigating how such processes played out over thousands of
years during past dramatic changes in climate. Then he came up
35 with a forecast for the future that accounts for both slow and
fast feedback processes.

Climate forecasts that use only fast feedbacks predict a
4.5 degree Celsius (8.1 degree Fahrenheit) change by the year
3000. But slow feedbacks added another 1.5° C—for a 6° total
40 increase, Zeebe reports. He also found that slow feedback events
will cause global warming to persist for thousands of years after
people run out of fossil fuels to burn.

"This study uses our understanding of how the climate works
to build an idea of what might happen in the future," Ana
45 Christina Ravelo told Science News. Ravelo is a climate scientist
at the University of California, Santa Cruz. She pointed out that
Zeebe's study also is conservative—which means it might greatly
underestimate the true boost in Earth's temperature.

My Thoughts

©Perfection Learning® • No Reproduction Permitted

FIRST RESPONSE: KEY IDEAS AND DETAILS

What does the author want readers to believe? Write your answer in your journal.

TECH-CONNECT

Find at least three facts about global warming. Post them on your class website, according to your teacher's instructions.

Focus on Defining Key Terms

In this article, the author uses technical vocabulary related to environmental science. Understanding these words is important to understanding the article. You may recognize and understand some of these terms, such as *global warming*. Others may be new. Complete the following chart. Use context clues to determine what you think each word means. Then check the definition in a dictionary. Some terms may not be found in the dictionary and will take a bit of online research to find the definitions.

Word(s)	What I Think It Means (from context and from what I already know)	Dictionary Definition
carbon		
fossil fuels		
carbon dioxide		

continued on next page

Word(s)	What I Think It Means (from context and from what I already know)	Dictionary Definition
global warming		
fast feedbacks		
slow feedbacks		

Speak and Listen Share your answers to the definitions chart with a partner. Discuss the following questions.

1. What is the difference between a fast feedback event and a slow one?
2. Why are both fast and slow feedback important to understanding global warming?

Second Read: Identifying Claims

A digital version of this text is available online at the Science News for Students website. Digital texts offer features such as hyperlinks to other articles, videos, and pictures. Try reading the article online and consider how the digital features enhance your understanding of the ideas.

Objective: Focus on the second paragraph. Identify each sentence with an F for fact or O for opinion.

©Perfection Learning® • No Reproduction Permitted

Focus on Identifying Claims

In this article, the author has an opinion, and he wants readers to agree with his opinion. To gain agreement, the author presents a claim.

A claim is

- a statement that an author is trying to prove is true.

- based upon an opinion.

- sometimes clearly stated and sometimes must be inferred.

Support for claims include the following.

- facts and evidence, such as statistics and quotations

- testimony from experts in their field

Answer the following questions to determine the claims and evidence in the article. Use your annotations of opinions and facts in paragraph 2 to help you answer the questions.

CONNECT TO ESSENTIAL QUESTION

How does taking care of the environment and animals help human beings?

REFLECT

Have you and your family made conscious choices to use alternative and clean energy sources?

1. In paragraph 2, what claim does the author make about global warming?

2. According to the last paragraph, how does the study of slow and fast feedbacks support the author's claim in paragraph 2? Support your answer by referring to lines in the text.

continued on next page

3. What can you infer about what the author wants people to think or do?

Speak and Listen With two or three classmates, discuss whether you find the claims made in this article convincing. Discuss the following questions.

1. How does the article support the central claim?
2. Do the science and the scientists seem believable, or credible? Why or why not?
3. *Bias* is a tendency to believe that some ideas are better than others, which usually results in treating some ideas unfairly. Is there any evidence that the experts in this story have any bias that might affect how they interpret facts?

Third Read: Integrating Information from a Text and a Graph

Study the following graph. Then read the article a third time.

Objective: Circle specific sentences in the article that relate to the information in the graph.

Climate Change: How do we know?

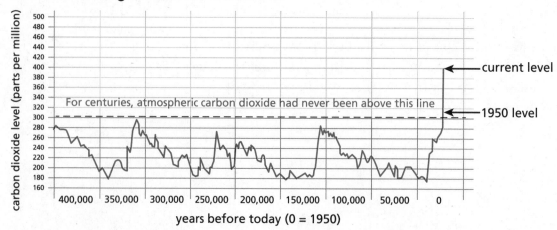

This graph provides evidence that carbon dioxide in the atmosphere has increased since the Industrial Revolution, which began in the late 1700s. Graph Source: http://climate.nasa.gov/evidence/. Accessed February 2017.

    ©Perfection Learning® • No Reproduction Permitted

Focus on Integrating Information from a Text and a Graph

Authors use a variety of support for their claims, including figures, charts, graphs, and other visual elements. Line graphs show how something has changed over time. They can track changes for short periods or long periods. Important parts of a line graph are the title, the x-axis, and the y-axis. The x-axis is horizontal (from side to side) and usually has numbers showing time. The y-axis is vertical (up and down) and usually has numbers for what is being measured. Look at the labels for the x-axis and y-axis to see what is being measured. Some graphs will also have a legend if two or more things are being compared.

Answer the questions to understand the graph and determine how it supports the author's claims in the article.

1. What is the graph's title?

2. What does the x-axis show?

3. What does the y-axis show?

4. What does the graph show about carbon dioxide? Use evidence from the graph in your answer.

continued on next page

©Perfection Learning® • No Reproduction Permitted

5. What does the article claim about carbon dioxide? Use evidence from the article in your answer.

6. How does the graph show support for this claim?

Speak and Listen Discuss your answers to the questions with a partner. Answer the following questions.

1. Is evidence from the chart and article used in the answers?
2. How convincing is the chart? Do you think it provides strong or weak evidence to support the author's point?

Language: Varying Sentence Patterns

Writing is more interesting to read when the sentences are different lengths and have different structures. Read the first paragraph from the passage.

> Earth is warming. Sea levels are rising. There's more carbon in the air, and Arctic ice is melting faster than at any time in recorded history. Scientists who study the environment to better gauge Earth's future climate now argue that these changes may not reverse for a very long time. Think millennia.

Count the words in each sentence, and underline the first word in every sentence. How many sentences begin with the same word? Also, notice how the sentence structures differ from sentence to sentence. Notice how the paragraph begins with short sentences and builds to a longer sentence. The final sentence is short again. What effect do shorter sentences have? Why would the writer use a longer sentence for the central claim of the paragraph?

In general, shorter sentences break up the flow of the writing, forcing the reader to slow down and think before moving on. Longer sentences flow more smoothly, making the pace of the writing more steady. When you write, try to vary the lengths and types of sentences to better communicate your ideas.

Rewrite the sentences below. Use the points shown to guide your rewrting.

- Combine or separate sentences to vary sentence length.

- Use different words to begin sentences so they don't all sound similar.

- Change the structure of sentences to make them more interesting.

REFLECT

Do you believe information more easily if it comes from an expert source, such as a doctor or scientist? Why or why not?

The four classmates sat at their table. They were waiting for their teacher. They were waiting for class to begin. Aditya glanced at Mary and grinned. Mary giggled quietly. José rolled his eyes. Yumi sighed. She wondered what the joke was.

Project-Based Assessments

Roundtable Discussion

Participate in a roundtable discussion about the following question.

Does the article "Climate Change: The Long Reach" present a strong argument that global warming will be even worse than currently predicted? Why or why not?

continued on next page

In a roundtable discussion, all students are equal and everyone participates. Arrange your seats in a circle so that all participants can see one another. The teacher or a discussion leader may sit in the middle. Come to the discussion with an open mind, and be prepared for a challenge! You will be evaluated on the following.

Expectations for Discussion	
Listening	**Speaking**
Listen respectfully.	Speak at least two times.
Look at the speaker.	Refer to the text to support conclusions.
Follow the text references. (Have the text open during the discussion.)	Ask questions about specific points made by the other speakers.
Take notes on what the speaker is saying.	Explain and give reasons to support your opinion.
Write down follow-up questions.	Invite comments.

Instructions for a Roundtable Discussion

1. The discussion leader (or teacher) begins by asking the question on the previous page.
2. Allow each member a chance to reply to the question.
3. Take notes on comments you disagree with or have questions about. Record what was said and who said it.
4. Go around the circle again and allow everyone to ask a follow-up question. Questions should be directed to the person who made the original comment. Try phrasing your questions or comments in this way:

   Explain what you mean by . . . .

   I agree/disagree with _____ because . . . .

5. Close the discussion by having everyone respond to the following question.

   > What do you think is the most important action to take to address global warming as a person, a state, or a country?

> **REFLECT**
>
> What might happen to humans and the world if global warming is not halted or reversed?

Use the following guidelines for your roundtable discussion.	
To receive the highest score (4.0), the discussion must meet all of these criteria.	During the discussion, you should • listen carefully when others are speaking: make notes about what they say. • offer thoughtful feedback and encourage everyone to participate. • share reasonable opinions and support your opinion with examples from the text. • demonstrate an understanding of the text. • speak to the question or point at hand in a clear, concise manner.

©Perfection Learning® • No Reproduction Permitted

Bringing Awareness Project

Using your own talents, bring awareness about climate change or another issue related to protecting animals or the environment. Choose from the options below.

Choose your project based upon your learning style.
Language/Musical
• Write a paper about the issue you researched, the action steps you took, and steps others can take to get involved.
• Create a digital presentation using images from the Internet or personal photos from your action steps. Include music or video clips to illustrate.
• Write and perform a song. Write lyrics to explain the issue and motivate listeners to change the problem. Record your song using digital software, or make a movie of yourself performing it.
• Create a public service announcement to raise awareness for your issue. Write the script, rehearse with actors, film it using your smartphone, and edit your video with computer software. Upload your commercial to the class web page or YouTube.
Body/Kinesthetic/Visual
• Produce an original piece of artwork that best expresses an environmental problem, and create an informational placard describing the significant elements. Upload an image of it to the class website.
• Create a dance or step routine to a song that addresses the issue you researched, and perform it for your class. Write an explanation of what it represents. Have a classmate record the dance, and post the video to your class website.
Interpersonal/Intrapersonal
• Work with others in your class on one of the projects listed above. Describe your feelings about working with others and about your personal connection to the topic by writing a blog entry on your class website. Respond respectfully to comments.
• Interview someone actively involved in protecting the environment, such as an environmental scientist or a local or a state government official. Before you do, prepare 5 to 10 questions to guide the interview. Write a newspaper-style article about the interview, or film the interview and edit it down to a five-minute video that you can show to the class.

Use the following guidelines for your project.	
To receive the highest score (4.0), the project must meet all of these criteria.	Your project • focuses on bringing awareness to an environmental issue. • creatively communicates details about the topic and ways the audience can get involved to change the current problems. • is appropriate for the audience. • is free from grammar, usage, punctuation, and spelling errors.

On Your Own: Integrating Ideas

1. NASA.gov claims that 97 percent of climate scientists agree that climate-warming trends over the past century are very likely due to human activities. What do the other 3 percent believe? Read articles discussing global warming trends from different viewpoints. Try these websites: www3.epa.gov, cfr.org, and climateclassroomkids.org.

2. Watch the documentary *An Inconvenient Truth*. What does the movie claim about global warming? What type of evidence is used to support the claims? Also, watch a video about climate change by Bill Nye the Science Guy at smithsonianmag.com. Does this video support the claims made in *An Inconvenient Truth*?

©Perfection Learning® • No Reproduction Permitted

Connect to Testing

In this chapter you practiced analyzing claims and supporting evidence. When you take assessments, you will be tested on these skills with questions like the following.

1. **Part A:** Which of the following best explains one of the central claims of the article "Climate Change: The Long Reach" by Stephen Ornes?

   A. Climate change is difficult to study and predict with accuracy.

   B. Global warming may be more severe and last longer than predicted.

   C. Scientific study of slow feedback is more important than the study of fast feedback.

   D. Too many studies focus on global warming in the next century.

   Part B: Which of the following provides the strongest support for the answer to Part A?

   A. *Earth is warming. Sea levels are rising. There's more carbon in the air, and Arctic ice is melting faster than at any time in recorded history.*

   B. *People burn fossil fuels like coal and oil for energy. That burning releases carbon dioxide, a colorless gas. In the air, this gas traps heat at Earth's surface.*

   C. *If current consumption of fossil fuels doesn't slow, the long-term climate impacts could last thousands of years—and be more severe than scientists had been expecting.*

   D. *"This study uses our understanding of how the climate works to build an idea of what might happen in the future," Ana Christina Ravelo told Science News.*

2. Use the list below to fill in the chart on the next page. Refer to the complete article as needed.

   melting of continental ice sheets
   snow and ice melting
   sunlight warming exposed ground and causing even more snow to melt
   migration of plant life
   6° C increase in global temperature
   rapid exaggeration of impacts

continued on next page

Fast Feedback	Slow Feedback

3. **Part A:** Summarize the central idea communicated by the line graph in the chapter.

©Perfection Learning® • No Reproduction Permitted

Part B: The graph provides the strongest support for which of the following lines from the text.

A. *Earth is warming. Sea levels are rising. There's more carbon in the air, and Arctic ice is melting faster than at any time in recorded history.*

B. *From a climate change perspective, "This century is the most important time for the next few generations," he told Science News. "But the world is not ending in 2100."*

C. *Melting of continental ice sheets and the migration of plant life—as they relocate to more comfortable areas—are two examples of slow feedbacks.*

D. *She pointed out that Zeebe's study also is conservative—which means it might greatly underestimate the true boost in Earth's temperature.*

4. **Part A:** The author includes the information about fast and slow feedbacks in order to:

A. explain why so much carbon dioxide is being released into the atmosphere in modern times.

B. provide examples of how the rate of climate change varies in different areas of the world.

C. give reasons why using fossil fuels is a danger to the environment.

D. give evidence for the claim that climate change may raise temperatures higher than expected.

Part B: Which of the following provides the strongest support for the answer to Part A?

A. *Scientists who study the environment to better gauge Earth's future climate now argue that these changes may not reverse for a very long time.*

B. *During that time, changes in the planet's environment could nudge global warming even higher.*

C. *Melting of continental ice sheets and the migration of plant life—as they relocate to more comfortable areas—are two examples of slow feedbacks.*

D. *Climate forecasts that use only fast feedbacks predict a 4.5 degree Celsius (8.1 degree Fahrenheit) change by the year 3000. But slow feedbacks added another 1.5° C—for a 6° total increase.*

Chapter 20

Analyzing Theme Through Sensory Language

Preview Concepts

Study the following picture.

Imagine you are at this carnival. Finish each of the sentence starters below with three descriptive phrases. Use words that appeal to the senses.

CHAPTER GOALS

In this chapter you will

- identify the theme of a work.
- analyze how sensory language communicates mood.
- analyze author's craft of opening an informational book with a fable..

I see
I hear
I taste
I feel
I smell

PREVIEW ACADEMIC VOCABULARY

fable

literary analysis

mood

plot

purpose

sensory language

setting

theme

Read your sensory descriptions to your partner. Ask him or her to identify which of your sensory phrases was most effective at communicating the experience of being at the carnival and to explain why it was his or her favorite.

Making Connections

Read the following Indian fable adapted by P. V. Ramaswami Raju.

The Raven and the Cattle

One evening, as some cattle were heading home, a raven rode on the horns of a bull in the herd; and as he approached the cottage, cried to the farmer, "Friend, my work for the day is over; you may now take charge of your cattle."

"What was your work?" asked the farmer.

"Why," said the raven, "the **arduous** task of watching these cattle and bringing them home."

"Am I to understand you have been doing all the work for me?" said the farmer.

"Certainly," said the raven, and flew away with a laugh.

Quoth the farmer with surprise, "How many there are that take credit for things which they have never done!"

---

arduous: difficult
quoth: said

What is a fable?

What other fables have you read before?

Explain the last line of the fable.

©Perfection Learning® • No Reproduction Permitted

> **MAKING CONNECTIONS**
>
> In this chapter you will be reading and analyzing a modern fable.

First Read: Identifying a Theme

Rachel Carson (1907–1964) was an avid student of nature and an ecologist long before ecology was an accepted science. Passionate about the natural world—and especially oceans—she became a marine biologist for the U.S. Fish and Wildlife Service. A scientist, scholar, and writer, she eventually wrote three well-respected books on ocean life. Her most famous and controversial book, *Silent Spring*, was published in 1962. In it she detailed evidence to support her claim that chemicals used to kill pests were hurting animals and people. Carson opened her book with the fable below.

   Objective: As you read, think about the events that happen and what readers are supposed to learn from them. Underline sentences that describe important events. Write questions you have about the fable in the My Thoughts column.

from

Silent Spring

A Fable for Tomorrow

by Rachel Carson

	My Thoughts
1 There was once a town in the heart of America where all life seemed to live in harmony with its surroundings. The town lay in the midst of a checkerboard of prosperous farms, with fields of grain and hillsides of orchards where, in spring, white	
5 clouds of bloom drifted above the green fields. In autumn, oak and maple and birch set up a blaze of color that flamed and flickered across a backdrop of pines. Then foxes barked in the hills and deer silently crossed the fields, half hidden in the mists of the fall mornings.	
10 Along the roads, laurel, viburnum and alder, great ferns and wildflowers delighted the traveler's eye through much of the year. Even in winter the roadsides were places of beauty,	

where countless birds came to feed on the berries and on

the seed heads of the dried weeds rising above the snow.

15 The countryside was, in fact, famous for the abundance and

variety of its bird life, and when the flood of migrants was

pouring through in spring and fall, people traveled from great

distances to observe them. Others came to fish the streams,

which flowed clear and cold out of the hills and contained

20 shady pools where trout lay. So it had been from the days

many years ago when the first settlers raised their houses, sank

their wells, and built their barns.

Then a strange blight crept over the area and everything

began to change. Some evil spell had settled on the community:

25 mysterious maladies swept the flocks of chickens; the cattle

and sheep sickened and died. Everywhere was a shadow of

death. The farmers spoke of much illness among their families.

In the town the doctors had become more and more puzzled

by new kinds of sickness appearing among their patients. There

30 had been several sudden and unexplained deaths, not only

among adults but even among children, who would be stricken

suddenly while at play and die within a few hours.

There was a strange stillness. The birds, for example—

where had they gone? Many people spoke of them, puzzled

35 and disturbed. The feeding stations in the backyards were

deserted. The few birds seen anywhere were moribund; they

My Thoughts

trembled violently and could not fly. It was a spring without voices. On the mornings that had once throbbed with the dawn chorus of robins, catbirds, doves, jays, wrens, and scores

40 of other bird voices there was now no sound; only silence lay over the fields and woods and marsh.

On the farms the hens brooded, but no chicks hatched. The farmers complained that they were unable to raise any pigs—the litters were small and the young survived only a few days.

45 The apple trees were coming into bloom but no bees droned among the blossoms, so there was no pollination and there would be no fruit.

The roadsides, once so attractive, were now lined with browned and withered vegetation as though swept by fire.

50 These, too, were silent, deserted by all living things. Even the streams were now lifeless. Anglers no longer visited them, for all the fish had died.

In the gutters under the eaves and between the shingles of the roofs, a white granular powder still showed a few patches;

55 some weeks before it had fallen like snow upon the roofs and the lawns, the fields and streams.

No witchcraft, no enemy action had silenced the rebirth of new life in this stricken world. The people had done it themselves.

. . .

60   This town does not actually exist, but it might easily have

a thousand counterparts in America or elsewhere in the

world. I know of no community that has experienced all the

misfortunes I describe. Yet every one of these disasters has

actually happened somewhere, and many real communities

65   have already suffered a substantial number of them. A grim

specter has crept upon us almost unnoticed, and this imagined

tragedy may easily become a stark reality we all shall know.

My Thoughts

_____

_____

_____

_____

_____

_____

_____

_____

FIRST RESPONSE: KEY IDEAS AND DETAILS

In your response journal, write a paraphrase of the moral of the fable.

Focus on Identifying a Theme

    The author introduces her nonfiction book with a story—a fable to be exact. In this fable, the setting, events, and characters all work together to communicate a theme. Often in literature, the theme must be inferred, but in a fable the theme is often explained outright so that the reader doesn't miss it.

    Refer to the sentences you underlined in the First Read. Fill in the following graphic organizer with key information from the passage.

TECH-CONNECT

Post your response on your class website, according to your teacher's instructions, or tweet it to your teacher.

Setting
Where does the story take place?
When does the story take place?

continued on next page

Characters

Who are the characters?

How are the characters described?

Plot

What happens in the story?

How does the story begin?

How does the story end?

What is the "white granular powder" that "had fallen like snow upon the roofs and the lawns, the fields and streams"?

What questions do you have that the story leaves unanswered?

©Perfection Learning® • No Reproduction Permitted

Theme
At the beginning, who is telling the story—an outside narrator or one of the characters?
How does the point of view shift in the final paragraph? Who is talking in the last paragraph?
What is the theme of the story—in this case, the lesson or moral?

Speak and Listen Share your answers in the chart with a partner. Discuss the following questions.

1. What is the lesson in the story?
2. How do the setting and events in the story reveal this lesson?
3. Do you agree with the lesson? Why or why not?
4. Why do you think the author is intentionally unclear about what has caused the deaths of the animals and people?

Write Write a short paragraph explaining the story's lesson. Use examples and details from the story to support your answer.

> **CONNECT TO ESSENTIAL QUESTION**
>
> What are some possible consequences for not protecting the environment?

Second Read: Analyzing Sensory Description

In the story, the author uses details that appeal to the senses to establish the setting, describe events, and create an emotional tone.

Objective: Read the story aloud with a partner. Underline words that appeal to the five senses. Label them with the words *sight*, *sound*, *taste*, *touch*, and *smell*.

Study this chart to learn more about sensory description.

Sense	Description
Sight	Writers often use the sense of sight to help the reader "see" the characters and setting: *a golden sunset; brightly colored autumn leaves; a wild riot of blonde curls; curling tendrils of mist.*
Touch	Touch can show pain or pleasure: *a soft, warm blanket; hot cocoa scalding your tongue; a bitterly cold wind; holding a small, wriggly puppy.*

continued on next page

Sense	Description
Sound	What you hear helps establish the setting and provides information about the characters: *flapping wings, the patter of quick footsteps, the thunder of heavy rain on the roof, the screech of nails on a chalkboard, the soft hoot of an owl, the rumble of an engine, a raspy voice, an infectious giggle.*
Smell	Smells can make you think of memories: *freshly brewed coffee, burned popcorn, freshly baked bread, sweaty socks, sunscreen.*
Taste	Taste can also trigger memories: *creamy mashed potatoes, salty French fries, cotton candy dissolving in your mouth, spicy chili, melted chocolate.*

Focus on Analyzing Sensory Description

Return to the story and find two sensory details that appeal to each of the senses listed and write them in the chart below. The first one has been completed for you.

Sense	Details from the Story
Sight	1. *In autumn, oak and maple and birch set up a blaze of color that flamed and flickered across a backdrop of pines.* (lines 5–7) 2.
Touch	1. 2.
Sound	1. 2.

©Perfection Learning® • No Reproduction Permitted

Carson uses sensory details to create the tone and mood of the work. Tone and mood can sometimes be confusing.

REFLECT

Which sense do you think you use the most? Which of your senses is the keenest?

- Tone is the author's attitude toward the subject. Words that describe the tone of a work include *humorous, sarcastic, angry, informal, serious,* and *matter-of-fact.*

- Mood is the feeling the work creates in the reader; it is the general atmosphere created by the author's words. Words that describe mood include *gloomy, joyful, suspenseful, mysterious, sad/melancholic,* and *hopeful.*

Answer the questions below about tone and mood.

1. How would you describe the author's tone toward her subject? Choose one of the tone words above.

2. What words or phrases from the fable best support your description of the tone?

3. What is the mood at the beginning of the fable?

4. What words or phrases from the fable best support your description of the mood at the beginning?

5. What is the mood at the end of the fable?

continued on next page

6. What words or phrases from the fable best support your description of the mood at the end?

Speak and Listen Share your answers to the questions with a partner.

Third Read: Analyzing Author's Craft

This fable is part of a larger work of nonfiction, but the fable tells a story using setting, sensory description, and other elements of fiction.

Objective: Read the fable a third time. Pay special attention to the images described. Think about why the author includes these descriptions in the story.

Focus on Analyzing Author's Craft

Silent Spring is about the hazards of using powerful chemical pesticides. Why would Rachel Carson open her book with a fable—a story? What was her purpose? How does the fable fit in with her idea? Answer the following questions.

1. How does the narrator describe the town in the first two paragraphs?

2. Why do you think the narrator never names the people in the passage?

    ©Perfection Learning® • No Reproduction Permitted

3. Why does the narrator describe the town and its natural surroundings in great detail?

4. What is the author trying to tell readers in lines 23–52?

REFLECT

The last paragraph states, "No witchcraft, no enemy action had silenced the rebirth of new life in this stricken world." Why does the author use the terms *witchcraft* and *enemy action* here to explain what did not cause the deaths?

5. What is the author's message in the last two paragraphs?

(Speak and Listen Share your answers to questions 1–5 with a partner. If you add to your answer based upon your discussion, use a different color pen for your additions.

▼Write Use your answers to the questions to write a paragraph evaluating Rachel Carlson's fable. Answer the following questions.

- How does Carson describe nature and the town to communicate her message? Why does she do this? Include specific examples from the fable.

Use these sentence starters to help you write your paragraph.

- Carson describes the town and its natural surroundings . . . .

- She describes . . . .

- She uses description to . . . .

Language: Commas Before Conjunctions

Notice how a comma is used in the following sentence.

On the farms the hens brooded, but no chicks hatched.

This sentence is called a *compound sentence* because it has two independent clauses. (See the underlined clauses.) An independent clause can stand alone as a complete thought. In other words, an independent clause is a complete sentence.

When two independent clauses are joined with the conjunction *and*, *but*, *or*, *nor*, *for*, *so*, or *yet*, a comma is placed before the conjunction.

Examples: Mammoth Cave is the longest known cave system in the world, and it stretches for more than 400 miles.   Then a strange blight crept over the area, and everything began to change.   Anglers no longer visited them, for all the fish had died.

In the space below, write three examples of compound sentences using three different conjunctions from the list above. Make sure you include two independent clauses in each of your compound sentences.

©Perfection Learning® • No Reproduction Permitted

Project-Based Assessments

Literary Analysis

An analysis is a careful study of something to learn how its parts are related to the whole. Throughout this chapter, you analyzed the details of the fable from *Silent Spring*. Write a multiple-paragraph analysis that answers the following question.

- How do the events, sensory language, and mood communicate the theme of the fable?

Here are some text frames to help you focus your ideas:

- Central idea (thesis) statement: The events, sensory language, and mood work together to communicate the theme that . . . .

- First, the events . . . . For example . . . .

- Next, the author uses sensory description to . . . . One example of this is . . . .

- The mood of the fable communicates the theme by . . . . At the beginning, the mood is . . . . Examples of this include . . . .

- At the end of the fable, the mood is . . . . In line xx, the author describes . . . .

- The theme (or lesson) of the fable is . . . .

Notice the underlined words and phrases in the text frames above. These transitional phrases indicate the relationship among your ideas. They act as signposts telling your reader where you are taking them next.

Use the following guidelines for your literary analysis.
To receive the highest score (4.0), the analysis must meet all of these criteria. Your literary analysis • has a clear main idea in a well-developed introduction. • clearly explains how events, sensory language, and mood communicate the theme of the fable. • contains ideas that fit together logically to create an understandable whole. • includes good transitional phrases. • maintains a formal style. • uses correct grammar, usage, punctuation, and spelling.

Write a Fable

Write your own fable. Your fable should have a lesson or moral. The lesson may be inferred or clearly stated.

To get ideas about what other fables are like, read a few of Aesop's fables. Many can be found online.

Here are some steps to help you:

- Begin by brainstorming ideas for the lesson or moral you want to communicate.

- Think about the types of characters you want to use in your story. Many fables use animals or simple characters that have one character quality.

- Choose a plot that includes events and character responses that communicate your lesson.

Use sensory language or description to engage readers.

CONNECT TO ESSENTIAL QUESTION

Do more animals harm humans or more humans harm animals?

Use the following guidelines for your fable.	
To receive the highest score (4.0), the fable must meet all of these criteria.	**Your fable** • has a clear, identifiable lesson. • includes characters, a clear setting, and a logical plot. • is appropriate for the intended audience. • uses sensory language to engage the readers and communicate the lesson. • uses correct grammar, usage, punctuation, and spelling.

On Your Own: Integrating Ideas

1. Read more of *Silent Spring* by Rachel Carson.

2. Read "How *Silent Spring* Ignited the Environmental Movement" at www.nytimes.com. Research Rachel Carson's life and find out what happened to her after *Silent Spring* was published.

3. Read other fables by Aesop and consider these questions: Are the lessons directly stated or inferred? Who are the characters? How well do they represent humans? Are the lessons worthwhile?

©Perfection Learning® • No Reproduction Permitted

Connect to Testing

In this chapter, you identified a passage's theme, explored sensory details and mood, and analyzed how a section of a text fits into the overall purpose of the text. When taking assessments, you will be tested on these skills. Answer the following questions.

Read this statement and the directions that follow.

1. The fable's lesson is that humans' use of man-made substances can be harmful.

   Choose the statement from the text that best supports the conclusion.

   A. *There was once a town in the heart of America where all life seemed to live in harmony with its surroundings.*

   B. *Then a strange blight crept over the area and everything began to change.*

   C. *These, too, were silent, deserted by all living things.*

   D. *The people had done it themselves.*

2. **Part A:** Which of the following best describes how the townspeople feel about the blight?

   A. persevering

   B. suspicious

   C. worried

   D. distracted

   Part B: Which of the following best supports your answer to Part A?

   A. *mysterious maladies swept the flocks of chickens*

   B. *Many people spoke of them, puzzled and disturbed.*

   C. *On the farms the hens brooded, but no chicks hatched.*

   D. *These, too, were silent, deserted by all living things.*

3. The fable shows the potential dangers of introducing chemicals into the environment

   A. by contrasting images of nature's beauty with sickness and death triggered by humans.

   B. by suggesting that humans are careless and greedy.

   C. by demonstrating that humans are better off without trying to improve their lives.

   D. by describing the way the townspeople lived peacefully for many years before the blight.

continued on next page

4. **Part A:** Which of the following best describes the change in mood from the beginning to the end of the fable?

   A. peaceful to gloomy

   B. joyful to rebellious

   C. lighthearted to angry

   D. uplifting to mysterious

   Part B: Provide two sentences from the text that support the answer to Part A.

5. **Part A:** How does the phrase *Some evil spell had settled on the community: mysterious maladies swept the flocks of chickens* in lines 24–25 of the fable contribute to the theme?

   A. It hints that the people were superstitious and uneducated and didn't have the advantages of modern technology.

   B. It implies that humans like to blame bad things on something other than their own choices.

   C. It explains the true cause of the dying animals.

   D. It blames the problems on the actions of a wicked witch.

   Part B: Which line from the passage best supports the answer to Part A?

   A. *The farmers complained that they were unable to raise any pigs—the litters were small and the young survived only a few days.*

   B. *In the gutters under the eaves and between the shingles of the roofs, a white granular powder still showed a few patches;*

   C. *No witchcraft, no enemy action had silenced the rebirth of new life in this stricken world. The people had done it themselves.*

   D. *Yet every one of these disasters has actually happened somewhere. . . .*

©Perfection Learning® • No Reproduction Permitted

Writing an Argument

O beautiful for smoggy skies, insecticided grain,
For strip-mined mountain's majesty above the asphalt plain.
America, America, man sheds his waste on thee,
And hides the pines with billboard signs, from sea to oily sea.

—George Carlin

In this unit, you read a fictional story, two nonfiction articles, a poem, and a fable all on the topic of protecting the environment and the creatures that live on Earth.

WRITING PROMPT

Humans are realizing that all of life on Earth is interconnected. Our actions impact the air we breathe, the water we drink, the food we eat, and the health we enjoy—or the illnesses we suffer from. Rachel Carson, author of *Silent Spring*, wrote, "In nature nothing exists alone."

As a final project for this unit, you will be writing an argumentive essay on a topic related to the environment. You may choose global warming, clean water or air, endangered species, or any number of topics. In your argument, make a claim and then develop reasons with evidence to support your claim.

Decide on your audience, or for whom your essay is written. Your audience might be your state or local community officials, your principal or your teacher, your classmates, or even your family. Include information from four reliable, up-to-date sources that you cite in your essay. Use a word processing program to produce a final copy of your essay. It should be one to three typed pages, double-spaced, using standard Times New Roman 12-point font. Include a Works Cited list of your four sources.

Prepare to Write

Carefully look at the prompt. Underline key words that explain the requirements of the task. Break it down based on purpose, audience, content, and additional requirements by filling in the chart on the next page.

continued on next page

Purpose	
Audience	
Content Requirements	
Additional Requirements	

▼ The Writing Process: A Plan for Writing

Brainstorm for a Topic

Your first step in the writing process is to decide on a topic related to ecology or the environment. To start, brainstorm a wide range of topics. Think about issues you've heard about in school, seen on television, or read about online. Talking with other students is helpful because they might have ideas that you wouldn't think of on your own. Create a chart like the following in your response journal or on your computer. List as many topics as you can think of in the left-hand column. Then write questions that you have about each topic that could be answered through research.

Environmental Topic	Questions
Alternative energy	What is alternative energy?
Electric cars	
Global warming	
Protecting endangered wildlife	

©Perfection Learning® • No Reproduction Permitted

Most of the topics listed on the previous page are probably too general to be covered in a two-page essay. For example, thousands of pages have been written on the topic of protecting endangered wildlife. An idea web will help you narrow down the topics.

Study the web below. These are subtopics of Alternative energy. Add two more narrowed subtopics to the web.

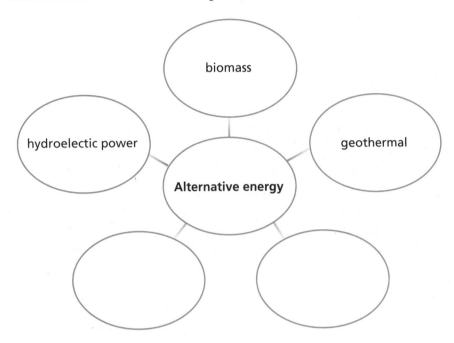

In your response journal, create an idea web with one of the topics you are interested in writing about.

Gather Information

Before you can have an opinion on a topic related to the environment, you will probably need to gather some information first. Then you can decide what your point of view is based upon facts. Use the Internet to find two or three websites on your narrowed topic. In your response journal, record your notes and the websites you used. Also write questions that this research raises.

Write a Claim

Decide on a major research question. Make sure it is clear and focused. The answer to this question will become the central claim of your paper.

In argumentative writing, your opinion is called a *claim*. Your claim should be debatable. In other words, people should have differing opinions about the statement. A claim should not be statement of fact.

continued on next page

Claims:

- Our state should ban the use of plastic grocery bags.

- Organic produce is a healthier choice than fruits and vegetables treated with chemicals.

- Our state should pass a law giving a ten-cent refund on plastic water bottles.

Not claims:

- Several species of sea turtles are endangered. (This is a fact.)

- Wind and solar power are clean energy alternatives to fossil fuels. (Also a fact.)

Many claims contain the words *should* or *must* in them. Others make a strong statement using *is* or *are*. Avoid using the phrases "I think" or "I believe." These are fine for informal writing but should not be used when writing a formal argument.

My claim: _____

_____

_____

- Is your claim an opinion?

- Is it a complete sentence?

- Is it debatable?

At this point, decide who your audience is. Your audience could be your parents, your classmates, or your congressperson. As you develop your essay, keep your audience in mind by choosing reasons and evidence that will be most convincing to them. Record your chosen audience below.

My audience: _____

©Perfection Learning® • No Reproduction Permitted

Conduct Research

You've already done some preliminary research to write your claim, but you'll need reasons and evidence to support your claim.

Consider the claim: Our school should install solar panels.

- reasons—statements that explain why your audience should agree with your claim. Here are two reasons in support of the claim.

1. Installing solar panels would save our school money.
2. Students could study solar energy as part of their science classes.

- evidence—facts, examples, expert opinions, personal experiences, and statistics that back up your reasons. Here are two pieces of evidence in support of the claim.

1. Sasha Johnson, an expert in solar panels, estimates that installing three solar panels could save our school $3,000 dollars a year.
2. At Roosevelt Middle School in Apache, Arizona, students daily monitor the energy collected by solar panels on the roof of their school.

Search the Internet and the media center for reliable sources. You are required to use four sources, but you may want to find more in case some of your sources don't contain the right type of information.

Taking Notes

As you find information for your essay, record it in your resource journal, in a word processing file, or with note-taking software. Always record the source of the information. For each source, record the following:

- name of the author (if provided)

- title of the article

- website name and address or title (if from a printed source)

- date (if provided)

- page number (if from a printed source)

Use your sources wisely. Don't cut and paste text from the Internet into your notes. Using text written by someone else is called *plagiarism*, and it is cheating. Instead, paraphrase the main ideas by writing them in your own words. If you find an interesting quotation from an expert or scientific data that is difficult to rewrite, make sure you put quotation marks around the text.

Follow your teacher's instructions for creating a Works Cited page that lists all of your sources.

> **CONNECT TO ESSENTIAL QUESTION**
>
> What could our planet look like in the future if current generations don't take care of the earth?

Organize Your Ideas

Essays are organized into three parts: (1) an introduction, (2) a body, and (3) a conclusion. Typically, a basic essay contains five paragraphs. The introduction is one paragraph, the body contains three paragraphs, and the conclusion is one paragraph.

Study this sample outline.

- Introduction—Introduce your topic, provide background, make a claim.

- Body—

    - Reason 1: Evidence: facts, examples, expert opinions, personal experiences, and statistics that back up your reasons

    - Reason 2: Evidence: facts, examples, expert opinions, personal experiences, and statistics that back up your reasons

    - Reason 3: Evidence: facts, examples, expert opinions, personal experiences, and statistics that back up your reasons

- Conclusion—Restate your claim, summarize your arguments, tell your audience what they should do.

Review your notes. Label information as reason, evidence, and background information. If you don't have enough information to support your claim, conduct more research. If you need to find more sources, narrow your search to more specific keywords so that you can find the information you need, for example: *evidence that solar panels save money.*

Here is an example of a sample outline of the body for the claim: Our school should install solar panels.

- Reason 1: Installing solar panels would save our school money.
  Evidence: Sasha Johnson, an expert in solar panels, estimates that installing solar panels at our school could reduce energy costs by 25 percent.

- Reason 2: Students could study solar energy as part of their science classes.
  Evidence: At Roosevelt Middle School in Apache, Arizona, students daily monitor the energy collected by solar panels on the roof of their school.

    ©Perfection Learning® • No Reproduction Permitted

- Reason 3: Using solar energy would be good for the environment.
  Evidence: Unlike fossil fuels, solar energy does not produce harmful emissions that hurt the environment.

In the space below, draft an outline for the body of your essay.

First Draft

Use your outline to write a draft of your argumentative essay. Here are some hints. Label this paper Draft #1.

- Refer to your notes while drafting.

- Write quickly. You will revise and proofread later.

- Write on every other line or double-space if working on a computer. This will make it easier to make revisions.

- If you take a break and then return to writing, reread what you have written before continuing. This will help you continue with your thoughts.

Revision

Having other students and your teacher read your essay will help you improve it. Listen carefully to their questions and comments on your writing. Applying their advice will help you refine your writing.

First Peer Review

This review will evaluate whether your ideas are interesting and whether they flow together in a logical order. With a group of two or three people, complete the following steps.

Steps for Peer Review

1. Select a timekeeper. Each writer gets 10 minutes. Respect the time limit.

2. One person begins by reading aloud his or her introduction while other members listen.

3. Pause. The same writer reads the introduction aloud a second time.

4. The writer asks, "Does the introduction of my essay make you want to know more? Is my claim clear?" Each member responds, as the writer takes notes on his/her draft.

5. The writer reads the entire essay, pauses, and then reads it again.

6. As the writer reads, members take notes.

7. The writer asks, "Is my argument convincing? Why or why not?" The writer jots down replies.

8. Repeat steps 1-7 with the next member, who becomes the writer.

As soon as possible after peer review, revise your draft based on your peers' questions and comments. Mark this paper Draft #2.

Second Review—Teacher/Parent

Ask an adult or older sibling to read your paper and respond to the following.

- Claim

  Is my claim clearly stated in the introduction?

- Content

  Are the reasons clearly stated?
  Are my reasons supported with strong evidence?
  What information or ideas are missing?

- Organization of Ideas

  Are the reasons logically organized—building up to the strongest reason?
  Are good transitions used between paragraphs? between ideas?

- Conclusion

  Does my conclusion restate my claim?
  Does it bring the paper to a satisfying close?

  When you finish the steps, mark the version Draft #3.

Final Peer Review

Ask another student to read your argumentative essay and rate it using the rubric below.

Use the following guidelines for your argumentative essay.	
To receive the highest score (4.0), the argumentative essay must meet all of these criteria.	Your argumentative essay • contains an introduction that makes a clear claim about the topic. • develops reasons that clearly support the claim. • includes strong evidence that supports the reasons. • wraps up the argument with a well-written conclusion. • is appropriate for the audience. • includes information from at least four reliable sources. • contains correct grammar, usage, punctuation, and spelling.

Proofread

As you prepare a final draft, make sure you have used correct grammar and punctuation. Proofread carefully for omitted words and punctuation marks, especially when using a direct quotation. If you used a word processing program, run spell-check but know that it won't catch every error. Proofread again to find the kinds of errors the computer can't.

Final Essay

Share your completed essay with your intended audience. Publish it online or send it in an email to state and local leaders. Upload your finished digital copy to your class website. If you have a school or personal blog or website, share it with your readers.

Practice Performance Task

A performance task evaluates your ability to comprehend selections of literature and informational text and then demonstrate your knowledge in writing. The task may begin with several multiple-choice or short-answer questions on key vocabulary and the central ideas of the passage(s). The task culminates with a writing assignment.

Complete the following performance task based upon selections from Unit 4.

Source #1

Read the following passage from *Flush* from Chapter 16 of this unit.

According to my father, Dusty Muleman was such a pathetic cheapskate that he wouldn't pay to have the *Coral Queen's* <u>sewage</u> hauled away. Instead his crew had standing orders to flush the waste into the basin, which was already murky. The tide later carried most of the filth out to open water.

"But why didn't Dad just call the Coast Guard?" my sister asked. "Wouldn't that have been the grown-up thing to do?"

"He told me he tried. He said he called everybody he could think of, but they could never catch Dusty in the act," I said. "Dad thinks somebody's tipping him off."

"Oh, please," Abbey groaned.

Now she was starting to annoy me.

"When wind and the current are right, the poop from the gambling boat floats out of the basin and down the shoreline," I said, "straight to Thunder Beach."

1. **Part A:** What is the meaning of the word *sewage* as it is used in the text?

   A. undrinkable water

   B. boat fragments

   C. human waste

   D. broken pieces

continued on next page

Part B: Which phrases from Source 1 best help the reader understand the meaning of the word *sewage*? Choose all that apply.

A. *that he wouldn't pay*

B. *his crew had standing orders*

C. *to flush the waste*

D. *into the basin*

E. *which was already murky*

F. *tide later carried most of the filth out*

Source #2

Read the following passage from "Saving Our Sea Turtles" from Chapter 17 of this unit.

Nevertheless, oil began to wash up on the beaches of Louisiana, Mississippi, Florida, and Alabama. Fishing was banned in a large portion of the gulf. Contaminated fish would be unsafe to eat and not just for humans. Small fish that ingested oil and were then eaten by other animals could send toxic chemicals all the way up the food chain. Birds could be covered in oil and drown, or ingest or inhale oil as they tried to clean their feathers. Sure enough, people began to discover birds, dolphins, and turtles that were oiled or dead.

The U.S. Fish and Wildlife Service was most worried about species that were already threatened or endangered. It listed 38 of them, from cranes to manatees to sturgeons. Some of the most worrying animals on the list were the sea turtles.

All five species of sea turtle that live in the Gulf of Mexico are threatened or endangered. Humans hunting them for meat, gathering their eggs, killing them for their shells, or accidentally catching them in fishing nets have made sea turtles rare. After the spill, a new threat faced these turtles, not just the ones swimming in oiled waters, but a whole generation that hadn't even hatched yet.

2. What is the main idea of the passage on the previous page? Write a two- to three-sentence summary below.

3. Based upon this passage, the reader can infer that the U.S. Fish and Wildlife Service was worried about sea turtles because they are

A. already in trouble.

B. the most valuable species.

C. difficult to locate.

D. important to human survival.

Source #3

Read the following passage from "Climate Change: The Long Reach" from Chapter 18 of this unit.

> Earth is warming. Sea levels are rising. There's more carbon in the air, and Arctic ice is melting faster than at any time in recorded history. Scientists who study the environment to better gauge Earth's future climate now argue that these changes may not reverse for a very long time. Think millennia.

continued on next page

People burn fossil fuels like coal and oil for energy. That burning releases carbon dioxide, a colorless gas. In the air, this gas traps heat at Earth's surface. And the more carbon dioxide released, the more the planet warms. If current consumption of fossil fuels doesn't slow, the long-term climate impacts could last *thousands* of years—and be more severe than scientists had been expecting. Climatologist Richard Zeebe of the University of Hawaii at Manoa offers this conclusion in a new paper. . . . in the *Proceedings of the National Academy of Sciences*.

Most climate-change studies look at what's going to happen in the next century or so. During that time, changes in the planet's environment could nudge global warming even higher. For example: Snow and ice reflect sunlight back into space. But as these melt, sunlight can now reach—and warm—the exposed ground. This extra heat raises the air temperature even more, causing even more snow to melt. This type of rapid exaggeration of impacts is called a "fast feedback."

4. **Part A:** *Fast feedback* is a term that refers to
   A. an increase in the amount of fossil fuels people use.
   B. the amount of carbon dioxide that is being trapped at Earth's surface.
   C. changes in the earth that magnify global warming effects.
   D. extra heat around the earth due to global warming.

Part B: Which of the following quotes from the passage explains a specific instance of fast feedback?

   A. *People burn fossil fuels like coal and oil for energy.*
   B. *the long-term climate impacts could last thousands of years—and be more severe than scientists had been expecting.*
   C. *Most climate-change studies look at what's going to happen in the next century or so*
   D. *as these melt, sunlight can now reach—and warm—the exposed ground. This extra heat raises the air temperature even more, causing even more snow to melt.*

Your Assignment

WRITING PROMPT

In this unit you read informational and fictional texts with environmental themes. Consider how the passages from this unit can help you formulate an answer to the Essential Question: *Why should we protect Earth and its creatures?* Write several paragraphs in which you respond to this question by making a claim about why we should be concerned with taking care of the environment. Refer to at least three passages from this unit to support your claim. Include direct quotations when appropriate.

Read the prompt carefully. Underline words that indicate what you must include in your answer.

Organize your ideas before you begin writing. Use the following chart to help you.

Essential Question: Why should we protect Earth and its creatures?		
Unit passage	What does this text say about caring for Earth and animals? How can this be written as a reason?	Support from text (paraphrase or direct quotation)
Flush		
"Saving Our Sea Turtles"		

continued on next page

"Song for the Turtles in the Gulf"		
"Climate Change: The Long Reach"		
Silent Spring		

©Perfection Learning® • No Reproduction Permitted

Use the chart you completed to plan your answer. Your writing will be evaluated on the following categories. Use these to check your writing before you turn it in.

Reading Comprehension
- Does your writing show that you understand the central ideas of the passages in this unit?
- Did you provide a paraphrase or direct quotation from the unit texts to support your answer to the essential question?

Writing Expression
- Does your writing address all elements required by the prompt?
- Does your writing state your answer to the essential question: Why should we protect the Earth and its creatures?
- Are your ideas well-developed and clearly organized?

Writing Conventions
- Does your writing follow the rules of standard, formal English with few or no spelling and punctuation errors?

Acknowledgments

Pages 10–12, Excerpt(s) from BUD, NOT BUDDY by Christopher Paul Curtis, copyright © 1999 by Christopher Paul Curtis. Used by permission of Delacorte Press, an imprint of Random House Children's Books, a division of Penguin Random House LLC. All rights reserved.

Pages 25–30, Excerpt from "Dirk" from My Life in Dog Years by Gary Paulsen. Copyright © Gary Paulsen.

Pages 47–48, WHY WE NEED FRIENDS NOW MORE THAN EVER by Lori Chandler. From http://bigthink.com.

Pages 62–64, Excerpt from REFLECTIONS ON TRUE FRIENDSHIP by Andrew O'Hagan. From From *The New York Times*, December 4, 2016, © 2016 *The New York Times*. All rights reserved. Used by permission and protected by the Copyright Laws of the United States. The printing, copying, redistribution, or retransmission of this Content without express written permission is prohibited.

Pages 76–80, "Damon and Pythias" by Fan Kissen from *LITERATURE*, Student Edition. Copyright © 2008 by Houghton Mifflin Harcourt Publishing Company. All rights reserved. Reproduced by permission of the publisher, Houghton Mifflin Harcourt Publishing Company.

Pages 112–114, SOMETIMES, THE EARTH IS CRUEL by Leonard Pitts, Jr. From *The Miami Herald*, January 14, 2010, © 2010 McClatchy. All rights reserved. Used by permission and protected by the Copyright Laws of the United States. The printing, copying, redistribution, or retransmission of this Content without express written permission is prohibited.

Page 126, "Mother to Son" from THE COLLECTED POEMS OF LANGSTON HUGHES by Langston Hughes, edited by Arnold Rampersad with David Roessel, Associate Editor, copyright © 1994 by the Estate of Langston Hughes. Used by permission of Alfred A. Knopf, an imprint of the Knopf. Doubleday Publishing Group, a division of Penguin Random House LLC. All rights reserved. Digital Rights by permission of Harold Ober Associates Incorporated.

Pages 171–177. Excerpt from "THE DAIRY OF ANNE FRANK" play by Albert Hackett, Frances Goodrich Hackett and Otto Frank. Copyright © 1956. Reprinted by permission of Random House, Inc.

Pages 202–203, Excerpt(s) from THE DIARY OF A YOUNG GIRL: THE DEFINITIVE EDITION by Anne Frank, edited by Otto H. Frank and Mirjam Pressler, translated by Susan Massotty, translation copyright © 1995 by Doubleday, a division of Random House LLC. Used by permission of Doubleday, an imprint of the Knopf Doubleday Publishing Group, a division of Penguin Random House LLC. All rights reserved.

Pages 210–211, "Words Free as Confetti" by Pat Mora from CONFETTI: POEMS FOR CHILDREN. Text Copyright ©1999 by Pat Mora. Permission arranged with LEE & LOW BOOKS, Inc., New York, NY 10016. All rights not specifically granted herein are reserved.

Page 223, THE POEMS OF EMILY DICKINSON, edited by Thomas H. Johnson, Cambridge, Mass.: The Belknap Press of Harvard University Press, Copyright © 1951, 1955, 1979, 1983 by the President and Fellows of Harvard College.

Pages 226–227, 229–230, Excerpt from OUT OF MY MIND by Sharon Draper. Copyright © 2010. Ahteneum Books for Young Readers, a division of Simon and Shuster.

Pages 246–250 From RED SCARF GIRL by Ji-Li Jiang. Copyright © 1997 by Ji-Li Jiang. Foreword copyright © 1997 by HarperCollins Publishers. Used by permission of HarperCollins Publishers.

Pages 267–268, "On to Victory in China" by Gloria W. Lannom from Calliope magazine, © by Carus Publishing Company. Reproduced with permission. All Cricket Media material is copyrighted by Carus Publishing Company, d/b/a Cricket Media, and/or various authors and illustrators. Any commercial use or distribution of material without permission is strictly prohibited. Please visit http://www.cricketmedia.com/info/licensing2 for licensing and http://www.cricketmedia.com for subscriptions.

Pages From *The Words We Live By: Your Annotated Guide to the Constitution* by Linda R. Monk. Copyright © 1993. Used by permission of Hachette Books.

Pages 310–314, Excerpt(s) from FLUSH by Carl Hiaasen, copyright © 2005 by Carl Hiaasen. Used by permission of Alfred A. Knopf, an imprint of Random House Children's Books, a division of Penguin Random House LLC. All rights reserved.

Pages 332–337, "Saving Our Sea Turtles" by Elizabeth Preston from Muse, © by Carus Publishing Company. Reproduced with permission. All Cricket Media material is copyrighted by Carus Publishing Company, d/b/a Cricket Media, and/or various authors and illustrators. Any commercial use or distribution of material without permission is strictly prohibited. Please visit http://www.cricketmedia.com/info/licensing2 for licensing and http://www.cricketmedia.com for subscriptions.

Page 353, "The Last Ocean" by Jamie Joseph. Reprinted with the author's permission.

Pages 354–355, Linda Hogan, "Song for the Turtles of the Gulf" from *Dark. Sweet.: New & Selected Poems.* Copyright © 2008 by Linda Hogan. Reprinted with the permission of The Permissions Company, Inc., on behalf of Coffee House Press, www.coffeehousepress.org

Pages 371–372, "Climate change: The long reach" by Stephen Ornes was originally published on August 22, 2013 in Science News for Students. Reprinted with Permission of Science News for Students.

Pages 388–391, "A Fable for Tomorrow" from SILENT SPRING by Rachel Carson. Copyright © 1962 by Rachel L. Carson, renewed 1990 by Roger Christie. Reprinted by permission of Houghton Mifflin Harcourt Publishing Company. All rights reserved.

Photo Credits: www.heatheronhertravels.com: p. 185; NASA: p. 370; Shutterstock: pp. 46, 254, 386 (middle); Thinkstock: all others